Studying Politics

Basic Concepts in Political Science

William A. Welsh, GENERAL EDITOR

STUDYING POLITICS, William A. Welsh, *University of Iowa*

SOCIALIZATION TO POLITICS, Dean Jaros, *University of Kentucky*

STUDYING POLITICS

William A. Welsh

PRAEGER PUBLISHERS

New York • Washington

BOOKS THAT MATTER

Published in the United States of America in 1973
by Praeger Publishers, Inc.
111 Fourth Avenue, New York, N.Y. 10003

Library of Congress Cataloging in Publication Data
Welsh, William A.
  Studying politics.
  (Basic concepts in political science)
  Includes bibliographical references.
  1. Political science. I. Title.
JA71.W44   320   77-189929

Printed in the United States of America

For my parents,
who have added new dimensions
to the concepts of Love and Understanding

Contents

Series Editor's Introduction

This book is one of a series of volumes, published and forth-coming, written for introductory and intermediate undergraduate courses in political science. In one sense, the purpose of these books is to introduce students to the field of political science. The core volume in the series, *Studying Politics,* presents an overview of the concepts, approaches, and subject matter of the discipline, together with an introduction to elements of critical thinking about the study of politics. Each of the other volumes in the series focuses on one or two central concepts used to describe major areas of political activity. These concept volumes provide definitions of important terms, summarize basic approaches, and describe what political scientists have discovered about the involvement of human beings in these activities—political socialization, the exercise of power and influence, conflict, policy-making, political leadership, the development of political culture, the formation and activities of political groups. By using various combinations of these relatively short books, instructors can structure, as broadly or as selectively as they wish, an introduction to the study of politics for undergraduate students.

In another sense, the purpose of this series is both less "academic" and more ambitious. For this series proceeds from the premise that what political scientists do *qua* political scientists has relevance well beyond the relatively narrow confines of a scholarly discipline. As political science has labored toward greater precision, rigor, and theoretical maturity, it has developed new ways of organizing and studying information about politics. By now, there is substantial agreement that these new approaches and techniques have—on balance—improved the scientific status of the discipline. But what of those who are not committed to becoming professional political scientists, but who nevertheless seek a sound, reliable understanding of politics, simply because political activity is so central to the management of human affairs? Does the development of systematic perspectives in the field of political science contribute only to the advancement of science, yielding no benefits for the thoughtful layman?

If one of the goals of science is to provide understanding of our environment, then scientists and nonscientists alike surely share that concern. If this is the case, then our progress as political scientists should hold the promise of improved understanding for nonscientists as well. In short, what political scientists have learned about how to study politics—especially about the close relationship between *what* we know and *how* we find out—ought to be useful to anyone who wants to understand politics. That belief constitutes the principal motivation for this series of books.

In pursuit of that goal, these books attempt to do four things. First, they introduce students to the language and approaches of political science—not merely as elements of a scholarly discipline, but as useful ways of looking at the world we live in. Second, relatedly, these books raise some basic methodological issues involved in studying politics—not as abstract issues in scholarship but as problems of how we obtain and critically analyze information available to us. Third, the concept-based volumes in this series introduce the student to concrete aspects of political activity through the use of unifying concepts that cut across both traditional subfields of the discipline and formal institutions, or structures, of government. They treat politics as a blend of several types of human behavior. Fourth, the books in the series attempt to overcome the student's natural parochialism—the limitations imposed by his much greater familiarity with the political practices and structures of the society in which he lives—by providing frequent examples of political activity from a variety of cultural settings. In short, the series seeks to be both systematic and concrete. It is designed to provide useful perspectives on an exciting area of human activity, and to present these perspectives in a way that is meaningful for students who are beginning their formal study of the subject.

The task is ambitious, and the accomplishment doubtless will be less than perfect. But the effort seems worthwhile, if we hope to establish the relevance of the discipline of political science not only to theory-building in social science but also to sound, reliable understanding of politics on the part of concerned citizens.

WILLIAM A. WELSH

Author's Acknowledgments

Many people have contributed a great deal to the genesis of this book and of the series of which it is a part. Marian S. Wood, formerly of Praeger Publishers, generated the early enthusiasm for the project, and her initial efforts have been carried forward with equal capability and verve by Denise Rathbun and Svein Arber. Much of the manuscript preparation was done by Barbara A. Gilbert, who somehow managed to bring both coherence to the typescript and relative calm to an author laboring to meet deadlines.

I owe some particularly great intellectual debts—a fact all the more frustrating because this book reflects those debts all too inadequately. My perspectives on the study of politics were profoundly influenced ten years ago by Richard C. Snyder, James A. Robinson, and Harold Guetzkow at Northwestern University. And my colleagues at the University of Iowa have created a remarkable environment for intellectual ferment and growth—warmly congenial, yet professional and motivating. Perhaps they will be willing to share much of the credit and a little of the blame for this book: credit, because they have clarified my thinking about the study of politics on numerous occasions and in numerous ways; blame, because they have been too kind to press on when my own biases did not permit me to see their points. It is difficult to imagine a finer group of colleagues.

Iowa City, Iowa
February, 1973

Studying Politics

1

What Is Politics?

For a good many years now most people have recognized that politics is ubiquitous in human circumstances. Political activity is all around us. Politics influences the lives of all of us, regardless of whether or not one participates in the political process.

This pervasiveness of politics led Aristotle to characterize man as a *zoon politikon*—a "political being." [1] Man cannot be otherwise. Politics is a necessary result of man's proximity to man and of the scarceness of resources available to meet the needs and desires of human beings. Wherever men perceive the need to organize for the purpose of pursuing material or psychic rewards, the political process comes into play.

Because politics is everywhere influential in the affairs of men, Aristotle regarded it as the "master science." In using that term, he was not suggesting that the conduct of political affairs is "scientific." Rather, he was trying to make the point that knowledge about politics is especially crucial for an understanding of our environment. In his view, therefore, the political dimension of man's existence was probably the most important dimension, in that politics decisively conditions the other circumstances in which we live. Politics, said Aristotle, "legislates as to what we are to do and what we are to refrain from doing." [2]

Consequently, we should not have much difficulty convincing ourselves that politics is something worth studying and understanding. Knowing that it is important does not, however, tell us

3

what politics *is*. Before we can understand politics, we need to try to define it.

THREE APPROACHES TO DEFINING "POLITICS"

Since it is difficult to study something if you do not know what it is you are supposed to be studying, political scientists have devoted a good deal of energy (perhaps too much energy) to trying to define "politics." Actually, much of the apparent disagreement on the appropriate subject matter to be studied by political scientists has been semantically trivial. There is, in fact, consensus on what constitutes politics, although the ways in which this consensus has been expressed have varied. Three types of approaches to defining politics may be sketched.

First, perhaps the most common approach has been to offer a single stipulative phrase designed to embrace the considerable variety of activities thought to be political in nature. Thus, for some, politics consists of those human behaviors that are centered on the institutions and practices of government. Others see politics as the process by which communities of human beings deal with their problems, that is, with the obstacles they perceive to exist between their present conditions and the goals they wish to pursue.[3] Still others find politics to be those human interactions involving the use, or threat of use, of power or authority. Another common perspective is that politics is the process by which scarce resources (human, material, and spiritual) are allocated within a social unit (be it a city, a state, a nation, or an organization) for the purpose of providing for human needs and desires.[4]

A second approach in defining politics has been to list the questions that should be asked and answered in understanding politics. The list of questions is formidable; a few examples, however, will suffice. Questions frequently cited are: (1) How do the artifacts of human organization (*e.g.,* formal groups, political parties, nation-states, international organizations) persist through conditions of stress and change? (2) How do particular individuals or groups achieve and maintain preponderant influence or power? (3) What social, cultural, and economic conditions nurture different types of political order (*e.g.,* anarchy, democracy, authoritarianism, totalitarianism)?[5]

It is worth mentioning that this second approach to characterizing politics does not actually offer a specific *definition* of politics. That is, it does not provide a phrase with which to complete the statement "Politics is . . ." Rather, this second approach urges that politics can be understood best by reflecting on some fundamental questions, the answers to which provide keys to the future shape of human society. If we can explain how individuals, groups, nations, and cultures achieve power, or persist over time, we will have gained an understanding of the forces that most basically shape the human order.

A third way to convey a sense of what politics is about has been to identify the major categories of activity, or behavior, that constitute politics. For example, some see *conflict* as the essence of politics. Conflict is a necessary characteristic of society. Human beings come from varying cultural backgrounds, have differing and complex sets of preferences, and articulate their concerns in different ways and with different intensities. Furthermore, the material, human, and psychic resources possessed by societies are limited and therefore generally insufficient to satisfy everybody's desires all the time. As a result, there is competition for access to, or control over, a society's resources. This competition manifests itself in conflict among individuals, groups, and organizations such as political parties.

Or, one might focus on the results of political competition and conflict, the emergence of certain individuals, groups, and organizations in positions of *power* and *influence*. Power and influence are terms used to describe certain relationships and activities that are part of politics. Students of politics have defined power in many different ways. But, in recent years, political scientists increasingly have agreed that political power is most usefully thought of as a *relationship between* people, rather than as a commodity or an attribute of one person. While it may make some sense to speak of military power in terms of absolute numbers of missiles, aircraft, ships, or infantrymen under a nation's control, political power is a rather more subtle phenomenon. Broadly speaking, it refers to the ability of A to make B do something that A wants him to do, regardless of whether B wants to do it. The means by which A exercises this ability determine whether we speak of his relationship with B as one of power or as one of influence. If A's ability to bring about desired behavior from B rests on the threat or use of *sanctions,* positive or negative, we say that this is a *power* relationship. If B follows A's lead without the presence of sanctions, we speak of a relationship of *influence.*

When we focus on political conflict, and on relationships of power and influence, we are reminded of another activity that is a central category of politics: *leadership.* When people decide to organize to pursue their desires and concerns, and to gain access to societal resources, they need leadership. Organizations with goals, and the need for specific action, cannot exist without leaders. Similarly, the existence of persons who have more power or influence than others suggests a distinction between leaders and nonleaders; between persons with greater and lesser access to the material and psychological resources necessary to mold, sustain, and change organizational structures and activities. Leadership, therefore, consists of the ability to mobilize human resources in the pursuit of specific goals. Like power and influence, it is a relationship between people; indeed, it refers to some of the same activities, since it may (but need not) involve power or influence.

One of the principal activities of leaders is *decision-making.* Consequently, this is another term we often use in describing the important activities involved in politics. *Decision-making* involves the selection, by persons in positions of power or influence, of a particular course of action from among two or more possible competing alternatives. When a chief of state determines to commit or withdraw a nation's military forces or to veto a piece of legislation, he engages in decision-making. When the delegates at a national political convention select a presidential candidate or adopt a series of platform propositions, they become involved in decision-making. And when the leaders of a labor union decide whether to support a political candidate, they are engaged in decision-making.

Conflict, power and influence, leadership, decision-making—these closely related activities are perhaps the central stuff of politics. Still other terms are used by political scientists to describe the essence of politics, and we shall encounter some of them later in this book. But the activities mentioned in the last few paragraphs have recognized importance in politics and serve to illustrate this third approach to defining politics.

At the risk of stressing a point that might seem obvious, we should emphasize that these sets of activities are by no means contradictory or exclusive; so that definitions based on these categories are also not exclusive. For example, one could define politics in terms of *conflict* among individuals and groups seeking *influence* over authoritative *decision-making*.

Although it might seem satisfyingly simple to assert that one of the above definitions of politics is the "best" or most "useful," the temptation to do so is worth resisting. Presumably, people who study politics are interested in understanding, not in imposed orthodoxy. Furthermore, strictly speaking, definitions are not "right" or "wrong"; they are arbitrary statements of how a person wishes to look at a given term and at the phenomena to which it refers. Each of us is free to define politics—or anything else—as he chooses.

Lest what we have just said be interpreted as an invitation to turn the study of politics into anarchic disarray, we should mention that the process of defining important terms is not wholly without rules or guidelines. While definitions are not "right" or "wrong," some definitions of a given term may be more useful than others. For example, definitions that seem grossly out of step with common usage are likely to introduce confusion into our conversations. Similarly, definitions that are highly abstract or obtuse may be difficult to apply concretely to objects in the real world that we wish to study. We shall say a good deal more about defining concepts in chapter 5. For now, we can be content to recognize that, in the absence of any orthodox dogma concerning definitions of politics, we need to define things in such a way that others are likely to understand us when we speak or write.

Finally, it is worth emphasizing that there is nothing inconsistent about the several definitions of politics that you have read. Politics is a frequently and widely observed phenomenon. There are numerous reasonable ways to look at the activities that constitute politics. It is not of great importance whether you choose to anchor your thoughts on a stipulative phrase (*e.g.,* "Politics is the process by which scarce resources are allocated within a social unit"), a series of central questions (*e.g.,* "How do political units such as parties or nation-states persist through stress?"), or a set of concepts referring to important political relationships and activities (*e.g.,* conflict, power and influence, leadership, decision-making). What is important is that you recognize that the political process involves an understanding of all these closely related things.

POLITICS AND THE POLITICAL SYSTEM

We have already suggested that politics, as defined above, is everywhere: Resources are allocated, influence and leadership are exercised, decisions are made in schools, in churches, in organizations, in governmental structures. Furthermore, not only are political activities carried on *within* large organizations, such as, for example, a trade union, but such organizations attempt to influence the political behavior that takes place through other structures in society, especially government.

To say simply that politics takes place everywhere does not say very much. Our effort to understand politics would be considerably enhanced if we could at least broadly identify the characteristics of the settings in which politics is found. By identifying the nature of these settings, or contexts, of politics, we can better grasp, also, the character of the social, cultural, and psychological factors that influence politics. That is, we want to be able to say, at least for purposes of our analysis, that politics takes place *some*where, not simply everywhere.

The "*some*where" of political activity we call a *political system*. We should hasten to emphasize that, although a political system is *where* the political action is, political systems are not to be found identified on political maps. That is, although we commonly use phrases such as the "American political system," the "French political system," or the "local political system," there is no *necessary* relationship between the boundaries of a political system and the political boundaries of an administrative unit such as a city, a state, or a nation. This is true for two reasons.

First, systems, and nations, are different, because the notion of "political system" is what political scientists call an *analytic construct*. It is a term used to make easier the analysis of certain concrete things. Systems do not exist in concrete form in the real world; rather, they are composed of selected aspects of the real world, which we abstract—pull out, if you will—to study more closely. To put this another way, "systems" exist in our minds and in our discussions about politics; they do not exist as such (*i.e.,* as systems) in the real world. To be sure, the objects that we include in our pictures of "systems" do have real-world existence.

A second reason systems are different from political units such as nations is that the existence of a system depends only on the presence of a certain type of *persistent pattern of human relationships*, while real-world political units have other requirements, such as territoriality and some measure of sovereignty, autonomy, or authority. Given the appropriate maps, we presumably could identify the physical (territorial) boundaries of Manhattan, Muskegon, Montreal, Munich, Montevideo, or Marrakesh. Similarly, motoring across Europe one can hardly miss knowing when he crosses a national border, since there will generally be border patrols, customs agents, and miscellaneous formalities to attend to. Thus, local and national boundaries are clearly observable in the real world.

By contrast, the boundaries of political systems generally do not have fixed territorial dimensions, since political systems are defined in terms of patterned relationships among people. We can define a political system as "any persistent pattern of human relationships that involves, to a significant extent, power, rule or authority." [6] Further, as we have already said, a political system may consist of *selected* aspects of any given situation that we wish to study. Thus, the Democratic Party may be viewed as a political system, as could be the United States Supreme Court or the Congress. With some reasonable specificity, we can identify the patterned relationships that are part of such systems. But to try to attach any notion of territorial boundaries to those systems makes little sense.

Characteristics of Systems

Systems—and, hence, political systems—have certain identifying characteristics. These characteristics distinguish *systems* from *sets* of objects and help us understand the picture political scientists draw of the political relationships in which they are interested.

A set is simply a number of objects that might be observed together, or considered together, for any reason. All the people living in a particular geographical area, for example, could be viewed as a set of persons, but this set would not necessarily constitute a *system*. In order for there to be a system, three characteristics would have to be present.

First, a system involves regularized *interaction* among its units or members. If we were to map out these interactions, we would discover that members of a system have, as a group, dense and mutual interactions with one another. That is, their interactions are not only frequent but also multilateral; most members of the system have some sort of interaction, direct or indirect, with most other members.

Second, the interaction of units or members of a system extends to a point of *interdependence*. By interdependence we mean that the actions of one member will influence the other members, or that changes in one unit will have an effect on the other units.

Third, a system has tendencies toward *self-maintenance*; it develops institutions and practices intended, in part, to preserve the existence and identity of the system. This happens because the existence of the system is somehow functional for its members. In the case of social systems, there is something about the pattern of relationships within the system that the members value and for that reason seek to maintain the system.

When we examine these characteristics of a system—interaction, interdependence, self-maintenance—in conjunction with the basic feature of politics—a central concern with power or authority—it becomes abundantly clear that not every collectivity of human beings constitutes a political system. In general, residential aggregates (people who live in a given area of a community), social groupings (from the Tuesday night bridge group to the folk dance club), and statistical social and occupational aggregates (*e.g.,* all white-collar workers, all persons of Irish descent) lack most, if not all, of the requisite characteristics of a political system. At the same time, it is clear, also, that most of these examples of *sets* of persons *could be organized* into what we might properly call political systems. Thus, neighborhood groups can form associations to oppose highway routes or to obtain improved community services. Occupational groups can form or join professional and labor organizations in order to pursue improved working circumstances. Persons with similar ethnic origins can organize to exert maximum influence, whether in domestic political matters or in their country's foreign policy toward their ancestors' homeland. In each of these cases, the organizations could involve interaction, interdependence, self-maintenance, and internal relationships of power or authority, as well as efforts to influence the exercise of power or authority by others. The possible range of locations in which political systems, or subsystems, can be found is great, indeed, and testifies to the pervasive character of politics in modern society.

Overlapping of Political Systems

There are several additional things about this notion of "political system" that we need to keep in mind. First, since the idea of a system is an analytical abstraction anyway, it is not surprising that political scientists use the term "system" to refer to sets of relationships that *overlap* in different ways. For example, one system may be wholly subsumed, or included, within another system. In this case, we usually refer to the smaller system as a *subsystem* of the larger one. A congressional committee may be viewed as a subsystem of the larger congressional system. In a slightly different sense of overlapping, important political institutions, groups, or individuals may be parts of several different political systems that overlap only in part. Thus, the President of the United States plays important roles in the party system, as the leader of his party; in the congressional system, as initiator and promoter of a particular set of legislative proposals; in the military hierarchy, as Commander-in-Chief of the armed forces; and so forth. Political systems overlap, then, sometimes wholly and sometimes only partially. This fact helps us to understand the abstracted, analytical nature of the concept of a political system.

Political Systems and Government

A political system is related to *government,* but the two are not identical. In the past, most of what was studied as part of the field of political science was focused on government. *Government* consists of the formal institutions and offices involved in making authoritative decisions for a political system. It is a "framework in which the executive, judicial, legislative and administrative business" [7] of a system is carried out.

In recent years, students of politics have come increasingly to recognize that many important aspects of political activity take place outside the formal structures of government—for example, in political parties, labor unions, schools, and interest groups. While part of the political system, these "informal" aspects of politics are not, to repeat, part of government; so that we can conclude that political systems comprise not only governments but numerous other patterns of relationships that influence government and, collectively, constitute the broader political process.

We should emphasize that the stuff of political activity cannot be understood by focusing entirely, or perhaps even primarily, on the formal structures of government. Simply studying the formal rules by which the executive, legislative, and judicial branches are constituted and function provides an inadequate, and often misleading, picture of what politics is all about. This certainly is not to say that the student of politics can ignore the formal structures of government; this would be patently absurd. But we must recognize that much of the activity that is important in shaping the policies pursued in society takes place outside the formal structures of government.

Relatedly, the formal structure of government itself is decisively influenced by outside factors. For example, we know that government is influenced by the attitudes held toward it by citizens, and that these attitudes, in turn, have been significantly affected by child-rearing practices, by interaction among members of peer groups, and by the nature of instruction in our schools. We naturally understand that what government does is influenced by the identity of the people who hold government positions. The recruitment of these government leaders is a complex process, influenced by a variety of economic and social factors that make it more likely that certain kinds of individuals will achieve positions of prominence in government and less likely that persons with other characteristics will hold such posts. We know that government is influenced by the activities of various groups in society, most of which represent organized concerns of clusters of citizens. And we know that the strength and vitality of the national economy may have an important impact on the functioning of government, as well as on the policies that emerge from governmental activity. In short, the formal structures of government may be viewed as important transmission belts in the process of politics, but they are only a few among numerous such transmission belts; indeed, the significance of government varies a good deal, depending on a number of situational contingencies.

Political System and Social System

Another central fact about a political system is that it does not exist in a vacuum. A political system is a subsystem of a broader social system and is substantially influenced by numerous essentially nonpolitical characteristics of that social system. These influencing characteristics may be cultural, economic, geographical, demographic, social, or psychological in nature.

Politics is conditioned, for example, by political culture; this consists of the basic values, beliefs, and attitudes of people toward the institutions and practices of politics. Especially in democratic systems, which encourage popular participation, the values, beliefs, and attitudes of individuals may represent significant constraints on both the means and the ends of politics.

If the influence of culture on politics varies a good deal with the extent of citizen participation in political activity, the impact of economic factors on politics appears to be substantial in all types of political systems; for one of the political system's principal functions is the allocation of material resources among competing groups or among alternative developmental goals.

Similarly, the availability of economic resources, as well as the health of the economy, may have a great deal to do with the success with which a government can pursue its diplomatic, military, social, and developmental goals. This degree of success, in turn, may have a great deal to do with whether the political leadership remains in power.

Geographical factors, too, influence politics. Physical barriers to transportation and communications, for example, have made the achievement of national political unity and a sense of national identity very difficult for some Latin American and African countries. And the "accidents" of political geography—such as the lack of warm-water ports—have sometimes exerted a powerful influence on the foreign policies of large and small nations alike.

Demographic features of a system also can have considerable influence on politics. The urban-rural distribution of the population, for example, can be consequential. Social scientists studying a variety of social systems have concluded that urban and rural life-styles are significantly different, and that, therefore, urban dwellers have attitudes toward politics substantially different from those of their rural compatriots. In large part, these varying attitudes result from the contrasting nature of social and economic problems and needs faced by urban and rural populations. These different problems often demand distinctly different responses from government.

Social and social-psychological characteristics of a system also may have an important impact on politics. The sets of social mores and norms that develop over long periods of time may include some fairly specific notions about how public officials should behave. For example, the degree to which bribery of public servants is accepted varies considerably among different societies. Likewise, recent research by political scientists has suggested that the stability of the political order may sometimes be related to the psychological "climate" of the system. In particular, some social scientists believe that the likelihood of civil strife, violence, and perhaps revolution sharply increases when the population shares a psychological sense of "deprivation," coupled with just enough material improvement to foment "rising expectations" that cannot be satisfied by government.

Many other examples of broader social-system influence on the political subsystem could be offered. What is important is that we recognize the complex intertwining of political and nonpolitical circumstances in any social system. Politics cannot be understood simply by focusing narrowly on manifestly political events. We began this chapter by asserting that politics might well be the most important dimension of man's existence, since political activity so clearly influences everything else. Yet, it is obvious that the relationships among politics, economics, geography, social mores, and all the other dimensions of human society are *reciprocal*; they influence one another in a complex and continuing set of processes. Thus, it is often suggested that politics is the *integrating* dimension of society—the subsystem through which the other dimensions of human activity are meshed.

We study politics, then, as it occurs in political systems. These systems are, in fact, abstractions of certain elements of the real world on which we choose to focus particular attention. They consist of persisting patterned sets of relationships among human beings, relationships that have to do with power, rule, or authority. Such sets of relationships, or systems, can be found not only in government but also in schools, churches, and social and professional organizations, as well as in nongovernmental but expressly political groups, such as interest groups and political parties. Because of its omnipresence, it is easy to understand that politics is substantially influenced by many elements of the broader social system of which it is a part.

Notes

1. It is worth noting that Aristotle's phrase was "political being" rather than "social and political animal," as St. Thomas Aquinas quoted Aristotle. See Herbert J. Spiro, *Politics as the Master Science: From Plato to Mao* (New York: Harper and Row, 1970), p. 7.
2. Aristotle, *Nicomachean Ethics*, Book I, 2; quoted in Spiro, *op. cit.*, p. 2.
3. This perspective is reflected in Herbert J. Spiro, "Comparative Politics: A Comprehensive Approach," *American Political Science Review*, LVI, no. 3 (September, 1962), 577–95.
4. This approach, which has become perhaps the most widely adopted

among students of politics, is exemplified by the work of David Easton. See *A Systems Analysis of Political Life* (New York: John Wiley and Sons, 1965).

5. See Michael A. Weinstein, *Systematic Political Theory* (Columbus, Ohio: Charles E. Merrill, 1971), pp. 7–11.

6. Robert A. Dahl, *Modern Political Analysis* (Englewood Cliffs, N.J.: Prentice-Hall, 1963), p. 6.

7. Robert E. Murphy, *The Style and Study of Political Science* (Glenview, Ill.: Scott, Foresman, 1970), p. 1.

2

The Systematic Study of Politics: Political Science

Now that we have in hand some notions of what constitutes politics, we can turn our attention to how we can study politics. One of the fundamental messages of this book is that how we look at something influences what we see. Political science provides the frameworks within which we can view political activity. Understanding the nature of our "what" (politics) requires an understanding of our "hows" (political science). In order to know what we can expect to see, we need to know something about the lenses through which we will be looking.

POLITICAL SCIENCE AS A SOCIAL SCIENCE

Since political activity is so clearly part and parcel of a broader social system, it is hardly surprising that political science is firmly embedded in a broader context of social inquiry, that is, in the social sciences. All the social sciences—anthropology, economics, social psychology, sociology, human geography, political science —are concerned in one way or another with the study of the behavior of human beings in social units, that is, with the study of patterns of human interaction. Thus, political scientists and sociologists, for example, gather some of the same kinds of information, organize their information around some of the same concepts and theories, and arrive at some very similar findings, or results. Likewise, political scientists, in recent years, have found it necessary to use a good deal of economic data in trying to understand governmental expenditure decisions. They have also begun to "borrow" theories from their colleagues in economics. For example, some political scientists have found it useful to think of political decision-making in terms of the "classical," rational, utility-maximizing model of man and his decision-making used for some time by economists.

Not only do political scientists find it necessary to include extra-political factors and approaches in their research, but other social scientists also give attention to political factors and develop theories of relevance to politics. Economists, for example, devote a good deal of attention to both the procedures and the results of government decision-making. Economists also have developed sophisticated theories of conflict and of bargaining, two activities that are of central importance in politics.

We should not be too quick to conclude, however, that political science is merely a hybrid offshoot of other social-science disciplines. Admittedly, political-science departments in American universities generally were carved out of other departments, usually history departments.[1] Some overlapping of subject matter between political science and the other social sciences clearly exists, which, indeed, is not surprising, given the importance of politics for nearly all societal activities. More important, political science as a scholarly field of inquiry shares with the other social sciences a commitment to scientific methods and standards (which will be discussed later). It is this common commitment that accounts, in considerable part, for the occasional similarity of approaches in several social-science fields.

What distinguishes political science is (1) its relative emphasis on relationships having to do with power and authority, and (2) the substantive content and structure of its explanations. First, while sociology and economics, for example, occasionally deal with power and authority relationships, the concern of sociologists with this subject is much less consistent or pronounced than is the concern of political scientists. This is a difference of degree, not of kind, but it is an identifiable and important difference. Second, and perhaps more important, political scientists are almost always interested in explaining the causes of political behavior and political relationships, while other social scientists frequently use political behaviors in an effort to explain the causes of nonpolitical (*e.g.*, economic or social) events. For political scientists, politics is what is to be explained; it is what we call the *dependent variable,* that is, the phenomenon that is viewed as being "dependent" on other factors. For economists and sociologists, by contrast, politics is frequently the *independent variable,* that is, the factor on which social and economic phenomena are "dependent," or from which they result.

Examples will serve to clarify this important distinction. One of the principal kinds of behaviors in which political scientists are interested is voting behavior. They wish to be able to say with reasonable certitude why different people vote as they do. Explanations of voting behavior generally refer to such factors as social class, education, income, religion, and ethnicity. These explanatory factors, or causes, are the independent variables. Generally speaking, the political scientist is interested in these independent variables only insofar as they help him to explain political voting, which is his dependent variable; he is not primarily concerned with explaining social class, for example. Why a person perceives himself to be upper class, middle class, or working class is of greater interest to the sociologist.

Conversely, an economist may be interested in political behavior because it helps him to explain economic developments. For example, for an economist to explain changes in growth rates in a less-developed African nation, or in a centralized economy such as that of the Soviet Union, he probably will have to include as one of his independent variables the nature of decisions made by the political leadership of the country in allocating the nation's resources. These political decisions have some effect on economic growth. The economist is less interested in the explanations for the political decisions than he is in the extent to which the political decisions help explain the economic growth rates. A political scientist, on the other hand, would tend to be more interested in explaining the political decision-making.

To sum up to this point, political science shares some important characteristics with the other social sciences. The trend in recent years has been toward an increasing amount of similarity and overlap, especially in the use of scientific methods and theories, but also in substantive interests. At the same time, political science has its own distinct identity, based both on its relative emphasis on relationships of power and authority and on its inclination to treat political behaviors as the dependent variables to be explained, rather than as independent variables to be used in explaining other (nonpolitical) phenomena. We shall say a good deal more about the structure of explanations in political science (*i.e.,* about the relationships between dependent and independent variables) later in this book.

Perhaps it is unnecessary to caution students against developing a fierce pride in their new-found competence as serious students of politics. Some of our best friends, after all, are sociologists, economists, and psychologists, and there is every reason to believe that there is intellectual territory aplenty to go around. That is, students of politics are increasingly recognizing that the overlapping of interests among social-science disciplines does not threaten any of us with intellectual extinction. Indeed, we may well learn a good deal from one another. Certainly, no serious student of American politics can afford to be ignorant of the dynamics of interracial strife in urban areas, a subject that sociologists have been studying for some time. And, if we believe, as many political scientists do, that psychological frustrations are major causes of some forms of civil strife and violence, then we cannot afford to overlook the very considerable research already done by psychologists on the sources of human frustration and aggression.

Nor does there seem to be any reason to fear that our colleagues in the sister disciplines will consume all the meaty intellectual dishes, leaving only the scraps for us. On the contrary, our common problem seems to be that there is so much to be learned about human beings and their relationships with one another, and that there are such limited resources with which to tackle the task. In short, the overlapping of the subject matter studied in the several social sciences is not only perfectly understandable, it is eminently desirable.

We have said that the social sciences share a focus on the behaviors of human beings in social units. There is another thread running through the social sciences, one that derives from their common desire to develop as *scientific* fields of study. This common thread has to do with procedures, not with any particular subject-matter focus. That is, the social sciences seek (as their label implies) to be scientific, and *science inheres in methods, not in substance.* That is, the distinguishing characteristics that set science apart from nonscience have to do with *how* things are studied, not with *what* is being studied. Thus, the social sciences share, in a broad sense, a common *substantive* focus on patterns of human interaction, and this common subject matter serves to set the social sciences apart from the natural and technical sciences. They also share a common *methodological* element: a commitment to scientific procedures of study. This commitment to the methods of science links the social sciences not only to one another but, at least in a general way, to the natural and technical sciences as well.

SCIENCE AND THE STUDY OF POLITICS

Broadly speaking, the purpose of scientific inquiry is to substitute knowledge for impressions.[2] Its purpose is to provide verified information and understanding in which we have confidence, and not merely faith. Science seeks reliable knowledge on the basis of which we can not only explain what has happened and is happening but also predict, with reasonable success, the likelihood of given classes or types of developments happening in the future.

It would be difficult to overstate the importance of developing this kind of reliable knowledge about politics. Given the central importance of political activity for much of what human beings do, an intelligent grasp of one's environment demands a sound understanding of politics.

Because politics is all around us, and because political activity receives a great deal of attention in our communications media, there is much "information" available about politics. Some of this information is reliable; some of it is not. The serious student of politics approaches all this information with healthy skepticism. He knows that careful study will confirm some of what he hears about politics, but will disconfirm another part of what he hears. Through this process of confirmation and disconfirmation, the serious student of politics will manage to substitute knowledge for the casual impressions which are so readily accessible.

Skepticism, Science, and Social Relevance

This attitude of healthy skepticism is fundamental to scientific inquiry. Significantly, it logically parallels an important development of recent years in the social consciousness of increasing numbers of people, especially young people, in a variety of societies. This attitude of social consciousness involves cutting through old myths and challenging conventional wisdom. It involves digging more systematically for a concrete understanding of how political and social institutions operate. And it involves an explicit separation of information and ideals—a distinction between the consideration of what *should be* and what *is*. It implies that the realization of political goals presupposes a systematic understanding of how political processes are conducted. Only after the "is" is carefully sorted out can the "ought" be effectively pursued.

Seen in this light, science is a necessary precondition for the notion of social relevance—not, as some have suggested, the antithesis of social concern. Science is a precondition for social relevance because the call for relevance is a call for discarding conventional assumptions and for finding out what the world is really like, and why. Finding solutions to the pressing political and social problems of the day will require considerably more than commitment. It will also demand solid, well-founded information, effectively organized, and viewed through meaningful frameworks for analysis. That is also what science is about.

Another way to make this important point is to say that political scientists and concerned citizens share a fundamental goal: Both wish to understand political activity as thoroughly and as precisely as they can. To be sure, not all the goals of the political scientist and the layman are identical, but they certainly are congruent. Generally, we may identify three professional goals that political scientists pursue.

Goals of Political Scientists

Citizenship Training. Political scientists contribute to the training of informed citizen-participants in politics. The extent to which citizens are encouraged to participate in public affairs by informing themselves about politics, and by taking part in the selection of public officials, varies a great deal among nations. In nearly all societies, broad citizen participation is officially sanctioned and, at least superficially, encouraged. Reality often is not reflected in legal statutes, however, and the extent to which mass participation is genuinely desired by governing elites actually varies a good deal. Similarly, citizen participation may be merely *pro forma* and devoid of real meaning. For example, voter turnouts of 95–98 per cent are not uncommon in some systems with Communist governments, but, until recently, voters had no choice of candidates on the ballot.

In essentially democratic systems, however (and these systems, perhaps not surprisingly, are the ones in which political science as an academic discipline is best established), citizen evaluations of political performance by officeholders are considered important to the continued stable functioning of the system. Such systems reject the proposition that politics and government are too complex for the average man to comprehend; indeed, it is an article of faith among them that most citizens can attain a reasonable understanding of the processes of government, an understanding at least sufficient to permit them to make intelligent judgments about political issues and about individuals who offer themselves for positions of public trust. Relatedly, democratic political systems are based on the premise that whatever fallibilities are reflected in such popular choices, they are less serious than the liabilities implied by the denial of public access to roles of influence in politics.

Obviously, such a premise is based on the assumption that citizen-participants will acquire reliable information about public affairs, will integrate that information into a reasonably coherent set of values, beliefs, and attitudes about politics, and will act with some identifiable measure of attention to this knowledge. To be sure, there is ample evidence to suggest that, even in those societies in which relevant information about public affairs is

easy to obtain, many citizens have remarkably little knowledge
about government and politics. One of the tasks for political
scientists is to contribute to an improvement of this situation
and, thereby, to a closer realization of one of the basic premises
on which democratic systems ostensibly are to operate.

Training Officeholders. A second task for political scientists,
and one closely related to the first, is to train political practitioners—men and women for whom politics and/or government
represent a professional undertaking. Here, the effort of political
scientists is toward contributing to more rational and effective
management of public affairs and public institutions. We hear a
good deal of discussion of the "quality of leadership" in different
political structures and in different societies. Sometimes, these
discussions center on the impact of leadership selection procedures on the caliber of leaders ultimately chosen. Thus, a commonly heard argument is that the relatively open, bargaining-
and-compromise presidential selection system in the United States
tends to elevate men of mediocre intellect and leadership capabilities to the presidency. Sometimes, the concern about quality of
public officials focuses on the lack of educational opportunities,
or avenues for acquiring relevant experience, for aspiring bureau-
crats and administrators. Such conditions have created distinct
problems in newly independent nations. Another situation in
which the quality of leadership has been an important political
issue has been that where the political system has experienced
crisis and subsequent radical change, such as in Germany after
1945. In this case, the necessity of recruiting large numbers of
new public officials from a shrunken manpower base posed special problems in the training of political practitioners.

In one sense, each of these three situations—the impact of
open presidential selection procedures, the lack of persons with
educational and professional experience in new nations, the need
to fill a professional manpower void created by war and resultant
political reorientation of the system—is a "special case." A more
broadly relevant issue concerns the quality of the political and
administrative personnel at local and other subnational levels
of government throughout the world who are in more direct,

day-to-day contact with citizens. These are city councilmen, administrators of housing and welfare programs, legislative ombuds-
men, perhaps members of a congressman's or a governor's staff.
They make some decisions themselves, of course; perhaps more
important, they must have a good grasp of the broader workings
of government, an ability to convey this understanding of government and politics to the citizens with whom they have contact, and, finally, an ability to understand and respond to, or
pass on to other officials, the concerns of the citizenry. These
abilities require a considerable schooling, both educational and
experiential, in political and governmental affairs. An important
part (but assuredly not all) of that schooling originates with the
efforts of political scientists to improve the storehouse of public
information and knowledge about politics.

These two pursuits of political *scientists* as professional people
are not, strictly speaking, goals of political *science* as a field of
scholarly inquiry. Rather, they reflect the social responsibility of
scholars whose work should provide them with particularly useful insights into a domain of human activity that is especially
important for the character of society in which men live.

Building Theory. The third goal of political scientists is more
directly part of political science as a scholarly field of study and,
indeed, is the central goal of all of science: the development,
testing, and verification of theory. Roughly speaking, theories are
sets of statements of relationships among things in which we are
interested. Taken together, the statements that are parts of a
theory purport to cover the most important aspects of the subject under study. And these theoretical statements either are
based on careful prior research or are susceptible to being verified
through subsequent research. In a sense, then, theories are simply
careful accumulations of the prior research and creative thinking
on a subject.

We shall have more to say later about the nature of scientific
theories and about the particular theory-building efforts of political scientists. For now, it is important to emphasize that theory-
building has, in a broad sense, precisely the same goal as that
which motivates the education of citizens and the training of

public officials: increasing reliable knowledge about politics. The search for reliable knowledge manifests itself most clearly in scientific theory-building.

Understandably, political scientists—because they are scientists —may sometimes use language that is not heard in everyday conversations and may sometimes judge their own efforts at generating knowledge against criteria that might seem harsh or demanding to others. One student of politics [3] referred to theory as "imaginative perspectives"—new ways of organizing and describing information about politics, original ways of orienting oneself toward political affairs. But the political scientist uses "technical" or "abstract" language not to obfuscate and confuse issues but, rather, to contribute to their *clarification* by making the study of politics as precise and as reliable as possible. Further, as we shall see, the language of political science is often neither as "abstract" nor as "technical" as it sometimes first seems to its new students.

WHAT DOES IT MEAN TO BE "SCIENTIFIC"?: AN INTRODUCTION TO THE PHILOSOPHICAL FOUNDATIONS OF POLITICAL SCIENCE

As we have already mentioned, the scientific character of a field of study, or of any given piece of research, is determined by the methods used, not by the nature of the subject matter being studied. In principle, any phenomenon, any event, which can be observed is susceptible to scientific treatment. Since human behavior in a variety of political situations can be observed, a science of politics is—in principle—possible.

To say that a science of politics is possible is not to assert that everything considered by reasonable men to be political in nature will be embraced in some theory of political behavior. Science has its limitations, to which we will return later in this book. These limitations include those of both scope and degree of certainty of predictions. But it is also the case that science, as a set of procedures for understanding what the world really is like, has considerably fewer limitations than do mere conjecture or intuition.

Of late, some authors of political science textbooks have been trying to "sell" science as a way of looking at the world by suggesting that we are all really scientists. This is not quite the case, although it certainly is true that the fundamental procedures of science are neither uncommon nor mystical activities. Perhaps the most accurate way to state the "You, too, can be a scientist" argument is to say that anyone who is careful about the ways in which he gathers, assimilates, and uses information is respecting the basic canons of science.

Broadly, scientific methods involve (1) making explicit, *in advance,* one's *assumptions and expectations* about what he is studying, (2) making explicit, *in advance,* the *rules* and/or guidelines by which he will proceed in his study, (3) making careful *observations* of the phenomena in which he is interested, (4) seeking, through one or more explicit frames of reference, to map the *relationships* among the things he has observed, (5) seeking to *explain* the relationships he identifies, (6) making verifiable (testable) *predictions* based on his explanations, and (7) *reporting* fully and clearly his *conclusions* or results in such a way that another scientist could, if he wished, repeat the study by making similar observations.

Prediction and Probability in Political Science

It is important to emphasize the modest character of the prediction in which political scientists are interested. When we talk about prediction in political science, we are talking about our ability to make *probabilistic* statements of *general conditions* under which certain types of political behavior are *likely* to occur. This kind of prediction has little in common with the "predictions" of seers, crystal-ball gazers, or mystics. Political scientists do not propose to "predict" specific events in the future, such as who will be elected President of the United States in 1984, or the date of the next attempted palace coup in a Latin American country. Such event-specific circumstances are subject to many influences of the moment and cannot reasonably be predicted.

Political scientists, however, are interested in attempting to specify the degree of probability that certain types of events will

occur, given carefully specified conditions. For example, a political scientist armed with the appropriate evidence might be prepared to predict that, given a high degree of economic deprivation among the population, the presence of well-organized revolu-
tionary groups, and the disorganization and ineffectiveness of
national security forces, there would be a high degree of probability that civil violence directed toward the overthrow of the
government in power would occur. Or, political scientists interested in studying the recruitment of political leaders might hy-
pothesize that the increasing complexity of public decisions will
result in a greater likelihood that national political leaders in
the Soviet Union will be recruited on the basis of their technical
and managerial skills rather than on the basis of their demonstrated ideological commitment.

The notion of probability is central to the character of prediction in the social sciences. If it is the case that political scientists
have increasingly shed their previous sense of mystique about
human behavior, it nevertheless remains true that "exceptions to
the rule" will continue to be demonstrably present in most dimensions of human activity. Furthermore, the great variety
of factors that can influence political developments suggests that
judicious scholars will acknowledge the tentativeness of their
predictions about politics. This sense of uncertainty and tentativeness is reflected in the probabilistic character of prediction in
political science. Our predictions do not purport to say that
specific events *will* occur; rather, they assert that the *likelihood*
of certain *types* of events is great, given specified conditions.

Probability is, of course, a matter of degree. Generally speaking, prediction in political science has not advanced far enough
to permit us to state, in advance, the precise degree of probability with which we expect an event. We tend to handle the
question of degree of probability *a posteriori*, that is, after the
fact. When we attempt to test, or verify, our predictions, we examine the relative frequency with which the prediction was
confirmed by real events. Just how frequently we need to be
correct in order to say that our predictions are confirmed is an
interesting, but obviously arbitrary, issue. Certainly, if we are
right only half of the time, that is not good enough. On the

other hand, it does not seem reasonable to expect that our predictions will always be correct. For the most part, political scientists have been willing to permit their judgments about the appropriate level of probability to be determined by certain statistical procedures that have been used for some time in the other social sciences. According to the most commonly used guidelines, predictions that are not supported by the evidence at least 90 or 95 per cent of the time are not considered to have been verified. Such guidelines are not only arbitrary but also rather demanding. For the very character of science requires that we be skeptical of our evidence and reluctant to accept that which we tend to believe is true.

Empiricism, Observations, and Values

In many respects, then, the care with which one makes and handles his observations is the pivot on which his scientific enterprise turns. Scientific observations are *empirical* observations, observations that can be verified. To be sure, the rules of evidence in the social sciences, as in law, can be complicated. About some events, there is little or no descriptive disagreement; about others, there may be considerable difference of opinion about what actually took place. Much like the jury in a court of law, the political scientist is sometimes called upon to make judgments of "reasonable doubt" about his evidence. If there is such reasonable doubt, the scientist rejects the information.

Once the scientist has empirical observations, he respects the impacts of those observations. That is, his analysis and his conclusions reflect the implications of his empirical evidence, rather than his own personal values, preferences, or presuppositions. Scientists, being, after all, human, have personal preferences about many objects and circumstances in their environment. Political scientists, in particular, have values that are directly relevant to the subject matter with which they work as professional scholars. Rare, indeed, would be the student of politics who had no political preferences. But, as a scientist, he must keep these personal values out of his scholarly analysis.

The reason for the need to exclude personal values and presuppositions from scientific study has nothing whatever to do with the propriety of scientists' having values. Rather, their exclusion is dictated by the importance of discovering and reporting to others what the world really is like. The simple fact of the matter is that the person who permits his feelings about what the world *ought to be* like to intrude into his observations of what the world *is* like runs a very great risk of misperceiving the real world and of reporting false information. The scientist —as a scientist—is interested in the "is" of things.

Doing Research and Using Research

It should be stressed that the exclusion of personal values from the *procedures* of scientific research itself does not necessarily extend to the *uses* that might eventually be made of that research. (Nor can values be excluded from the *selection* of research topics, a problem to which we turn in chapter 7.) If the social sciences are to make contributions to the betterment of the circumstances in which human beings live, the results of social-science research surely will have to be taken into account. If political scientists, for example, can discover, with some certainty, the causes of politically relevant civil strife and violence, then this should help us to determine how to eliminate that strife.

It is worth emphasizing that any discussion of "betterment" of the human condition implies a set of values, a set of criteria, by which circumstances can be judged. In the case of civil strife and violence, for example, suggesting that social research into the causes of such behaviors might help eliminate them implies the value judgment that strife and violence are undesirable and *should* be eliminated. Most people probably would accept that value premise. Other value judgments to which political-science research is relevant may, however, be less universally accepted. Even one of the cornerstone value premises of a liberal-democratic philosophy—the judgment that broad mass citizen participation in politics is desirable—is not fully accepted in democratic societies, to say nothing of elitist systems. Consequently, the possible value implications of political-science research that identifies the causes of apathy and disinterest toward politics are not at all clear. Some people might propose that, knowing the causes of apathy, we should move forthwith to eliminate apathy. Others might wish to cultivate the sources of apathy in order to keep the number of persons involved in political activity to a more modest level.

For our purposes, there are three important points to be made about this distinction between the *conduct* of scientific study and the *use* of the *results* of scientific studies. First, personal values must necessarily be excluded from the former but, by contrast, provide the basis for the latter. Second, scientific research is *conducted* by scientists, but it may be *used* by scientists and nonscientists (especially, political practitioners) alike. And third, the value questions that provide the bases on which scientific research may be used, though obviously central in the conduct of human affairs, are outside the realm of science. This in no sense devalues value judgments. Nor does it make science either more "pure" or less "noble" because of its exclusion of these values. The simple fact of the matter is that such values must be excluded from scientific study, because their inclusion would, perhaps ironically, endanger the potential contribution of science to the improvement of the lives of human beings and the realization of whatever higher values a given society might seek to achieve or maximize. Our grasp of what "is" can serve well our achievement of what "ought to be," but only after the "is" has been rigorously and thoroughly established.

What we have been saying about the distinction between "is" statements and "ought" statements is sometimes characterized as the *fact-value distinction*. In this terminology, facts are empirically verifiable statements of what the world is like. Values are "should" or "ought" propositions, indicating what the person making the statement values or prefers. Value judgments are sometimes called *normative* propositions, to be contrasted with factual propositions.

As we have suggested, normative and factual propositions have wholly different statuses in science. Since factual propositions are empirically verifiable through observation, factual propositions are appropriately part of scientific research. Normative propositions, however, cannot be empirically verified. It is not possible to make observations that tell us whether a normative proposition is "right" or "wrong." Rather, normative propositions have to do with the "proper" way of *evaluating* facts.

Many different evaluations of the same observation could be made, depending on one's personal values. As a result, normative propositions are not part of science. They are, however, very relevant to the *use* of scientific research.

Science as a Procedural Value

There is a different, more subtle, sense in which a certain kind of value judgment is inherently part of scientific research. To this point, when we have talked about values, we have been referring to what might be called *substantive* values. These are normative judgments about real-world objects that are being studied. Hence, substantive value judgments might state that the seniority system in Congress is good or bad, that the electoral-college provisions of the U.S. Constitution should or should not be changed, or that the Soviet military intervention in Czechoslovakia in 1968 was right or wrong.

There is, however, another kind of value judgment that does not refer to substance, that is, to objects in the real world. These are *procedural* value judgments, that is, normative judgments about what should be the appropriate procedures by which real world objects are studied. To say that politics should be studied by using scientific procedures is to make a procedural value judgment. It should be recognized that some people who study politics do not agree with this value preference for scientific procedures, believing, instead, that an intuitive sensing of political reality is to be preferred to the more cautious, and often laborious and time-consuming, procedures of science. This book is not the place to rehash the debate between scientifically and nonscientifically oriented students of politics. But it is important to acknowledge that the selection of any given set of procedures by which knowledge is to be generated involves the making of a procedural value judgment. In this special sense, the preference for science itself is an important normative proposition.

Comparison and Science

One other dimension of science is especially important to understand. At the heart of science—indeed, at the heart of meaningful communication—is *comparison*. At each step in the process of theory-building—and at each step in the process of communicating ideas among human beings—comparison is crucial. We can illustrate the importance of comparison by looking briefly at the principal steps involved in constructing scientific theory.

First, it is difficult to talk about something if you do not have agreed-upon terms, or concepts, to describe what you want to talk about. In science, this process of deciding what terms to employ, and to what phenomena the terms will apply, is called *concept-formation.* Comparison is the basis of concept-formation. We assign a particular label (term or concept) to things that seem similar to one another; for example, we call organizations that present programatic statements of goals and offer candidates for public office "political parties." We also separate "political parties" from organizations that also have specific goals, but which do not offer their own candidates; the latter we might call "interest groups." Obviously, in order to decide what distinctions to draw between these two concepts, we have to compare the phenomena to which the concepts refer.

Second, comparison is the basis of *classification.* Once we have decided that we are going to talk about political parties, we need to determine what characteristics of parties we want to use as bases for classifying them. How we decide to classify our concepts depends largely on our theoretical interests, that is, on what we are hoping to explain. We might decide, for example, to explain differences among political parties in terms of their ideological positions and the nature of their appeals to voters. Hence, we might choose to classify these parties, first, into categories of liberalism-conservatism and, second, into categories of pragmatic, doctrinal, and personal campaign appeals. In order to decide what classificatory categories would be useful, and in order to determine which political parties fall into each category, we would have to compare them to identify similarities and differences among them.

Once we have determined our concepts and our categories of classification, we can set them into whatever *theoretical framework* we are using. A theoretical framework is really just an explicitly stated set of expectations and hypotheses about how we think certain selected aspects of reality operate. These expectations and hypotheses must be *verified*, of course; in effect, they must be compared with reality. This process of comparing our expectations and hypotheses with reality must be repeated many times, and in different settings, in order to insure the accuracy of our findings. Here, too, comparison is crucial. It is important that the numerous "tests" of our hypotheses be done with similar (comparable) procedures, and that we be aware of the similarities and differences between the settings in which the hypotheses are examined. Otherwise we could not feel confident that our results were reliable.

When we want to make a generalized statement of a relationship between political phenomena, we presumably do so on the basis of the accumulated knowledge from many observations of that relationship. Knowing that there is, in the United States, a positive relationship between personal wealth and support for the more conservative political party would not be enough to generalize such a relationship for all political systems. Many more observations, made in a variety of environmental settings, would be required. This process of deriving general statements of relationships between phenomena from numerous specific case studies is called *induction*. Comparison is an important part of induction, because the numerous specific observations, or cases, must be compared in order to determine whether (and to what degree) they actually support the general statement of relationship.

After tentative findings based on a number of cases have been developed, the scientist is interested in further testing or refining his knowledge. At this point, he must work back from his generalized statements of relationships (generalizations) down to additional specific case studies. The logical process of moving from a more general statement to a more specific one is called *deduction*. When political scientists state specific hypotheses designed to test, or verify, general propositions, we say that they have "deduced" these specific statements about what will be observed. For example, a political scientist interested in testing the general proposition that there is a positive relationship between wealth and support for more conservative political parties would need to deduce specific statements that could be tested in given settings. He might deduce the statement "Persons in the Federal Republic of Germany with annual incomes of more than 30,000 Deutsche Mark tend to support the Christian Democratic Union." Obviously, comparison is crucial to deduction, since the validity of using any given deduction to test a general proposition depends substantially on the degree of comparability between the concepts of the general statement and the concepts of the specific statement. If DM 30,000 is not really a high income, or if the Christian Democratic Union is not really a conservative political party, then the specific statement would not represent a valid test of the general proposition. The way to determine whether the more specific statements are valid as a test of the general proposition is by comparing the meanings of the concepts in the two statements.

This discussion of the central importance of comparison in science carries an important practical message about how we understand politics. One of the most common, and unfortunate, characteristics of human thinking is the tendency to generalize from the relatively limited, narrow range of experiences that each of us has. What we personally experience tends to be seen as the "usual," the "normal," and sometimes, normatively, the "best." Things that differ from our usual experience are frequently viewed as aberrations or oddities.

Europeans, whose geography and political history have brought about much greater exposure to widely different political, social, and economic practices, often contend that Americans are particularly guilty of this kind of narrow, parochial way of looking at the world. It is undeniable that Americans have relatively little knowledge of political circumstances in other political systems, much less, for example, than most Europeans have of the American political order. This is unfortunate, because the increasing amount of interaction across national boundaries demands a considerable understanding of the political practices of others. Furthermore, it can well be argued that a person fully understands his own political system only when he understands how that system compares with others around the world.

To say that a country has a "liberal-democratic" system of government means little if we do not understand the workings of governments that are not liberal-democratic. To say that a fundamental feature of politics in the United States is our two-party system is not especially interesting until we understand why so few countries have two-party systems. An understanding of the significance of a presidential system rests on a comprehension of how it differs from nonpresidential (*e.g.,* parliamentary) systems.

The message is clear and vital. The study of politics must proceed with attention to how political behaviors and relationships vary under different conditions. Political science, like any science, is fundamentally comparative in nature. We should stress that the comparisons that give meaning to our understanding of politics are not necessarily comparisons between the political systems of different countries, although they sometimes will be. We are interested in comparing *political systems*—and political systems, after all, are not necessarily congruent with nation-states, as we have seen. Our comparisons may focus on different organizations, or within different regions, of the same country. In addition, we may wish to compare the same political system at *different points in time;* in effect, to compare a political system "with itself" over time. But, whatever the form or framework, comparison is essential to our understanding of politics.

NOTES

1. A useful discussion of the origins and emphases of political science programs in the United States can be found in Malcolm B. Parsons, "Perspectives in the Study of Politics," in Parsons (ed.), *Perspectives in the Study of Politics* (Chicago: Rand McNally, 1968), pp. 1–22.
2. An effective, practical discussion of this process of substituting knowledge for impressions or opinions is contained in Sotirios A. Barber, Robert E. Johnston, Roger M. Nichols, and Janice B. Snook, *Introduction to Problem Solving in Political Science* (Columbus, Ohio: Charles E. Merrill, 1971).
3. Michael A. Weinstein, *Systematic Political Theory* (Columbus, Ohio: Charles E. Merrill, 1971), p. 5.

3

Political Science as Subfields of a Discipline

As we have seen, there is breadth and diversity in the subject matter covered by political science; and, notwithstanding the increasing commitment of political scientists to scientific methods in general, a great variety of concepts, approaches, models, theories, and techniques are in use in the field today. That is, there are many different ways to approach the study of politics and numerous ways in which information about politics can be organized and analyzed.

In this and the following two chapters, three different ways to divide up the intellectual pie will be described. Other strategies for describing the content of political science doubtless could be devised, but these three are probably the most commonly used. This chapter views political science in terms of the major *subfields* into which teaching and research in the field are divided. Chapter 4 characterizes the field in terms of some more general *frameworks* (or approaches and models) that can be used to organize and integrate information about many different aspects of politics. Chapter 5 suggests that political science can be viewed through several major *concepts,* some of which were introduced briefly in chapter 1, and which describe important categories of political activity.

Each of these types of perspectives on what constitutes political

37

science can be useful to the student of politics. In a broad sense, it is possible to encompass the subject matter of political science within each of these perspectives. In that sense, these different perspectives accomplish the same thing.

Yet, despite the fact that these three perspectives appear to do the same thing in different ways, they do have different implications, or consequences, for the way we understand politics. For example, as we shall see, these perspectives imply distinctly different degrees of integration, or interrelationship, among the substantive areas of study in political science. This, in turn, is closely related to the issue of whether there can be *a* theory of politics or, perhaps, many *theories* of politics. Furthermore, the perspective one takes on the nature of the field has a good deal to do with the concepts he will tend to use in his studies. That is, one's view of the nature of the subject matter has a considerable influence on the language one uses in talking about that subject matter.

SUBFIELDS OF POLITICAL SCIENCE

One way to look at the subject matter covered in political science is in terms of the subfields, or research and teaching specializations, of the field. This has been, and continues to be, a common approach in describing and organizing political science as an academic discipline. Most university curricula in political science are organized around a reasonably common set of subfields, as are the formal requirements for graduate and professional degrees in the field. Furthermore, the more specialized journals, which carry reports of new research and analysis, tend to be oriented toward one or another of the major subfields of the discipline.

As might be expected, the listing of subfields in political science varies a good deal, for example, among different colleges and universities. Some schools have developed particular instructional and research strength in relatively specialized subfields and have therefore elevated these subfields to positions of unusual significance in their curricula. For the most part, however, there is at least a broad similarity among the subfields recognized by most political scientists. The following discussion probably includes a larger number of subfields than would be found in any given college catalogue, but each of these areas has acknowledged significance in many curricula.

It is possible to separate the major subfields of political science into three categories. This threefold breakdown is not common in college curricula, but it is particularly useful for our purposes here. The first category includes subfields that usually are identified largely or wholly on the basis of *spatial* (*i.e.*, territorial or geographical) criteria. The second category embraces subfields identified primarily in terms of *types of activity,* or types of behavior. The third category consists of subfields focusing on the *analysis of ideas* about politics.

SPATIALLY IDENTIFIED SUBFIELDS

There are four subfields of political science that usually are identified spatially or geographically. These subfields are comparative politics, international politics, the politics of a single nation, and the politics of subnational political units.

Comparative Politics

Broadly, we may say that comparative politics is the study of political processes and relationships in a variety of environmental settings. It attempts to explain similarities and differences in political behaviors in terms of differences between the settings in which these behaviors take place.[1]

From the point of view of science, comparative politics is probably the most important subfield in political science. Yet, because of the great difficulty of developing genuinely comparative, reliable knowledge about politics in a wide variety of settings, it has been slow to develop according to scientific criteria. Perhaps paradoxically, recent improvements in the scientific quality of research in comparative politics have been accompanied by increasing confusion about the boundaries of this subfield and what it actually includes.

The subfield of comparative politics used to be called "comparative government." In those days, there was relatively little dispute about what the subfield involved. In fact, it might well have been called "foreign governments," since the field excluded any study of one's own nation. Research was focused primarily on the formal structures of government in the larger Western democracies. Other governments that were studied were viewed as deviations from the norms of these Western systems. There was little interest in nongovernmental activities that are part of the broader political system, nor was much attention given to non-Western or nondemocratic countries.

Since World War II, things have changed considerably in this subfield. There is growing recognition that informal processes outside the structures of government are often highly significant in determining political outcomes. And, in keeping with the growing respect for, and use of, scientific perspectives in the study of politics, specialists in comparative politics have come to understand that the research done on any given country needs to be closely comparable with similar research done on other countries; there has been increasing concern with the use of comparable research procedures and the identification of political concepts that have similar significance in a variety of political systems. In many ways, then, the change from the study of "foreign governments" to the study of "comparative politics" involved a very considerable broadening of that subfield of political science.

Not surprisingly, the broadening of the subfield has made it much more difficult to identify any precise boundaries for it. As we have suggested, most college curricula show the existence of subfields such as parties and interest groups, public administration, public law, and electoral behavior in the field of political science. Yet, it is obvious that the new comparative politics involves the study across national boundaries of all these things. Even more important, the existence of a separate subfield concerned solely with a single state has become more and more difficult to reconcile with the existence of this substantially broadened subfield of comparative politics. If it is the case that reliable knowledge depends so fundamentally on an understanding of political relationships in many different societies, why should the political system of any one country be singled out for such emphasis? If our goal is to understand politics, its processes and its relationships, then why not compare one's own political system with others?

As we shall shortly see, there are some powerful arguments advanced in support of retaining a focus on one's own system of politics as a separate subfield of political science. But we should acknowledge that, from the point of view of developing scientific theory, there is little justification for giving separate status to the study of any single country. This point helps us to understand why the boundaries of the field of comparative politics are increasingly difficult to specify. If comparison is a fundamental part of all science, then comparative politics must be a fundamental part of all of political science.

Indeed, a good many contemporary political scientists suggest that there is no sense in speaking of comparative politics as a subfield at all. According to them, comparative analysis is pervasive throughout the discipline of political science, so that to pick out one subfield of the discipline and attach to it the adjective "comparative" is misleading. From this point of view, it is more appropriate to think of comparison as a *method* to be used in studying all aspects of politics rather than as a subfield of the discipline of political science.

International Politics

International politics is a relative fledgling in the nest of political science, but it is a subfield that has developed rapidly since 1950. It also is a subfield that, like comparative politics, has somewhat vague intellectual boundaries. In the case of international politics, however, the overlap of subject matter historically has been with some of the other social sciences, rather than with other subfields of political science.

Strictly speaking, international politics is part of a cross-disciplinary specialization called international relations. The study of international relations—literally, the various relations between national units—includes a good many phenomena that are not expressly political. That is, nations interact with one another economically, militarily, and culturally as well as politically. These extrapolitical reationships are part of international relations, but not strictly part of the subfield of international politics.

Matters are not quite that simply resolved, however. Historically, the cross-disciplinary specialization of international relations has been taught almost entirely in political science departments. As a result, political scientists who worked primarily in the international-politics subfield found themselves concentrating as much on the explanation of nonpolitical interactions as on that of political interactions. Since 1950, however, specialists interested in the various aspects of international relations increasingly have tried to be explicit in distinguishing international politics from other forms of interactions among nations. Nonetheless, much of the instruction and research in all facets of international relations is done by specialists in international politics.

Because international politics involves the study of interactions between national units, most of which are by definition "foreign countries," students sometimes are not sensitive to the difference between international politics and comparative politics as subfields. The difference is distinct. Comparative politics involves the study of political relationships *within political systems* (not necessarily nation-states) and the comparison of these relationships across systems. International politics, by contrast, involves the study of relationships *between national units.*

The one area of research with which comparative-politics specialists and specialists in international politics have both dealt with some consistency is the study of foreign-policy-making. The overlapping of interest is understandable, since the origins of foreign policy are to be found in both domestic politics and international relations. An understanding of a nation's foreign policy implies a grasp of the domestic cultural, economic, and political factors that influence the decisions of leaders. It also involves an appreciation of the ways in which past relations with other nations have influenced a nation's current foreign-policy stance. Comparative studies of the domestic origins of foreign policy fall, strictly speaking, into the subfield of comparative politics. Studies of past relations with other nations fall, again strictly speaking, into the subfield of international politics. Yet, many of the most distinguished students of international politics have in fact concentrated much of their research broadly on foreign policy, including the domestic sources of the foreign policies of nations.

Politics of a Single Nation

Almost everywhere, political scientists display particular interest in the politics of their own states. This concern can be explained in the same sort of terms as are used below to explain the interest of American political scientists in their domestic political system, notwithstanding the historical emphasis in the United States on its own affairs and concerns.

Despite the intellectually anomalous nature of this subfield, there are persuasive reasons why it has continued to exist in, and in many respects dominate, the field of political science in the United States. In the first place, as we have pointed out, two of the principal tasks of political scientists are the training of citizen-participants in politics and the professional training of political practitioners. In the United States, these goals understandably are focused on the American political process. (To be sure, the importance of citizens and political practitioners alike having a basic understanding of non-American systems and practices is clear.)

A second reason for the central importance of the subfield of American politics is the accessibility of these phenomena for study by American political scientists. Doing systematic research in other countries involves obtaining leave from one's own college, as well as travel and research funds, and, perhaps, having foreign-language competence and professional contacts in other countries. Obviously, it also involves developing a sound understanding of the historical and cultural factors of relevance to one's research. By contrast, research in this country is relatively less expensive as well as less demanding of time and training.

It might be emphasized that the post-World War II trend toward empirical, scientifically acceptable research also tended to promote interest in American politics among researchers in this country. That is, the emphasis on direct and repetitive observations of political phenomena encouraged scholars to conduct their studies where such direct and repetitive observations were most easily facilitated. For American political scientists, this implied research on American politics.

A third, very pragmatic reason for the continuing autonomy of the subfield of American politics has been the requirement in many state statutes of courses in American government as part of both teacher-training and general education programs. One of the results of this kind of requirement has been the tendency for colleges to make courses in American government serve as the introductory course in political science. There are intellectual liabilities in such a curriculum decision; as we have noted, politics in America is quite different from politics in many parts of the world. Understanding *American* politics is of vital importance, but it may not be the most effective way to introduce students to politics *in general*, that is, to politics as a generic kind of human behavior. In recognition of this, an increasing number of colleges are beginning to offer courses that, like their counterparts in the other social sciences,[2] introduce students to the basic principles and concepts of the field, using examples of political activity from a variety of settings.

Politics of Subnational Units

You are not likely to find the phrase "Politics of Subnational Units" on a course description or in a college catalogue. The phrase is a very general one, intended to encompass several similar categories of instruction and research carried on in political science. The most commonly found versions of this category are State and Local Government, Urban Politics, Community Politics, and Federalism. They share the common feature of focusing on political activity in political units *within* larger national units.

In the United States, the study of subnational government and politics has concentrated heavily on this country. Only very recently have American scholars paid much attention to, say, local government in other parts of the world. A recent development, however, has been increasing interest in problems of local government in less-developed countries in Africa, Southeast Asia, and Latin America. A few American scholars also are interested in problems of federalism, that is, relations between national and subnational units of government, in countries with histories of regional cleavage and conflict, as, for example, Yugoslavia.

What, among other things, sets subnational political units apart from national units is their relatively greater dependence on a larger administrative unit. That is, states can be viewed as subsystems of a nation, and communities can be viewed as subsystems of states. This relatively high degree of dependence on a larger, inclusive unit exerts considerable influence on the politics of subnational units. States and localities, for example, may be substantially dependent on the national government for the financing of roads, certain educational programs, disaster relief, and mass-transportation systems. This financial dependence implies a reduced degree of decision-making autonomy for the public officials of states and communities. It also may affect electoral activity within the states. For example, a senatorial candidate from the President's party may be able to argue that his election will result in more favorable economic treatment for his state.

ACTIVITY-BASED SUBFIELDS

Five subfields of political science are identified primarily in terms of activities, or behaviors. These types of activity, or of behavior, can be studied in a variety of settings, although, again, political scientists in the United States have tended to emphasize the American experience. These subfields are (1) public opinion and voting behavior, (2) political parties and interest groups, (3) public administration, (4) public law and judicial behavior, and (5) politics and the economy.

Public Opinion and Voting Behavior

The subfield of public opinion and voting behavior was the first in political science to experience change in the direction of more precise, scientific methods of research. Apparently, this happened for two reasons. First, the data dealing with these subjects were easy to quantify, and quantification, because of its precision, is helpful to science. It is easy to tabulate votes and expressed opinions. Second, survey research (*i.e.*, asking people about their political preferences) provides the opportunity for careful, direct "observation" of the "behavior" in question (*i.e.*, the expression of an opinion by a person being interviewed). Relatedly, some political scientists considered surveys preferable to many other methods of observing "behavior," because surveys permitted the researcher to seek actively just the information he was interested in by asking specific questions. Rather than passively observing political events, the student of politics could, with survey research, actively ferret out whatever he wanted to know about a citizen's perspectives on politics.

In liberal-democratic societies, the expression of public opinion, especially through voting, is viewed as the most basic indication of the citizens' feelings. Public opinions about politics have both factual and normative dimensions; that is, they include both how citizens perceive the political world and evaluations of specific individuals or political practices based on personal values and attitudes. These values and attitudes are often complex and stem from a variety of sources.

Through the identification of public opinion and the study of electoral behavior we can gain some clue concerning the ideological tenets (*i.e.*, the fundamental evaluative criteria against which public personalities and their acts are judged) of a political culture. One of the things that political scientists have learned is that the ideological attachments of the majority of citizens in many societies are primarily to abstract symbols and slogans. People tend to respond to simplified pictures of politics and to build their opinions about politics from a fragile informational base. One of the manifestations of this lack of attention to specific practices is the absence of active involvement in politics on the part of a majority of persons in most societies. In the United States, interest even in presidential elections is relatively low and active electioneering is engaged in by a very small percentage of the population. What we have learned about public opinion and subsequent political participation suggests a substantial degree of political misinformation and apathy on the part of citizens in many different cultures.

The study of public political opinions has tended to emphasize explanations for why people hold the opinions they do. Only recently has concern been shown for the impact of public opinion on the decisions reached on authoritative decision-makers. Political scientists have also come to recognize that it is important to explain not only the apparent origins of votes and other expressions of public opinions but also the *lack* of opinions, informational apathy, and electoral inaction. That is, we have begun to realize that there may be special explanations for the failure to develop coherent political opinions and the disinclination to participate even in the most basic political activities.

The careful reader will notice that, in characterizing public opinions, we have referred to them as "behaviors" but have consistently placed the word "behavior" in quotation marks. We have done this because there is some debate among students of politics about whether an opinion is actually a behavior. We shall return to this issue later in this book, for the debate is far more important than as a mere semantic difference of opinion. For the moment, we should simply mention that, when a person expresses an opinion to an interviewer, it does not necessarily mean that he intends to engage in any specific political act as a result of holding that opinion. In fact, his actions may seem to be inconsistent with his expressed opinions. He may tell an interviewer that he prefers the Democratic candidate for President and intends to vote for him, but he may not end up doing so. Some of the problems presented by this kind of situation will be discussed in subsequent chapters.

Political Parties and Interest Groups

For many people, political parties *are* politics. Parties are, indeed, central to the political process in nearly all systems. In liberal-democratic societies, they function as vehicles for the resolution of conflicts and for the representation of interests in society. Much of the political competition within such systems is competition within and between political parties. Furthermore, a good deal of the political activity engaged in by citizens of liberal-democratic systems is carried out through the structure of the major political parties. Party attachments provide the basis for the voting behavior of large numbers of people, and political parties generally are able to define the issues that will be debated in the political system, especially around election time.

In liberal-democratic systems, political parties aggregate and represent the interests of groups of individuals. We therefore tend to think of parties as important agents in the process of keeping public officials responsible to the mass citizenry. Yet, there are many societies in which political parties are primarily agencies of government itself, instruments for implementing the decisions made by the political leadership. In view of this, one of the important tasks for scholars has been to identify differences among the functions performed by political parties in different systems, to explain the reasons for them, and to assess their impact on the internal organization and operation of the political parties themselves.

The study of political parties is one of the subfields of political science in which comparative analysis has progressed furthest. This comparative research has illuminated differences in the internal characteristics of political parties in different settings, as in the relationships between party leaders and their followers. It has shown differences in the structure and conduct of conventions, congresses, and other general meetings of party members and their representatives. Comparative research has also identified differences in campaign strategies, in ideological positions, and in the bases of support in society enjoyed by political parties of different kinds. Relatedly, a good deal of comparative research has focused on the differences between party *systems*. In particular, important work has been done contrasting single-party, two-party, and multiparty systems.

We may group the study of interest groups into this same subfield with the study of political parties. In modern society, the direct representation of the desires and needs of all segments of the population to the agencies of government is understandably impossible. Consequently, the political order develops institutions and practices that serve as intermediaries between the public and the authoritative decision-makers. Broadly speaking, the purpose of these intermediary practices and institutions is to serve as input channels, conveying the interests and opinions of citizens into the political process.

It is quite clear, however, that not all interests shared even by large numbers of citizens are equally or adequately represented in the political process. Furthermore, the extent of autonomy from governmental control enjoyed by interest groups varies a great deal between different political systems. Even in those systems where interest groups enjoy substantial autonomy, some groups have influence disproportionately greater than the size of their constituencies.

The study of interest groups has focused not only on the means by which they are organized and through which they gain and maintain support but also on the tactics used by them in attempting to influence political decision-makers. These interest-representing activities are carried on in a variety of ways and are directed toward many different points in the political process —for example, toward various agencies and personalities in government.

Public Administration

The study of public administration is one of the subfields of political science that have undergone considerable change in recent years. Formally, public administration involves (a) the application and execution of the laws and regulations enacted by authoritative decision-makers, and (b) the performance of the various public services provided by government.

Recent studies in this subfield have tried to explain the consequences of different organizational and administrative practices or styles for the effectiveness of administrative structures. Efforts are also being made to acquire a precise understanding of the "policy process," that is, the process by which formal decisions are translated into actual policy, with consequences for the lives of human beings.

This distinction between *decisions* and *policy* is important. When authoritative decision-makers (*e.g.,* the Congress, the President, the Supreme Court) select a specific course of action from among the available alternatives, they are making a decision. Decisions, however, have to be carried out, administered, and enforced. Not infrequently, these formal decisions cannot be, or are not, translated faithfully into practice. *Policy* refers to the actual state of affairs, the result of whatever efforts have been made to carry out the decision. The gap between decision and policy is referred to as the *slippage* in the policy process. For example: The position of the Supreme Court and of the Congress on the unconstitutionality of racial discrimination and segregation in public facilities is clear. But a trip through the American South, or, indeed, through many cities throughout the country, suggests that the letter of these decisions has not been translated faithfully into policy. In recent years, the study of the reasons for this kind of slippage in the policy process has been one important focus in the subfield of public administration.

Public administration also includes the study of bureaucracy. Some people argue that the single most important change that has occurred in developed political systems in the twentieth century is the bureaucratization of politics. Because the scope of governmental activity has expanded greatly and the elements of the social order in which government is involved—*e.g.*, the economy—have become tremendously more complex, governmental bureaucracy has expanded as well. Similarly, nongovernmental political organizations, such as parties, have often taken on increasingly complex structures and functions. Public-administration research is investigating how the bureaucratization of political activity has affected other elements of political life.

Public administration as a field of study has displayed an interesting blend of empirical and normative elements. In their efforts to contribute to more efficient and rational management of public affairs, students of the administrative process not only have attempted to identify how that process takes place but have offered numerous suggestions for improving it, as well. Indeed, some of the leading scholars in the subfield of public administration are strong advocates of a normative role for themselves and for their colleagues. They believe that the writings of students of public administration should go beyond the description, explanation, and prediction of those elements of politics having to do with administration and should, additionally, embrace specific recommendations on how the policy process could be improved.

An important concomitant of the recently renewed call for blending empirical and normative elements in public administration has been a growing interest in the study of human relationships within complex organizational structures. One of the frequently asserted characteristics of a growing bureaucratization of political life is a substantial dehumanization of personal relationships. Complex organizational structures, perhaps especially in large corporations and in government, are generally thought to have a depersonalizing and numbing effect on the persons who work in them. Relatedly, it is often asserted that citizens who must deal with these bureaucracies find little responsibility or responsiveness among public servants. Specialists in the subfield of public administration recently have shown a great deal of interest in this problem and have devoted considerable energies not only to identifying its dimensions but also to making recommendations on how it might be alleviated.

Public Law and Judicial Behavior

The study of public law is the study of the constitutional and legal bases for the existence and interrelations of political entities as well as for the relationships between political entities and individuals. As recently as forty years ago, much of what was labeled "political science" in both American and European universities was actually the study of public law. And what has come to be called a "legalistic tradition" exerted great influence on the study of politics until very recently.[3]

There is little doubt that the student of politics must understand constitutions and legal prescriptions. The legalistic tradition in political science emphasizes the study of these formal prescriptions and laws and de-emphasizes the "informal" aspects of politics not explicitly dealt with in constitutions or in bodies of law. Thus, a legalistic perspective on the American Congress or the Presidency would focus on the constitutionally granted powers of each. Similarly, a legalistic approach in comparative government would emphasize the comparison of the constitutions of major countries.

In recent years, the more restrictive, legalistic approach has been broadened, and the subfield of public law has increasingly come to be called judicial behavior, or law and politics. This change reflects the recognition that the content of laws, as well as the mechanisms by which laws are interpreted and legal disputes adjudicated, are very much part of the broader political process. Consequently, an understanding of the content of laws demands the study of the institutions, people, and processes involved in judicial activities.

Recent trends in the field of law and politics, or judicial behavior, have stressed that the essence of the judicial process is decision-making. In this sense, the judicial process has much in common with other elements of the political system. The features shared by other elements of politics and the judicial process sometimes need to be emphasized, because many citizens somehow believe that the court system is "nonpolitical." In some senses, of course, judicial decisions are different from legislative or executive decisions. Still, despite the restrictive framework of law and precedent within which it operates, the essence of the judicial process is decision-making. Further, judicial decision-making is an integral part of the political process: Not only do decisions of the courts have important political repercussions, but, conversely, the judicial process is not insulated from the influence of social and political elements.

For example, one of the important societal functions of the courts is to resolve conflicts. In order for their conflict-resolving influence to be maintained, the courts must attract support for their decisions by making them at least broadly consistent with dominant social and political values in a society. Thus, the political culture exerts influence on the content of judicial decisions. Furthermore, an understanding of the judicial process suggests a need for research on the people who make judicial decisions as well as on the procedures by which they make them. A good deal of research is now being done into the personal and professional backgrounds of members of the judiciary at different levels, and in different kinds of courts, in a variety of political systems. This knowledge has been found useful in predicting the kinds of decisions they are likely to make.

One of the most important elements in the relationship between the judicial process and the broader political process concerns the adjudication by the courts of issues dealing with the legitimate means by which political activity can be carried out.

For example, one of the most difficult problems for any political system is how to define the boundaries of acceptable political dissent. In a democratic system, the presumption is that these boundaries must be broad and reasonably flexible. The courts in several countries have consistently held that, in times of war or other national crisis, individual liberties, especially the right to vigorous political dissent, may be curtailed in the national interest. In deciding upon such questions, the courts perforce become deeply embedded in politics. Judges in these circumstances must make sensitive judgments about the impact of political behavior on the political system, and their decisions will sometimes have great impact on the political future of specific groups within the system.

Politics and the Economy

A subfield of political science that has not frequently enjoyed separate status in the United States, but has been an important field in European universities, is politics and the economy. In Europe, this area of study has been subsumed under the heading "Political Economy."

The study of the relationship between political and economic activity is important for political scientists because public officials—persons selected through, and participating in, the political process—make important economic decisions. That is, government is deeply involved in economic controls and activity in most countries of the world. Governments manipulate the flow of money and the cost of credit, subsidize and tax economic concerns and activities, regulate the degree and nature of relationships between businesses through antitrust legislation and action, regulate public utilities and public communications facilities, and attempt to control aspects of economic production and prices. Such activities clearly are crucial to the affairs of a nation, and the procedures through which governments engage in such activities demand careful study.

The greater attention given to political economy in European universities has been due largely to the historical importance in Europe of political thinkers who stressed the close relationships between politics and economics. For example, Marxian concepts and theories, which stress the interdependence of politics and economics, have been given much more systematic attention in Europe than in the United States. Nevertheless, there has been growing attention in this country to topics that concern government's role in the economy and, conversely, the impact of economic conditions on political behavior.

"THEORETICAL" SUBFIELDS

Two subfields of political science focus on the analysis of ideas about politics rather than on the substantive elements of politics itself. Loosely speaking, these two subfields constitute the "theoretical" side of political science.

It cannot be overstressed that "theory" and "substance" (or "facts") are very closely related to one another. Indeed, *without a blending of both "theory" and "facts," there can be no understanding* of politics or any other subject. This is the most fundamental message of this book. We shall therefore, return to it often.

For now, however, we shall introduce our brief survey of these last two subfields of political science by stressing two senses in which "theory" and "substance" are closely intertwined. First, there is, in fact, theory in every one of the subfields we have already described. There are theories that attempt to explain things about political parties, election behavior, and the judicial process. There are theoretical frameworks for explaining a variety of differences between political systems. There are theories for explaining, and interpreting, international politics.

Second, quite aside from the existence of many theories in political science, theory and substance are *logically* dependent on one another. Theories are frameworks, structures for looking at things. Without substance—without facts to put flesh on the skeleton—theories are not particularly interesting for people who want to understand what the world is like. Conversely, facts are rather like people who desire political influence: Without careful organization, they have little meaning or consequence. Unorganized information is not very useful. More specifically, any given "fact" is more important in understanding reality when it is related to an increasing number of other "facts." Memorizing "facts" is not the basis of understanding. In order to understand factual information, we need to be able to select those facts that are most relevant and important for our purposes, and to collect these important facts together in some kind of meaningful frame of reference and analysis. Theories are designed to provide these frameworks of analysis. Theories help us to *select* information that is relevant and to *organize* that information in such a way that we can better understand the subject at hand.

Empirical Political Theory

As a subfield of political science, empirical political theory involves the study of approaches and techniques by which scientific theories of politics can be constructed. It is concerned both with the development of such approaches and techniques and with their evaluation against the guidelines of scientific inquiry.

We stress the phrase "as a subfield of political science" in the last paragraph. There are, after all, empirical theories—theories based on observational data—of many aspects of politics. As we emphasized above, theory and substance go together. The study of American politics, international politics, public administration, and so forth would not progress very far without theory. In this broader sense of the term, "empirical theory" is a characteristic of all subfields of political science, rather than a distinct subfield. In a narrower sense, however, the phrase "empirical theory" has been used often to describe the analysis of the *methods* by which we attempt to build substantive theories. Because of the focus of this subfield on *methods* of building theory, it is sometimes called *methodology*. Similarly, the important questions that are raised about the ways in which we study politics are usually referred to as methodological issues.

Some examples will serve to clarify the sorts of things that are done in the subfield of empirical theory, or methodology. An assessment of the extent to which Marxian theory accurately and adequately explains relationships between economic and political change would be the concern of empirical political theory. (Note, however, that an assessment of whether Marx was "justified" in his criticisms of nineteenth-century capitalists would be a *normative* concern and, hence, not part of empirical political theory.) An examination of the adequacy of the definition of "power" given in chapter 1 for describing and analyzing Presidential-congressional relations would be a task for empirical political theory. An examination of the usefulness of utility-maximizing models of human behavior (developed in economics and assuming highly rational, goal-oriented behavior on the part of human beings) for understanding voting would be done in this subfield. More generally, methodological work involves efforts to clarify the assumptions behind, and the implications of, commonly used approaches and theories of politics. Students working in empirical theory, or methodology, try to provide guidelines for, and evaluations of, the substantive work of their colleagues who are studying particular aspects of politics.

Methodological concerns also include developing and refining *techniques* by which information about politics can be gathered, organized, and analyzed. For example, one of the ways we obtain information about politics is by conducting surveys, or interviews with selected samples of citizens. A methodological perspective gives attention to such matters as how the sample of persons should be drawn so that it will be representative of a larger population, how the questions in the interviews should be stated and organized, and how the results of the survey can be best tabulated and analyzed. Similarly, methodologists are interested in developing information-gathering techniques such as content analysis, which we may explain through an illustration: Suppose that a student of the American Presidency wanted to know more about the kinds of oratorical appeals used by different Presidents. A principal way to study this subject would be to select some speeches of each President and conduct a similar examination of each speech. This is called content analysis. From a methodological point of view, the student would need to be concerned with such questions as which speeches should be selected and why, how many speeches would be needed for the analysis, what sorts of words should be searched for, and how the significance or importance of different words or phrases should be assessed.

Each of these issues in empirical theory, or methodology, clearly illustrates the inevitable link between theoretical, or methodological, issues and substantive issues. No serious researcher interested in understanding public opinion can ignore methodological issues having to do with the structuring and organization of his questionnaire. Nor can he simply turn over the questionnaire design entirely to someone who knows a good deal about psychological responses to different sorts of questions but nothing about the subject matter of the questions to be asked in this particular study. No student of presidential speeches can ignore the "technical" details of learning how to set up a content-analysis study. At the same time, he cannot reasonably leave the selection of words to be looked for to someone who knows a great deal about semantics and the technique of content analysis but little about presidential politics or American history. Every study requires *both* substantive knowledge *and* a knowledge of the theoretical and technical issues of how the study should be conducted. Although this implies the acquisition of an increasingly broad range of skills by students of politics—and, therefore, some extra effort—the effort seems both necessary and worthwhile. To a certain extent, every student of politics needs to be his own methodologist; that is, students of politics must learn a combination of substantive and methodological skills.

At the same time, political science is not unlike many areas of science, in that technical and theoretical innovations are developing at least as rapidly as, if not more rapidly than, our substantive understanding of things. Because of the importance of trying to keep up with these technical developments, a considerable number of students of politics undoubtedly will concentrate their efforts in the subfield of empirical theory and methodology.

Normative Political Theory

For many years, and certainly until the third decade of the twentieth century, normative political theory, or political philosophy, was one of the dominant segments of the field. It continues to have vitality, although its importance vis-à-vis some other subfields has declined at most American universities.

Courses in "political theory" still usually deal primarily with normative theory, a fact that emphasizes the traditional importance of normative concerns (*i.e.,* values, or "should" and "ought" propositions) among students of politics.

There are two identifiable strains in the subfield of normative political theory. The first consists of the analysis of the normative propositions advanced by prominent political philosophers of both past and present. The purpose of such study is to clarify the origins and implications of their political preferences, that is, of their "ought" statements about politics. This first strain is *explanatory* and *analytical,* in that it seeks to understand why and how certain political philosophies developed, and what impacts these philosophies had on subsequent political activity.

The second strain in the subfield of normative political theory is itself *normative* in nature, rather than explanatory. In this case, the purpose is to evaluate given philosophies, or the apparent real-world ramifications of putting these philosophies into operation, against some set of normative criteria. Philosophies are evaluated in terms of having been (or of being) good or bad in their political effects or right or wrong in their fundamental premises and propositions. Not infrequently, this strain of normative political theory involves evaluating the relevance and propriety of certain philosophical points of view for the solution of contemporary social problems.

It should be emphasized that most college courses in "political theory" involves both of these strains, that is, both explanatory and normative treatments of selected political philosophies. Indeed, some such courses also deal with what we have called empirical political theory, in that they assess the extent to which the *predictions* (as opposed to the preferences) of important political thinkers have proved to be accurate. A blend of normative and analytical perspectives is often present in these courses.

Concern with normative political theory is understandably important for students of politics, as we have already suggested. The political process is central to the management of human affairs, and it involves a multitude of judgments by many persons on the basis of their own preferences, their own normative feelings of what the world should be like.

At the same time, it must also be acknowledged that the normative strain in this field—*i.e.*, the practice of evaluating given political philosophies against normative criteria—is outside the accepted definitions of science and, therefore, is not, strictly speaking, part of political science *as a science*. Yet, this normative strain in political theory has recognized importance in college curricula, and there is no reason to believe that the growing orientation of the study of politics toward scientific goals will result in an exclusion of normative concerns from courses taught in the discipline.

NOTES

1. Precisely what the subfield of comparative politics is trying to explain, and how it should structure these explanations, has been the subject of a great deal of recent discussion among political scientists. An especially interesting perspective is presented in Adam Przeworski and Henry Teune, *The Logic of Comparative Social Inquiry* (New York: John Wiley and Sons, 1970).
2. Part of the impetus for this reorientation of introductory political-science courses seems to have come from the recognition that most introductory courses in the other social sciences are broad, concept-based, and not restricted in focus to any particular country or geographical area, *e.g.*, "Introduction to Sociology" or "Principles of Economics."
3. See Frank J. Sorauf, *Perspectives on Political Science* (Columbus, Ohio: Charles E. Merrill, 1966), pp. 9–21.

4

Political Science as Approaches and Models

As we have seen, one way to divide up the discipline of political science is by looking at the principal *subject matter* covered in the field. Another way is by developing a sense of what political scientists are up to, which one can do by distinguishing some of the major *approaches* used in studying politics; that is, by identifying the perspectives or frameworks from which students of the field see political activity. As has been pointed out, *how* we look at things influences *what* we see, and this chapter gives attention to some prominent "hows" of political science—some important approaches and models used in studying politics.

Just about everybody who studies politics talks about the "approaches" that he or others use. Most political scientists also talk about "models"; unfortunately, however, few of them stop to make even rudimentary distinctions between the two terms. An *approach* is a set of concepts, categories, or terms that serves to focus attention on particular aspects of politics. Usually, an approach is based principally on one central concept that is thought to be especially useful in studying the basic features of politics. The other terms used in the approach derive their usefulness from their relationships with the central concept. The central concepts around which the most prominent approaches to studying politics have emerged are *system, function, communication, decision-making,* and *development.*

Sometimes, but less frequently, approaches are based on *techniques,* that is, on procedures by which we gather and analyze information, rather than on concepts describing the substance of politics. In such cases, a variety of central concepts might be used as part of the approach; the basic feature is the technique. Prominent examples of technique-based approaches to studying politics are *simulation* and *game theory.*

Models can be thought of as refined and more specific versions of approaches. The principal characteristic distinguishing a model from an approach is the presence of explicitly stated relationships among the concepts, or terms, being used. Approaches are sets of concepts. These concepts are viewed as being somehow connected with one another, but the nature of these connections is not made explicit. Models, however, specify relationships among the terms used.[1] When a student of politics adopts an approach, he is simply saying, in effect, "Here are some useful terms which direct our attention to important elements of politics." When he advances a model, he is saying, "Here is a hypothesized series of relationships among some important elements of politics." Because approaches are more general, and less explicit, it is not surprising that more than one model can be developed within a given approach. There is one systems approach; there are several models using a systems approach. There is one functional approach; there are several models based on a functional conception of politics.

It might be mentioned that several prominent political scientists, perhaps out of a sense of modesty or scholarly tendency toward understatement, refer to their models as approaches. David Easton, for example, refers to his "systems approach"[2] and Herbert J. Spiro describes his issue-processing model in terms of a "comprehensive approach."[3] To be sure, the statement of relationships among terms is a matter of degree and, therefore, the distinction between approaches and models, also, is a matter of degree. Because skepticism is an important part of a scientific perspective, some of these prominent scholars tend to be skeptical about the sophistication of their own work. Nevertheless, we shall discover that the extent to which relationships among concepts is made explicit in the work of students of politics such as

Easton, Spiro, and others is substantial enough to warrant considering their work to represent models.

We also should make explicit the connection between approaches and models, on the one hand, and the subfields of political science, on the other hand. Approaches and models are intended to serve as bases for organizing information about most or all aspects of politics. Some models purport to cover more of the political terrain than others do, but the thrust of the development of approaches and models is toward general perspectives capable of embracing a wide range of information about politics.

Consequently, approaches and models overlap the subfields of political science. It is hoped they are useful in studying political parties, bureaucracies, government structures, and interest groups in a variety of systems. Approaches and models thus attempt to *integrate* the substance of politics by cutting across the traditional distinctions among subfields. The use of these relatively broad, inclusive perspectives implies that there may be common features of political activity and behavior in many different institutions and circumstances, and that it may be fruitful to use a common vocabulary in describing political behavior, regardless of where that behavior takes place.

APPROACHES TO THE STUDY OF POLITICS

A Basic Strategic Distinction—Behavioral vs. Institutional Approaches

Before we can examine some of the common concept-based and technique-based approaches used in studying politics, a basic strategic distinction needs to be drawn. This is the distinction between focusing on the political *behaviors of people* and focusing on the *characteristics of (political) institutions*.

There are two reasons why it is important to draw this distinction. First, the trend away from an institutional perspective and toward a behavioral perspective has been one of the most noticeable changes in the field of political science in the last thirty years. Second, the study of government and politics in elementary and secondary schools has been heavily concentrated

on the institutions of government rather than on political behaviors. As a result, most students enter college with an institutional perspective toward public affairs. If this distinction between institutional and behavioral perspectives is made clear,
perhaps the thrust of many college political-science courses will
become more apparent.

The *behavioral* perspective (or "persuasion," [4] or "approach," [5]
or strategy) involves both a particular substantive focus and
a particular intellectual orientation.[6] In terms of substantive
focus, it means emphasizing the political behavior of individuals
rather than the characteristics of institutions such as legislatures,
executives, or judiciaries. In terms of intellectual orientation,
it rests on the conviction that there are discoverable regularities
in political behavior occurring in all settings, and that these
regularities can best be understood by careful, systematic (*i.e.,*
scientifically acceptable) study. If there are such regularities, or
similarities, in political behavior, the study of politics naturally
requires some general approaches and models that will help us
to identify and explain these regularities. That is, you cannot
discover common features in different situations if you do not
have a common, broadly relevant framework for looking at
those different situations.

Whenever we contrast two things, most of us seem invariably
to assume that the two are somehow polar opposites. Our tendency is to make contrasting items of a pair ("dichotomies," social scientists call them) into wholly distinct, irreconcilable opposites. The tendency to simplify our environment into black-
and-white, good-and-bad, hero-and-villain contrasts is powerful.
It is also worth resisting because such simplifications are almost
inevitably grossly misleading. Let us, therefore, begin describing
the institutional perspective by emphasizing that it is *not* the
"opposite" of the behavioral perspective, that "behavioralists"
and "institutionalists" are more than cordial to one another, and
that, in fact, most students of politics use *both* behavioral and
institutional strategies at one time or another.

The *institutional* perspective involves an emphasis on the
study of institutions and their structural characteristics. It is less
inclined toward broad generalization, because it emphasizes the

structural differences between institutions found in different political settings and the great influence of varying cultures on the political institutions that operate within them.

It cannot be emphasized too strongly that the comparative study of institutions in a variety of political settings is a vital and increasingly common part of political science. For example, the comparative study of legislatures is an area of considerable importance in the field. A focus on legislatures is an institutional focus; yet, the comparative cross-national study of legislatures necessarily involves a search for broad approaches, or frameworks, within which many different legislatures can be compared. Consequently, when we say that the institutional perspective is not as inclined toward generalization as the behavioral, we are referring to an *observed tendency,* but not to a *necessary* characteristic, of the institutional perspective.

Someone studying legislatures can, however, adopt either a behavioral perspective or an institutional perspective (or, indeed, both), depending on what aspects of the legislature he wishes to study. Legislatures, after all, like other institutions in human society, are composed of people. When we focus on the actions of the individuals who make up legislatures—on their votes, their speeches, their initiatives in drafting legislation, their interactions with their colleagues—we are studying legislatures from a behavioral perspective. In effect, we are studying *legislative behavior.*

By contrast, one may also study legislatures by focusing on the powers granted to them in constitutional documents, their formal relationships with other branches of government, their organizational structure (*e.g.,* committee structure, membership requirements and composition), or the nature of their outputs (*e.g.,* how many bills are passed and on what subjects). This would be an institutional perspective; the study would be one of *legislative institutions.*

Because of the trend of recent years toward behavioral perspectives in the study of politics, most of the approaches and models commonly referred to are largely behavioral in orientation. As we shall see, however, the study of political institutions is not ignored in some of these approaches.

Concept-based Approaches

Five concept-based approaches to the study of politics will be briefly distinguished. These approaches are centered on the concepts of *system, function, communication, decision-making,* and *development.*

The Systems Approach. Without doubt, the systems approach has become the most popular way of looking at political activity. Its importance is suggested by our early attention to the concept of a political system in chapter 1. Much of the current writing by American political scientists uses, to one degree or another, a systems perspective in describing and analyzing political activity. Furthermore, most of the other approaches that we shall discuss shortly are based on some of the same premises as is the systems approach.

As we have already seen, the concept of a system implies patterned relationships involving frequent interactions and a substantial degree of interdependence among the members of a system, as well as established procedures for the protection and maintenance of the system. The systems approach focuses on sets of political relationships that have these characteristics. The systems perspective thus is concerned primarily with individual behaviors and with the relationships that develop between human beings. It is less concerned with the characteristics of social institutions.

A principal concern of the systems approach is to explain how given political systems maintain their existence over time. In particular, attention is focused on the causes of stability or instability in political systems. Political systems are seen as responding to demands, threats, or supports directed toward them. They must manage these demands, threats, and supports in such a way as to maintain their existence.

In a national political system, for example, individuals, groups, and organizations both make demands upon, and offer support for, government and its occupants (*i.e.,* the persons and political groups occupying authoritative decision-making positions). In addition, the national political system may be faced with demands or threatening circumstances originating outside that system. These demands and threatening circumstances may originate with other national political systems or with capricious developments in the environment. Such external threats may take the form, for example, of military coercion or invasion, economic boycotts, or devastating storms or floods. The national political system must respond to both internal and external demands and supports and must manage these "inputs" by utilizing as efficiently as possible the human and material resources at its disposal.

The systems approach usually implies some concern with the notions of *order, change,* and *goal-realization.* That is, the systems perspective suggests that the maintenance of a system's integrity depends on its ability to maintain order. This involves fashioning regularized procedures by which society's scarce resources can be distributed in such a way that the members of the system are sufficiently satisfied that they will not permit order to collapse and chaos to develop.

Similarly, the systems approach is concerned with how political systems meet the inevitable challenge of change in their environments. No one doubts that the pace of technological and economic change has accelerated tremendously in recent human history. A major problem in the management of social systems is how to adapt human institutions and practices to the real and anticipated material changes in the environment. Adjusting to change is difficult, because change is simultaneously both difficult to contrive and impossible to avoid; that is, human beings have a demonstrated propensity for that which is familiar and instinctively resist conscious efforts to bring about changes in their life-styles. At the same time, human society is faced with the need to adapt to technological and other environmental changes that are, at least in part, beyond its collective capacity to control. Thus, there is a substantial conflict between the necessity of responding to change and the difficulty of engineering specific changes that might seem desirable in human attitudes and behaviors.

The systems approach also suggests the importance of looking at *goal-realization* as a central aspect of what happens in political systems. A principal reason human beings organize themselves into persistent patterns of interaction and interdependence—*i.e.,* into systems—is in order to pursue certain goals they feel are important. Some students of politics who use the systems approach have suggested that no political system can exist over a substantial period of time without articulating and pursuing identifiable goals. The processes by which these goals come to be defined for the system as a whole, and by which members of the system pursue these goals, are important foci in the systems approach.

The Functional Approach. Broadly speaking, the functional approach emphasizes studying the *functions* performed by and within political systems. More specifically, the functional approach looks at institutions and practices in society and asks what purposes these institutions and practices serve for the political order. Because functional analysis gives considerable attention to what particular structures (*e.g.,* political parties, government agencies, interest groups) do (*i.e.,* what functions they perform), this approach is sometimes called the *structural-functional approach.*

The functional approach shares several characteristics with the systems approach, although these two perspectives can be distinctly identified. Functional analysis is similar to the systems approach, especially because it gives considerable attention to the functions that must be performed in order for systems to maintain themselves, and to the extent to which different structures within political systems depend upon one another in order to perform their functions.

The functional approach, however, gives more attention to the nature of the functions that are performed within political systems. It asks what functions, or activities, are necessary in order to keep the system alive and to satisfy the needs and desires of citizens. The lists of functions that have been developed by the various students of politics using this approach understandably vary a good deal. But there is some broad agreement that all systems must, among other things, inculcate supportive values and attitudes in the minds of citizens (political socialization), recruit new political leaders, resolve political conflicts, provide for the representation and organization of the interests of concerned citizens, and make, as well as enforce, authoritative decisions designed to maintain public order. The functional approach attempts to identify activities such as these, as well as the structures, or institutions, in society that perform these functions; to explain the persistence of both the functional activities themselves and the institutions performing them; and to identify the relationships among the various functions that are performed. For example, it seems clear that political socialization and leadership recruitment are closely related, since the availability of a pool of potential leaders committed to maintaining the system depends substantially on the success of the educational and cultural institutions of that system in inculcating supportive values and attitudes in the minds of most citizens.

It should be emphasized that, although the functional approach gives considerable attention to formal structures in society, it takes a behavioral (as opposed to an institutional) perspective on these structures. Indeed, one of the important contributions of a functional approach to the study of politics has been its capacity to focus attention on what institutions *do* rather than on what institutions' characteristics *are*. An important implication of the functional approach is that a given political function may be performed by many different institutions; conversely, a given institution may be involved in performing several different political functions. That is, the functional approach helps us to understand that there is not a one-to-one relationship between functions and structures in society. Many studies done in the late nineteenth and early twentieth centuries implied that legislatures made laws, the executive administered and enforced laws, and the judiciary resolved conflicts about the interpretation or application of laws. By now, we know that such a picture of the functions of political structures is greatly oversimplified. The executive, in the U.S. for example, may make laws, in addition to administering and enforcing them. The judiciary, through procedures of judicial review or legal reinterpretation, can, in effect, make social policy as well as influence the ways in which laws are enforced. The legislature sometimes enacts laws designed, directly or indirectly, to modify the impact of judicial decisions. The legislature may also influence the nature of executive activities by withholding financial appropriations for certain kinds of projects or by appropriating additional sums of money to encourage the executive toward action in areas where it has dragged its feet. The functional approach focuses on this overlapping of structural and functional features of a political system and thereby substantially improves our ability to understand the complex political world in which we live.

The Communication Approach. The basis of all social interaction is communication. Most of the human behavior in which we are interested is communication of one sort or another. To interact with one another, human beings must be able to communicate. Concerned citizens must be able to communicate their needs and desires to government; political leaders, in turn, must be able to communicate to the concerned citizenry the reasons for their decisions, in order thus to provide some basis for public support. More broadly, any kind of organization rests centrally on communication. Consequently, it is not surprising that some students of politics feel that the most useful way to understand the basic features of political activity is to conceptualize that activity as a series of communicative acts.

It should be emphasized that the term "communication," as used in this approach to the study of politics, involves more than merely written and oral speech. One scholar defines communication as "all the procedures by which one mind may affect another." [7] Obviously, then, various behaviors other than speech can have substantial effects on the thinking of others. The study of politics, from the point of view of the communication approach, involves the study of all of those behaviors, including, but not limited to, written and oral speech, that communicate information from one political actor to another. This approach focuses on such things as the channels through which communications among political actors flow, the procedures and rules governing communications within a political system, the instruments that are used in the communications process, the kinds of information contained in these communications, the intensities of feeling that are associated with given messages, and the kinds of responses that can be expected from various political actors who receive specific types of messages.

It should be mentioned that the communication approach, like the functional approach, makes use of the concept of system. Indeed, the theoretical basis for the communication approach centers around the notion of a *feedback system*. Political systems are viewed as organisms that have a specific desired state of affairs, or set of conditions, toward which they are working. They also have barometers, so to speak, that permit them to measure the conditions in which they are operating at any given time. There is always a difference between where political systems are and where they want to be. Political systems must, then, act to reduce the gap between their *actual* state of affairs and their *desired* state of affairs.

If a system is striving to achieve full employment, zero population growth, rapid industrial growth, minimal pollution levels, or an all-volunteer army, it must have communication channels that are sensitive and efficient, so that it knows the extent to which it has achieved any of these objectives. The system must then be able to respond to these communications by allocating its resources in such a way as to maximize the achievement of its goals. This process of responding in a systematic way to the difference between its desired state of affairs and its actual state of affairs is referred to as a feedback process. Systems in which this process takes place can therefore be referred to as feedback systems. The feedback is the information about the state of the system as well as about its previous actions that is returned to it through regularized communication channels. By means of a continuous flow of such information, it is possible for political decision-makers to have a more or less current picture of the success or failure of their actions and of the relative adequacy of their efforts at goal-realization.[8]

Thus, the communication approach to the study of politics may be seen as the study of those communications relating to the goals of the system that are transmitted among important individuals, groups, organizations, and government structures, of the processes by which these communications are transmitted, and of their results.

The Decision-Making Approach. One of the most frequently used approaches to the study of politics in recent years has been the decision-making approach. This is hardly surprising, for the making of decisions is a fundamental part not only of politics but of every other human activity. The concept of decision-making, therefore, has been accorded great importance in nearly all the social sciences, and not just in political science.[9]

Even the principal advocate of the systems approach in political science, David Easton, can be said to use the decision-making approach. That is, he suggests that politics is the "authoritative allocation of values" for a society. Now, as another political scientist, William Riker, has suggested, the notion of "allocation" refers to the process of deciding how resources shall be distributed.[10] That process of deciding is, of course, reasonably viewed as political decision-making. To be sure, Easton's view of the nature of politics from the systems approach involves rather more than the study of decision-making, but it seems clear that decision-making is central to his view of political activity.

Thus, decision-making may be seen as the selection by authoritative political officials of one specific course of action from among two or more alternatives. The study of this act of choice has variously focused on the *origins* of the decision (where the issue that had to be resolved came from in the first place), the *procedures* by which the decision was made, the influence of the *backgrounds of the decision-makers* themselves on the choices they make, the influence of the institutional or organizational *environment* on the decision, and the *content* of the decision itself.

It should be noted that the study of decision-making is part of, but not identical with, the study of policy-making. As we have already suggested, the term "policy" refers to the result of trying to enforce authoritative decisions. Policy describes the actual state of affairs; decision refers to the prescriptions made by public officials concerning what is supposed to be done about something. Strictly speaking, the study of decision-making stops at that point at which an authoritative choice of action to be executed has taken place. The study of policy-making goes further and attempts to explain any differences between the decision and the policy.

The possible usefulness of the decision-making approach seems clear, given the ubiquity of decision-making in the political process. Citizens' votes, selections of candidates by political parties, votes of legislatures are all decisions; the signing of executive orders or treaties by a President constitutes decision-making. The decision-making approach, therefore, makes an important contribution to our understanding of politics, by focusing attention on various aspects of this important kind of behavior.

The Developmental Approach. It is an old notion that the one great constant is change. We know of few societies or political systems that are not changing. Both technological developments and ideological currents create great pressures for fundamental changes in the circumstances in which human beings live.

The developmental approach to the study of politics reflects a special concern for one important dimension of societal change, namely, politicoeconomic development. According to this perspective, economic development brings increasing economic and social complexity and, hence, specialization. To oversimplify, economic development involves the change from a situation in which one artisan or craftsman made many things to an assembly-line situation in which many men are needed to make one thing. Economic modernization is industrialization, specialization, and organization. It has distinct impacts on social relationships. Occupation-based groups and associations are formed, the social class system becomes more complex, and the social and economic role of government becomes broader and vastly more complicated.

Generally speaking, the impact of these fundamental economic and social changes on the political system force it to change from a set of undifferentiated structures to a set of highly differentiated structures. To explain, let us cast this developmental change in terms of extremes: It can be said, for instance, that primitive societies have a very limited number of institutions, which are formally responsible for nearly all aspects of governance; religious, familial, economic, and political functions are performed by the same persons, groups, or institutions. In modern industrial societies, by contrast, we observe a very specialized set of institutions, or structures, performing a highly differentiated set of functions; that is, religious, economic, and political functions are here performed by different structures. Indeed, so diverse and complex have become the political functions that many different structures are required, in turn, to perform them; and hence the existence not only of distinct branches of government (executive, legislative, judiciary) but of political parties, interest groups, and communications media, as well.

It is on the processes by which this structural differentiation takes place, and on the accompanying proliferation, or elaboration, of political functions and structures, that the developmental approach to the study of politics focuses. The developmental approach, therefore, concentrates on such questions as: How does the political system respond to increasing complexity (and, often, conflict) in the social and economic spheres? What new political functions must be performed in response to social and economic changes? How do new political structures, or institutions, develop in response to changing societal needs?

The developmental approach to the study of politics is important not only because of the central significance of change in human society; it is important, as well, because it explicitly provides a *temporal dimension* for the study of politics. That is, the developmental approach explicitly recognizes that things are different today from what they were yesterday and are likely to be different tomorrow from what they are today. It therefore calls on us to think specifically about how political functions and structures are changing; for, to ignore the phenomenon of change is to limit our understanding of politics.

Approaches Based on Techniques

The fact that a useful, well-developed approach to the study of politics could be based on a technique for gathering and analyzing data, rather than on a substantive aspect of politics, is itself a new and rather remarkable development. Until very recently—certainly before the mid-1960's—the notion that a method can be important enough to generate a whole way of looking at politics would have been laughable. That *several* methods are now accorded such significance in political science is an indicator of the remarkable methodological progress made in this field in recent years.

There are several possible technique-based (or method-based) approaches to the study of politics that might be discussed here, but we will content ourselves with two prominent examples: *simulation* and *game theory*. One of the important reasons for choosing these two approaches is that they are related to one another; indeed, are sometimes even confused with one another. But we shall see that, though related, they are, in fact, quite distinct approaches.

The Simulation Approach. One of the difficulties in political science, in contrast to the natural and technical sciences, is that it is very hard to study politics experimentally, that is, in a controlled laboratory situation. For example, a physicist can easily create a vacuum in which he can compare the velocity of a falling feather with that of a lead ball let drop; a chemist can examine the results of combining several mixtures under controlled conditions in a laboratory. But it is a far different matter to conduct a controlled, experimental analysis of human political behavior. President Truman's Cabinet and political advisers cannot be reassembled in the laboratory to find out under what conditions they might have decided not to drop atomic bombs on Japan; nor can the Republican national convention of 1940 be reconvened to ascertain under what sorts of stimuli the choice might have been someone other than Wendell Willkie. In a very real sense, then, human behavior is both highly complex and intimately time-dependent; its "re-creation" in the laboratory seems an overwhelming, if not impossible, task.

Nevertheless, political scientists continue in their attempts to subject political behavior to laboratory study. They do so because they recognize that controlled experimentation has been crucial to the development of every scientific field. Since the basic purpose of scientific inquiry is to specify the likelihood that certain types of events will occur under specified conditions, it follows that being able to study precisely different sets of environmental conditions and their effects is central to science. And the only sure way to control these environmental effects is by studying them in a laboratory situation, where the researcher can experimentally manipulate the conditions under which behavior takes place.

The simulation approach is the closest thing to laboratory experimentation that political science has come up with. Simulations are "operating models"; they are "physical representations of sociopolitical processes." [11] In short, they are efforts to create, under at least partially controlled conditions, working systems that correspond roughly with what goes on in the real world. They are "selective abstractions from reality";[12] that is, they include only a simplified version of what happens in real-world political systems. But what they do include, it is hoped, represents accurately the most important features of that reality. Given the flexibility of such simulations, the researcher is free to manipulate in accordance with need, and in this lies, perhaps, their chief advantage.

A more concrete illustration will serve to sharpen our sense of what simulation involves. One of the best-known simulations in political science is the Inter-Nation Simulation (INS),[13] developed by Harold Guetzkow and others at Northwestern University.[14] The purpose of INS is to re-create certain elements of internation relations in a partially controlled setting and to observe the effects of controlling certain parameters, or boundary conditions, of these relations in particular ways. For example, the researchers operating INS were interested in what would happen to relations among these "simulated nations" if the distribution of military and economic resources were altered in certain ways, or if the "decision-makers" in these "nations" were told that they had certain ideological differences with other "nations" in the simulation.

The "decision-makers" in these simulations usually have been either college students or enlisted military personnel. They have been given imaginary nations (*e.g.*, Erga, Utro, Omne) on whose behalf to act, along with "scenarios" describing the history and contemporary circumstances of their "nations." And, most important, they were given a set of resource capabilities and national goals from which to work. They could enter into alliances, declare war, or sign economic-development or -integration pacts. They could also lose office through election or revolution if they did not satisfactorily meet the needs and demands of influential "groups" within their countries. In short, they were faced with conditions thought to be roughly comparable with those faced by real-world decision-makers.

The behaviors of these simulate "decision-makers" were carefully observed by the researchers running INS, who also introduced quasi-experimental dimensions into the simulations by "creating" economic, military, and political crises. That is, they were able to imitate experimental scientific conditions by manipulating some of the environmental conditions under which the "decision-makers" were operating. In one simulation, for example, the researchers "re-created," as closely as they could, European internation relations as of the beginning of 1914. They then wanted to see whether World War I would occur. It did not!

By controlling the environmental conditions of these political interactions, and then observing the behavior of the simulate "decision-makers," the researchers learned some things about political behavior that they could not otherwise have discovered. We should not hesitate to acknowledge that many scholars have criticized simulations on several grounds, especially on the ground that they usually fail to "reproduce" reality very faithfully.[15] These criticisms have merit; simulation enterprises have problems to overcome, and the process of refining these quasi experiments may be costly and time-consuming. But it also seems clear that simulation has considerable potential as an approach to the study of politics, especially in view of our virtual inability to control and manipulate real-world political events for purposes of scientific study.

The Game-Theory Approach. Game theory, a mathematical technique for studying conflict, was developed originally in economics. It focuses on the selection of rational strategies in situations where two or more parties involved in interaction with one another have at least partially incongruent goals; that is, for one party to accomplish his goals, at least one of the others cannot accomplish his. Situations such as this, of course, are, as we have seen, the cornerstone of politics. A popular way to describe politics has been in terms of the allocation of scarce resources, that is, in terms of decisions specifying who will get what at the expense of whom. Because game theory seems so relevant to this basic characteristic of politics, a good many students of politics have wondered whether it might not serve as a useful approach in political science.

The "classical" form of game theory developed in the early 1940's has been modified, refined, and expanded, so that it is now relevant not only to the choice of strategies in conflict situations but also to the study of *bargaining* and *coalition-formation*. Bargaining, considered by some social scientists to be one of the central social and political processes,[16] may be thought of as the "control of leaders by other leaders"; that is, the process by which two or more persons in positions of power or authority adjust their at least *partially* inconsistent goals in order to arrive at a mutually acceptable course of action. This bargaining process is characteristic of much of the interaction among leaders in political parties, government, and interest groups.

Coalition-formation is also an important aspect of political activity. Political parties, for example, usually are coalitions of different groups and organizations. The Democratic Party in the United States since the early 1930's has been thought of as a coalition of labor unions, ethnic and religious minorities, and intellectuals. The questions of how particular coalitions come to be formed, and how the benefits accruing from the coalitions are divided among the coalition's members, can be studied by using some central concepts and ideas from game theory.

The study of coalition-formation also has been applied to an understanding of decision-making by justices, usually on the Supreme Court. From this perspective, justices are seen as entering into changing coalitions with some of their colleagues in order to maximize their own individual influence and, often, to influence the court's decisions in ideological directions congenial to their own points of view.

The game-theory approach has been applied in several ways to the study of international politics. One way has been to describe the major features of an international conflict in terms of the concepts of game theory and then to see whether analyzing the conflict through the use of the theory itself adds to our understanding of the conflict. For example, one effort involved applying game-theory concepts to the Soviet-American confrontation during the Hungarian revolt of 1956.[17] A result of this study was to suggest that the Soviet Union followed essentially the strategy "predicted" by the game-theory model, while the United States did not. That is, the model suggested that it would have been rational for the United States to exhibit greater support for the uprising, even to the point of threatening (but not carrying out) military intervention. On the other hand, the Soviet military intervention that actually took place in 1956 was essentially the course of action "predicted" by the model. Such a finding, in turn, leads the student of international politics to ask additional questions about the ways in which foreign-policy decisions are made and carried out.

Game theory, it should be noted, is not the same thing as simulation, although both are sometimes called "gaming." Simulation, as we have seen, involves efforts to "re-create" real-world situations by using human subjects (or computers) in a quasi-controlled laboratory situation. Game theory does not "re-create" events; rather, it is a mathematical framework into which information about real-world events can be fitted. This mathematical framework provides a basis for predicting what would be rational strategies for the participants in the real-world conflict (or the "players" in the "game") under given conditions. Simulation is an "operating model" based on experimental foundations. Game theory is an analytical approach, based on assumptions about what constitutes rational behavior in conflicts.

MODELS IN THE STUDY OF POLITICS

As we have noted, most of the approaches to the study of politics are sufficiently broad that each has spawned several models. Models, it will be recalled, are elaborated and refined offshoots of approaches. In particular, they involve the positing of specific relationships among their concepts.

We shall not attempt to cover the considerable variety of

models now in use in political science. In fact, it would be a lengthy undertaking even to summarize the most prominent models that are representative of the several approaches discussed above. Our strategy shall be to look at three models that are frequently used or referred to in studying politics. Easton's input-output model [18] will serve to illustrate the popular systems approach. The model advanced by Almond and Powell [19] combines the functional and developmental approaches, as well as making use of a systems perspective. And Spiro's issue-processing model [20] embraces elements of the decision-making and system approaches. These three models do not, by any means, exhaust the very considerable intellectual creativity of the model-building clan in political science. But they do represent three distinctly different, and yet in a broad sense intellectually compatible, models. each of which has proved to be useful in studying politics.

Before launching into our discussion of these three models, we should pause to take a general overview of the model-building enterprise in political science. Two of the striking things about the study of political science in recent years have been (1) the considerable number of new models offered, and (2) the substantial degree of basic similarity in the assumptions and general approach of these numerous models.

Broadly, we may say that models used in studying politics share the following tendencies: [21]

1. To emphasize the *influence of social, cultural,* and *economic factors* on politics
2. To use concepts that characterize politics as a series of *actions,* or *behaviors,* involved in meeting changing environmental demands
3. To conceptualize political activity in a *systemic* way, with particular attention to the *goals* of political systems
4. To deal, implicitly or explicitly, with the *requisites* (or prerequisites) *for effective operation* of a political system
5. To assign very considerable influence to the activities of *groups* in the political system (a tendency toward what has been called a "group perspective" in looking at politics)
6. To be presented in such a way as to imply their *general*

relevance for the study of politics (*i.e.,* their applicability to politics wherever it is observed)

To a considerable degree, the three models we have singled out for attention here reflect these six tendencies. In this regard, too, they are appropriate to focus our attention on, because they are broadly representative of recent model-building efforts in political science.

Easton's Input-Output Model

Easton's input-output model is based on a systems approach to the study of politics. As we have seen, this approach involves looking at politics in terms of patterned relationships among human beings. For Easton, the interactions that are part of a political system are those interactions through which scarce resources ("values") are authoritatively allocated for a society.

In addition to the concept of *system*, Easton's model is centrally based on the concepts of *input, demands, supports, output, decisions,* and *feedback*. By examining each of these terms and the ways in which they are used by Easton, we can gain a general sense of the characteristics of this model.

Figure 4.1 shows how the elements of Easton's model are related. The political process may be viewed as beginning with a series of *inputs* into the political system. Easton's notion of inputs is a very broad one, encompassing all activities and events that may have an influence on the way that society's scarce resources are allocated. The principal categories of inputs are demands and supports. *Demands* involve statements by individuals or groups in the society to the effect that societal resources, or values, should be distributed in a particular way. Usually, these demands reflect representations by groups of citizens who are interested in increasing their relative share of the values distributed by government. It should be noted that, without the existence of demands, there would be no need for a political system; that is, if everyone were satisfied with the extant distribution of resources, no need would arise to make decisions about who would receive them.

Inputs also include *supports*. The concept of support is also defined broadly by Easton. This term refers to any of the various

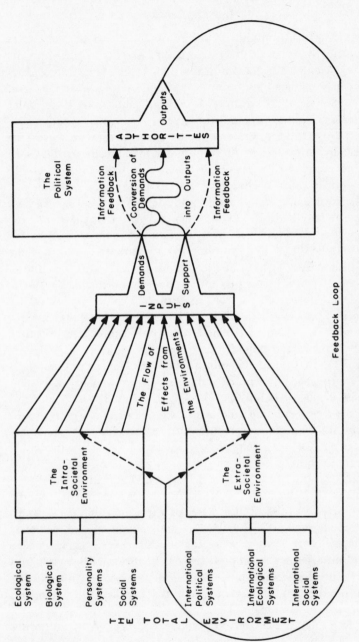

FIGURE 4.1 Easton's "Dynamic Response" Model of a Political System. From *A Framework for Political Analysis* (Englewood Cliffs, N.J.: Prentice-Hall, 1965). p. 110.

ways in which individuals or groups may orient themselves favorably toward a political object; that is, ways in which people support elements in the political system. These favorable orientations may include expressions of opinion or specific actions, and they may be directed toward political objects such as other persons, groups, specific political goals, or given political institutions. In particular, Easton's model suggests that we should be especially interested in those supports that are directed toward the norms, or basic rules of the game, by which political activity is conducted in the system, or toward the specific occupants of authoritative decision-making positions. According to Easton, supports may be diffuse or specific, positive or negative. *Specific* support is that which is given in return for the fulfillment of demands. *Diffuse* support consists of an orientation toward the political system as a whole, its norms, or its authorities and is not associated with any perception that one's demands have been satisfied or attended to. *Positive* support is what we would ordinarily think of as implied by the notion of support: that is, attitudes or actions on behalf of a political object. *Negative* support is, in fact, opposition.

It should be noted that this analysis of demands and supports can be couched in terms of a discussion of how political systems persist through conditions of stress. Since contemporary political systems face increasing amounts of stress, this is one of the most important questions for Easton and, in fact, for the systems approach as a whole. Demands are viewed, in Easton's model, as the basic sources of societal *stress*; supports are the principal mechanisms by which stress is managed and abated. If the system cannot fulfill demands, or perhaps even process them, support for the system will decline. One of the important messages in Easton's argument is that the nature and volume of demands made by citizens must be regulated through the development of cultural norms that place limits on the inputs of demands into the political system. Thus, Easton believes that members of a political order must learn to limit the number and intensities of demands that they make.

The results of demands and supports processed by authoritative decision-makers in the political system are referred to as *outputs.* Outputs consist of authoritative allocations of values, that is, of resources. They are decisions made by authorities concerning the ends toward which the human and material energies of a society will be directed. Outputs may therefore be viewed as the results of having met, managed, or subdued demands through the use of supports and societal resources.

The concept of *feedback* in Easton's model refers to the process by which the political system informs itself about the consequences of its outputs. It is clear that the outputs of the system will have influence on the broader societal environment. Some individuals and groups will be pleased; others will not. As a result, some new supports for the political system, and for the holders of authoritative positions, will be generated. At the same time, some demands will not have been met, and new demands may even be created as a result of the outputs of the political system. In order for the system to understand the changing character of the demands and supports that result from its outputs, it must develop mechanisms by which such information is fed back into the system. These mechanisms are part of the feedback function. The fidelity and effectiveness of the feedback process have a great deal to do with the success with which a political system will meet the challenges and stresses brought to it from the environment. Consequently, feedback has great influence on the likelihood that the system will maintain its integrity and persist through time.

Almond and Powell's Functional-Developmental Model

What Almond and Powell call their "developmental approach" in fact combines elements of a systems approach, a functional approach, and a developmental approach. As such, this model represents a kind of amalgamation of the most recent conceptual thinking in political science.

This developmental model focuses on the functions performed by political systems. The Almond and Powell notion of "political system" is very close to that presented in chapter 1 of this book and similar to Easton's. Almond and Powell introduce a slight variation by giving greater emphasis to the concept of *roles* within political systems. They agree that systems involve interactions among their members, but they look at these interactions as involving *roles* rather than simply persons. Just as a family "system" is made up of the interacting roles of father and mother, husband and wife, brother and sister, so the political system is made up of the interacting roles of voters, legislators, administrators, judges, and so on.[22] These roles involve not only *behaviors* but also *expectations* about the appropriate behaviors to be engaged by oneself and by others performing given roles.

The Almond-Powell model also deals with political *structures*. Structures are sets of roles that are related to another. A legislative seat implies a role; and a legislature is an interacting set of roles, that is, a structure.

This developmental model also places emphasis on the concept of *political culture*. The political culture includes the values, beliefs, attitudes, and skills present in the population. It is important in influencing the ways in which political functions are performed.

Three aspects of the functioning of political systems are discussed by Almond and Powell. The first aspect consists of a system's *capabilities,* its capacities to mold its social environment. Four types of capabilities are mentioned: *regulative, extractive, distributive,* and *responsive*. Regulative capabilities involve being able to coerce the behavior of members of the system. Extractive capabilities permit systems to draw maximum resources from their populations by focusing human energies on a limited number of specifically defined goals. Totalitarian systems, then, have high regulative and extractive capabilities. Distributive capabilities involve being able to shift societal resources from some groups in the population to others, that is, to redistribute resources. Responsive capabilities reflect the extent to which demands from different societal groups are consequential in shaping the regulative, extractive, and distributive activities of the system.

A second area of functioning takes place *within* the political system. Almond and Powell refer to these activities as the *conversion functions*. The six conversion functions are crucial to this developmental model. They are

1. *interest articulation*: how demands are formulated
2. *interest aggregation*: how interests that have been articulated are then pulled together (often, by political parties) in such a way as to provide major alternative courses of action on important political issues (*e.g.,* alternative platforms and candidates in elections)
3. *rule-making*: how laws are formulated and decided upon;
4. *rule application*: how laws are applied and enforced;
5. *rule adjudication*: how the application of laws is interpreted and adjusted in individual cases (*e.g.,* in the event of disagreement over the proper mode of application of a law)
6. *communication*: how the other conversion functions of the systems are communicated to members of the system and to the system's environment, including other systems

The third set of systemic functions in the Almond-Powell model involves *system-maintenance* and *system-adaptation* activities. These functions are *political socialization* and *recruitment*. Political socialization is the process by which members of the systems are taught values, beliefs, and attitudes that are supportive of the system. Recruitment is the process by which persons are brought into the political roles that must be performed. Obviously, these two functions are essential if a system is to maintain itself in existence and adapt to changing environmental conditions.

Although we have been referring to the Almond-Powell model as a "developmental" one, we have said little so far about the study of development, which is a central feature of this model.

Broadly speaking, Almond and Powell propose that we study the development of political systems by focusing on the *changing relationships among* the three types of *functions* and on the *changing relationships between structures and functions.* As we noted earlier in this chapter, political development involves, in part, a change from a situation in which very few structures perform many functions each to one in which there is a proliferation of many specialized structures, each performing only certain aspects of a limited number of functions. Or, as Almond and Powell indicate, development results when existing structures within the political system are unable to cope with given problems or challenges without introducing further structural differentiation.[23] As we have already pointed out, the tremendously increased economic, technological, and social complexity of modern society assures that change will continue to be a central feature of politics. The Almond-Powell developmental model is useful in getting an intellectual handle on that change.

Spiro's Issue-Processing Model

The Spiro issue-processing model combines some elements of the systems approach and the decision-making approach. But it goes beyond either of these and is therefore generally more difficult to categorize. The issue-processing model has received less attention by students of politics than have the Easton and Almond-Powell models, perhaps because it seems, at first glance, to be more complex or involved than the other two. As a result, it requires a lengthier introduction to students who have not used it before, which is worth the effort, considering how useful this model can be to students trying to organize their ideas about politics.

For Spiro, a political system is a community of individuals processing (*i.e.,* trying to define and do something about) *issues.* The existence of "community" is dependent upon the presence of persons who consciously pursue a finite set of *goals.* Thus, community rests fundamentally on the notion of *goal consensus.* One type of community is a political system. A political system, however, is based on the existence of some measure of *dissensus* on the *means* by which a set of common goals should be achieved. This dissensus manifests itself in political *issues.* Therefore, political systems exhibit goal consensus, but dissensus on the procedures by which these goals can best be realized.

In addition to the central concepts of *issues* and *goals,* the Spiro model also focuses on, and interrelates, the concepts of political *problems,* political *styles, decision-making ("resolution"),* and *policy ("solution").* It should also be mentioned that the Spiro model depends on the concept of *system,* since the goals, issues, problems, styles, and behaviors with which Spiro is concerned are those of systems.

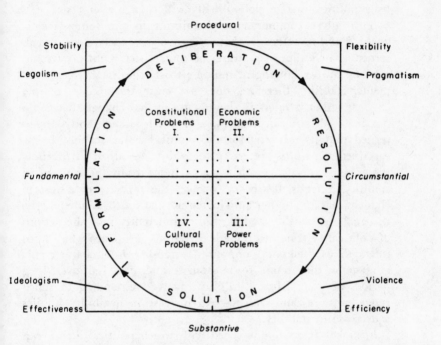

FIGURE 4.2 A Diagrammatic Representation of Spiro's Model for the Comparative Analysis of Political Systems. Adapted from *American Political Science Review*, LVI (September, 1962), 580.

According to Spiro, all political systems pursue, with various emphasis, four basic goals: *stability, flexibility, efficiency,* and *effectiveness.* (See Figure 4.2) A political system probably will emphasize the pursuit of one or two of these goals at a given point in time. Furthermore, the principal goal or goals being pursued by a political system undoubtedly will change over time.

Spiro gives common-sense definitions to the four systemic goals. *Stability* refers to the absence of unexpected or unpatterned change. Spiro is aware, of course, that political systems are constantly changing in response to changes in their environments. Stability, therefore, does not mean the absence of *any* change; rather it refers to the absence of that change that could not reasonably be anticipated, and which is sufficiently unpatterned that its meaning for the political system cannot be ascertained. *Flexibility* refers to the ability to adjust to precisely those kinds of changes that are excluded from the concept of stability. That is, flexibility involves the capacity to adjust to changes that are neither anticipated nor patterned. Consequently, the goals of stability and flexibility inherently pull the actions of political systems in different directions. They are what Spiro refers to as "temporal opposites": stability is a characteristic of systems that tends to be sought and achieved over long periods of time; while flexibility involves responding to short-range pressures and changes. An increase in flexibility implies a decrease in stability.

Efficiency refers to the speed with which political action can be taken. It explicitly excludes any consideration of whether the action will have the desired effects in the long run. *Effectiveness,* by contrast, refers to the long-range staying power of political action. It refers to the extent to which enacted policies provide lasting solutions to the issues and problems toward which those policies were directed in the first place. Efficiency and effectiveness, then, also may be viewed as "temporal opposites." Emphasizing efficiency is likely to decrease the long-range effectiveness of political action. A successful emphasis on effectiveness is less likely to be achieved through efficient (*i.e.,* rapid) action.

Spiro's model takes a more moderate, and less absolute, posture toward goal realization than do some other models in use in political science. Specifically, this model recognizes that a system may fail to realize fully one or more of its basic goals without ceasing to exist. Spiro's model focuses on the evaluation of the *"relative* success of political systems . . . by the degree to which they manage to sustain a dynamic equilibrium among the four basic goals." [24] Ideally, political systems will give attention to all goals all the time; but, practically, this is unlikely to be the case. A variety of environmental pressures, coupled with a limited amount of material and human resources, will tend to focus the attention of the political system on one or two goals at a given time.

The nature of the goals pursued by political systems determines the character of the issues that will be processed by the system. Political issues, according to Spiro, can be identified along two dimensions. The first is the *fundamental-circumstantial* dimension. Issues are said to fall somewhere between a fundamental character and a circumstantial character. *Fundamental issues* are recurring, long-range concerns that have always been with us and probably always will be. An example would be the issue of how to keep the food supply and the population roughly in balance. *Circumstantial issues* are those that arise on short notice, perhaps have not arisen before, and may not arise again. A stark example of a circumstantial issue confronting the decision-makers of a political system would be the presence of unidentified blips on a radar screen. It should be emphasized that the fundamental-circumstantial dimension is a temporal dimension, and is not necessarily related to importance. That is, the basis of deciding the extent to which an issue is fundamental or circumstantial rests on the longevity of the history of the issue in question. Circumstantial issues are every bit as significant for a system as fundamental issues.

The other dimension along which issues can be described is the *substantive-procedural* dimension. *Substantive* issues are "what" questions; they contain the substance of what should be done. *Procedural* issues are "how" questions; they concern the methods by which action should be taken.

It should be stressed that these issue dimensions are continua, and that a given issue must be placed at some point between

the two extremes on each dimension. For example, Spiro suggests
that there are few issues that are wholly fundamental or wholly
circumstantial; generally, they fall somewhere in between. Similarly, there are few issues that are wholly procedural or wholly
substantive. Even a cursory examination of the legislative proposals before the U.S. Congress, for example, would show that
questions of "what" and "how" are closely intertwined. Whether
we decide to do something depends, in part, on whether we
believe we have the legal mechanisms and resources available to
do it. That is, the "what" of political choice is substantially influenced by the "how" of practical politics.

An examination of Figure 4.2 shows the relationship that Spiro
posits between the goals that a system pursues and the issues
that it must process. When a system concerns itself with the goal
of stability, it is processing fundamental-procedural issues. When
a system concerns itself with the goal of flexibility, it is processing procedural-circumstantial issues. When the focus is on the
goal of efficiency, the issues are substantive and circumstantial.
And when the goal is effectiveness, the issues are substantive and
fundamental.

These goals and issue dimensions are, in turn, related in a
specific way to the sorts of problems encountered by political systems. Again, a glance at Figure 4.2 reveals Spiro's position on
these relationships. *Constitutional and legal* problems are said to
be associated with the pursuit of the goal of stability and with the
processing of procedural-fundamental issues. *Economic* problems
are supposed to be associated with the goal of flexibility and with
the processing of procedural-circumstantial issues. Problems having to do with the distribution and exercise of *power* are associated with the pursuit of efficiency; these power problems surround the processing of circumstantial-substantial issues. Problems of *cultural conflict* are associated with the pursuit of the
goal of effectiveness; these cultural conflicts have to do with
the processing of fundamental-substantive issues.

Similarly, the political *styles* exhibited by a system are linked
to the nature of the problems with which it must deal. Constitutional problems are tied to a style of *legalism*. That is, when
a system is excessively concerned with constitutional problems,

to the exclusion of others, we say that it has a legalistic style. When a system preoccupies itself with economic problems, its style would be called *pragmatic*. When problems concerning the distribution and use of political power become central, Spiro asserts that the style of the political system is likely to be *violent*. And when cultural conflicts constitute the principal problems confronting a system, the style of that system is likely to be *ideologism,* that is, a preoccupation with ideological concerns.

While, at first glance, these relationships among issue dimensions, goals, problems, and political styles might seem complex, they are, in fact, simple. Indeed, one of the characteristics of the Spiro issue-processing model is that the relationships among its major concepts are deterministically stated; that is, it is not possible for the relationships among these concepts to vary in different political systems. Stability is always associated with constitutional problems, fundamental-procedural issues, and a legalistic style. Efficiency is always associated with power problems, circumstantial-substantive issues, and a style of violence; and so forth.

Although it is accurate to assert that the relationships among these concepts in the Spiro model are deterministically stated, there is considerable face validity, or reasonableness, to what the model suggests. For example, Spiro's argument that the goal of stability is generally linked with constitutional and legal problems in society is fully consistent with what students of politics have been saying for many years. Some of the most important sources of systemic stability are thought to be the agreed-upon legal and constitutional documents specifying the rules under which political activity can be conducted. In a similar vein, it is reasonable to link the goal of flexibility with the economy, since the economy reflects the dynamics of technological change, and these changes, perhaps more than any other dimension of human activity, demand flexibility in the responses of authoritative decision-makers. Given Spiro's definition of efficiency (in terms of the rapidity with which political action can be taken), it is also logical to link the goal of efficiency with problems in the distribution and use of power. It is often the case that the only efficient way to reach controversial political decisions in a complex, modern society is through the fairly bold application of political power.

We could go on exploring the logic of the relationships that Spiro suggests, but it does not seem necessary here. The general point to be made is that the relationships offered in this model seem reasonable and provide a relatively simple handle by which students of politics may grasp the relationships among the principal elements of political activity.

The Spiro issue-processing model also hypothesizes a four-stage process by which issues are resolved and solved. This process involves the common-sense notion that issues must first be formulated, then deliberated and decided upon, and, finally, solved through the enforcement of these authoritative decisions. For our purposes, what is especially important is that the Spiro model explicitly recognizes the difference between *decision* (resolution) and *policy* (solution). According to Spiro, there can be substantial slippage between the formal prescriptions of decision-makers and the actual policies carried out in the real world. This slippage is brought about by two kinds of circumstances, both of which are depicted on the lower part of the scheme (see Figure 4.2), where the solution phase is located. The circumstances leading to decision-policy slippage have to do with the power held by persons responsible for enforcing decisions and with the values, beliefs, and attitudes that constitute the political culture of the persons to whom these decisions must be applied. If the authorities responsible for enforcing a decision do not have adequate power at their disposal to overcome opposition to the substance of the decision, there will be a greater degree of slippage. Similarly, if the persons to whom the decision is to be applied have values that are directly contradictory to the substance of the decision, it will be more difficult to bring about compliance on their part. Hence, the Spiro scheme also suggests important relationships between the different phases of the policy-making process, on the one hand, and the other dimensions of political systems—*i.e.,* goals, political problems, and styles—on the other hand.

One of the interesting implications of the Spiro model is that a given issue may change in its basic characteristics while it is being processed. That is, as an issue moves from formulation, through deliberation, to resolution and solution, it may take on different characteristics, although the substance of the issue may remain essentially the same. As an illustration, we may look at conflicts surrounding race relations in the United States. An examination of Figure 4.2 should help to guide us in pursuing this point.

Race-relations issues are initially problems of conflicts within the culture, that is, of conflicts between the values, beliefs, and attitudes held by different groups of citizens. As the issues of how to handle race relations are better formulated, and as they move into the deliberation stage, legal and constitutional questions arise. That is, it is necessary to ask what the existing laws and constitutional provisions say about race relations and to consider the possible changes in these legal and constitutional prescriptions that might improve the basis for handling race relations. As deliberation on this issue progresses, there is increasing recognition that some of the most important manifestations of racial difficulties are economic in nature. That is, some of the ways in which discrimination has most graphically affected minority groups are reflected in their relatively underprivileged economic circumstances. At the same time, the substantial number of persons of minority group status in the United States creates an economic impetus to attempt to resolve issues surrounding race relations. Minority groups represent important segments of the country, and their continuing subsistence economic circumstances clearly create economic difficulties for the system as a whole. In addition, the resolution stage of handling this issue must increasingly give attention to questions of political power. Voter-registration drives among American blacks, for example, and the increasing militance of some minority groups in pursuing their social, economic and political concerns, brought decision-makers to realize the implications of racial problems for the distribution of political power. This twin recognition of the economic and political importance of race-relations problems served as important spurs toward concrete action on the part of authoritative decision-makers.

Once a series of these decisions had been made, the substantive problems involved in enforcing those decisions became apparent. These problems had to do with the ability of enforcement agencies, for example, to carry out faithfully prescriptions against discrimination and segregation. They also had to do with the extent to which the values, beliefs, and attitudes of significant groups of citizens were consistent with the new governmental prescriptions on this issue. That there has been considerable slippage between resolution and solution is clear. This exercise of examining the changing character of an important political, social and economic issue in the United States illustrates the usefulness of the Spiro scheme in relating the policy-making process to other aspects of the political system.

Approaches, Models, and the Study of Politics

There is no such thing as a person interested in politics who does not use an approach, or a model, in organizing the information he has. As we have noted, unorganized "facts" are not very helpful in understanding things. When we discover something new, we ask ourselves, "What does it mean?" What it means is determined by how it fits into what we already know. And we cannot decide how it "fits" unless we have something to fit it into. This something is an approach to, or a model of, politics.

Consequently, what sets Easton, Almond, Powell, and Spiro apart from most of us is not that they would like to be "abstract" or "theoretical." On the contrary, it is that they are trying to be explicit and concrete about how they understand politics. Each of us should do as much. No one proposes that every student of politics devise his own approach or model. That is not only impractical but undesirable. For, if reliable knowledge is based on the accumulation of comparable information from many different studies, then we ought to be working toward a few common frameworks, rather than proliferating numerous, disparate ones.

But it is important for each of us to be explicit about the assumptions with which we approach the study of politics. Let us hope that our assumptions and frameworks will be sufficiently close to one or more of the sets of ideas advanced in this chapter that we will feel comfortable adopting a framework that has already proved useful. In any case, we should disabuse ourselves of any notion that "theories" are for "eggheads." Without frameworks—approaches or models—within which we can accumulate and relate information, there is no understanding. This simple fact testifies to the importance of familiarizing ourselves with prominent approaches and models in political science.

NOTES

1. For a review of literature discussing the general characteristics of models, see Robert T. Golembiewski, William A. Welsh, and William J. Crotty, *A Methodological Primer for Political Scientists* (Chicago: Rand McNally, 1969), pp. 427–48.

2. The original version of Easton's approach appeared in David Easton, "An Approach to the Analysis of Political Systems," *World Politics*, IX, no. 3 (April, 1957), 383–400.

3. Herbert J. Spiro, "Comparative Politics: A Comprehensive Approach," *American Political Science Review*, LVI, no. 3 (September, 1962), 577–95.

4. See Heinz Eulau, *The Behavioral Persuasion in Politics* (New York: Random House, 1963).

5. Behavioralism is viewed as an "approach" by many writers, including James C. Charlesworth, "Identifiable Approaches to the Study of Politics and Government," in Charlesworth (ed.), *Contemporary Political Analysis* (New York: The Free Press, 1967), pp. 1–10.

6. See David Easton, "The Current Meaning of 'Behavioralism' in Political Science," in James C. Charlesworth (ed.), *The Limits of Behavioralism in Political Science* (Philadelphia: The American Academy of Political and Social Science, 1962), pp. 1–25.

7. This usage is from Warren Weaver. See Claude E. Shannon and Warren Weaver, *The Mathematical Theory of Communication* (Urbana: University of Illinois Press, 1959), p. 95.

8. Richard C. Snyder, H. W. Bruck, and Burton M. Sapin, *Decision-Making as an Approach to the Study of International Politics* (Princeton, N.J.: Organizational Behavior Section, Foreign Policy Analysis Project, Foreign Policy Analysis Series No. 3, 1954), p. 88.

9. See James A. Robinson and R. Roger Majak, "The Theory of Decision-Making," in Charlesworth (ed.), *Contemporary Political Analysis*, pp. 175–88.

10. William Riker, *The Theory of Political Coalitions* (New Haven, Conn.: Yale University Press, 1962), p. 10.

11. Richard A. Brody, "Some Systemic Effects of the Spread of Nuclear Weapons Technology: A Study through Simulation of a Multi-Nuclear Future," *Journal of Conflict Resolution*, VII, no. 4 (December, 1963), 671.

12. Richard C. Snyder, "Some Perspectives on the Use of Experimental Techniques in the Study of International Relations," in Harold Guetzkow, Chadwick F. Alger, Richard A. Brody, Robert C. Noel, and Richard C. Snyder, *Simulation in International Relations: Developments for Research and Teaching* (Englewood Cliffs, N.J.: Prentice-Hall, 1963), p. 4.

13. INS has subsequently been renamed the Simulated International Processes (SIP) project. Most of the published discussions of this project, however, refer to INS.
14. A good overview of INS can be gleaned from Guetzkow *et al.*, *Simulation in International Relations,* especially chapters 2 and 5.
15. A discussion of this and other problems with the INS project can be found in Golembiewski, Welsh, and Crotty, *A Methodological Primer for Political Scientists,* chapter 9.
16. See, especially, Robert A. Dahl and Charles E. Lindblom, *Politics, Economics, and Welfare* (New York: Harper, 1953).
17. William A. Welsh, "A Game-Theoretic Conceptualization of the Hungarian Revolt: Toward an Inductive Theory of Games," in Frederic J. Fleron, Jr. (ed.), *Communist Studies and the Social Sciences: Essays on Methodology and Empirical Theory* (Chicago: Rand McNally, 1969), pp. 420–65.
18. See Easton, "An Approach to the Analysis of Political Systems," *op. cit.;* Easton, *A Systems Analysis of Political Life* (New York: John Wiley and Sons, 1965); and Easton, *A Framework for Political Analysis* (Englewood Cliffs, N.J.: Prentice-Hall, 1965).
19. Gabriel Almond and G. Bingham Powell, *Comparative Politics: A Developmental Approach* (Boston: Little, Brown, 1966).
20. Herbert J. Spiro, "Comparative Politics: A Comprehensive Approach," *American Political Science Review,* LVI, no. 3 (September, 1962), 577–95.
21. For a discussion of the common features shared by several frequently mentioned models of politics, see Golembiewski, Welsh, and Crotty, *A Methodological Primer for Political Scientists,* pp. 241–61.
22. Almond and Powell, *Comparative Politics: A Developmental Approach,* pp. 19–20.
23. *Ibid.,* p. 34.
24. Spiro, "Comparative Politics: A Comprehensive Approach," p. 578.

5

Political Science as Basic Concepts
of Political Activity

A third way to view the content of political science is through some basic concepts describing important political activities. Since, however, students of politics are far from agreed on what the most central, or salient, aspects of politics are, the list of such concepts is potentially interminable. In this chapter, we shall sample only a few of the most commonly used ones.

CONCEPTS AS HANDLES

The German word for "concept" is *Begriff*, from *Griff*, meaning "handle." A concept, therefore, is a kind of verbal handle we use to grasp and communicate the essential features of something in which we are interested.

As is the case with much of the apparatus of science, there is not universal agreement on what the notion of a "concept" itself means; one writer [1] has identified six distinct ideas about the nature of concepts. For our purposes, it is sufficient to adopt what seems to be the most straightforward of these notions, namely, that a concept consists of the verbal *label* we attach to something, plus the *verbal definition* we give to that label. Thus, a concept of "influence" might consist of the definitional statement, "Influence is A's ability to bring B to do something that A wants him to do, regardless of whether B wants to do it."

Concepts are the cornerstones of human communication. The effectiveness of our communication with others depends a great deal on the clarity with which we convey our concepts, that is, on the clarity of the definitions, or meanings, we attach to the terms we use.

At the same time, conceptual definitions are suited primarily for general, verbal discourse and are less useful when we decide to take a closer look, for example, at a specific political object or situation. Suppose we want to discover the extent of influence exerted on a congressman by certain presumably powerful interest groups. Talking in somewhat abstract terms about "A getting B to do something" does not focus our attention very effectively. A more precise notion of "influence" is required.

We call this more precise notion an *operational definition*. Any concept that is to be used in a concrete study must have an operational definition. The purpose of this operational definition is to indicate what specific information will be accepted as constituting evidence of the occurrence of the phenomenon to which the concept refers. Or, to put this another way, an operational definition specifies the activities ("operations") necessary to identify—in our last example—"influence." In the case of interest-group influence on a congressman, we might *operationalize* "influence" in terms of the number of times the congressman changed a previously stated position in order to vote as the interest group had urged him to vote on legislative bills. This more precise rendering of the concept of "influence" would be consistent with the more general conceptual definition but would permit us to examine "influence" in a specific, concrete situation.

We shall say more about the relationship between conceptual and operational definitions in subsequent chapters. For now, it is enough to recognize that concepts are general, verbal definitions that ultimately require more precise operational definitions to become useful in studying politics.

As might be expected, the most important concepts used in the study of politics have been given various definitions, both conceptual and operational. That is, not all students of politics agree on the verbal definition, for example, of "power," and there has been an even greater variety of operational definitions used in various studies. We offer here some common conceptual and operational definitions, without, however, asserting that they are more, or less, useful than other possible ways of looking at these important concepts.

INFLUENCE AND POWER

We suggested in chapter 1 that influence and power are closely related terms. More specifically, we indicated that power is a special case of influence. That is, power relationships meet the general criteria for influence, but power additionally includes a more specific factor, the threat or use of *sanctions*. Let us explore the nature of these two concepts more explicitly and make the relationship between power and influence more explicit, as well.

We have suggested that A influences B to the extent that A gets B to do something that B would not otherwise do. This includes not only situations where A induces B to undertake an action but situations, also, where A influences B to go on doing something that B is now doing, and which B would stop doing if it were not for the influence of A.

The astute reader no doubt already recognizes that influence is much easier to define conceptually than to measure operationally. It is one thing to talk in general terms about A's influencing B; it is quite another thing to go into the real political world and discover the precise nature of relationships of influence. Two sorts of problems present themselves to the student of influence. One is that it is sometimes difficult to find the appropriate evidence to support our ideas about people influencing one another. For example, determining, in a reliable way, whether Congressman Snort voted for a farm-subsidy bill because of the influence of powerful agricultural lobbies, or out of spite, because his estranged wife urged him *not* to vote for the bill, can be very difficult. Similarly, discovering whether the good congressman would have voted for the bill in any case, even without the encouragement of interest lobbies, can present research problems. A second problem is that statements about influence and power really are interesting only if they provide a basis for *comparing* the influence exercised by different individuals or groups: It is only marginally interesting to be able to make noncomparative statements about the influence of a single political figure or interest group; it is much more interesting and useful when we can compare the relative amounts of influence exercised by a variety of political actors. Saying that the National Association of Manufacturers (NAM) is "very influential" is not nearly as meaningful as saying, for example, that the NAM exerts more, or less, influence than does the AFL-CIO on wage-price legislation. As we have said, comparison is crucial to understanding and meaning.

Measuring Influence

Robert A. Dahl, the political scientist who perhaps has contributed more to our understanding of the nature of influence and power than any other student of those subjects, has suggested five bases on which students of politics might try to measure and compare amounts of influence.[2] Dahl suggests the following:

1. *Identify the amount of change in the position of the person being influenced.* This idea rests on the assumption that a person may be influenced to change his ideas or his behavior only a little bit, a good deal, or a great deal. To illustrate, let us take the hypothetical case of a long-time Democrat who favors the presidential candidacy of one of his party's most conservative leaders throughout the primaries. As primaries come and go, it becomes clear that his preferred candidate does not enjoy widespread support and, thus, does not have a chance to gain the party's nomination. Sensing this, two of this old Democrat's friends decide to persuade him to change his allegiance to one of the two principal contenders for the party nomination, one of whom is considered a "moderate," the other, very "liberal." If the supporter of the more liberal candidate for the nomination can persuade his conservative friend to switch his allegiance, then a greater amount of influence will have been exercised than would have been the case if our conservative Democrat had changed his allegiance to the moderate, or middle-of-the-road, Democratic candidate.

2. *Examine the "subjective psychological costs of compliance."* This idea for measuring influence rests on the assumption that it is psychologically more difficult for some people than for others to make the same sort of change in attitude or behavior. For example, we have every reason to believe that it was relatively easy for some Democrats to switch party allegiance and support Richard Nixon for President in 1972, while other Democrats found such a switch psychologically very difficult. For some people, switching party allegiance in a presidential election is not a difficult matter. For others, it can be psychologically and emotionally very unsettling.

3. *Identify the scope of the influence exercised.* Some people are able to exercise influence on the actions of others in many different areas of human activity. Other persons may be highly influential along one or two dimensions of human activity but have no influence whatever in other areas. For example, in many local communities economically powerful individuals may exert a considerable influence not only on economic activity but on the political and social structure of the community, as well. On the other hand, a clergyman may influence his congregation on matters having to do with religious doctrine and ethics but may have no impact whatever on their economic, political, and social behavior. Such difference in the scope of influence of leaders is one of the most important means of distinguishing totalitarian, authoritarian, and pluralistic political systems. In totalitarian systems, as the root of that word ("total") implies, the political authorities attempt to influence nearly all aspects of the daily lives of citizens. In authoritarian systems, the political leadership attempts to exercise influence over all aspects of politics as well as over those other elements of individual behavior that are considered relevant to politics. In pluralistic systems, by contrast, the political authorities seek influence only over those aspects of human existence that are defined by the citizenry itself as being relevant for authoritative action. That is, in pluralistic systems government presumably acts at the behest of the politically active segment of the population and exerts authoritative influence only where this politically active citizenry believes authoritative influence should be exercised.

4. *Identify the number of persons who respond to an act of*

influence. A straightforward approach to measuring influence is to identify the number of persons who are influenced by a given act. An example of this approach can be applied to local machine politics as traditionally practiced in some large cities in the United States. One of the important elements of machine politics has been the capacity to "deliver" blocs of votes. The ward- or precinct-level political leaders are thought to be able to "produce" sizable numbers of votes; yet, some of these leaders evidently can produce more votes than others. It is reasonable to assert, then, that the person who can "influence" the largest number of voters has more influence than other leaders, whose influence does not embrace as many voters.

5. *Measure the size of the difference in "probabilities of compliance."* In this case, Dahl suggests that we focus on the likelihood that an attempted act of influence will be successful. We know that the President of the United States is frequently in touch with principal congressional leaders on questions concerning important pieces of legislation. He may speak with important committee chairmen, for example, on several occasions during each session of Congress. But how likely is it that a given committee chairman will yield to the President's wishes? Will he probably change his position and go along with the President three times out of four? Seven times out of eight? Nineteen times out of 20? Taking this approach to the measurement of influence recognizes that even very powerful political leaders will not always be successful in their efforts at influencing political outcomes. It is therefore important to try to establish the *probability* that their efforts at influence will bear fruit.

Power and the Powerful

As we have said, power is a special case of influence. A power relationship is present if the influence being exercised rests on the threat or use of sanctions, positive or negative. Another way of putting this is that power is *coercive influence.* Coercion, it should be noted, can be negative or positive. Negative coercion is based on the threat of punishment, whereas positive coercion is based on the prospect of gain.

One of the more interesting questions concerns who really has political power. Several different approaches have been used to determine who the powerful persons in a political system are. We shall briefly mention three of these approaches here.

First, the easiest way is probably to assume that the powerful are those who *occupy important positions in political institutions.* Because of the great powers at the disposal of the chief executive, one can simply assume that a President, a Prime Minister, or a Chancellor has a very high degree of power. (A similar assumption might be made at the local-government level about a mayor or a city manager.) Or, because of the judicial-review powers of the U.S. Supreme Court, it might be assumed that any man holding appointment to the Court could exercise a lot of power.

This simple and straightforward approach is likely to avoid any sort of confusion or argument about what persons should be studied. Official hierarchies are usually pretty well defined. The occupants of positions can be clearly identified, and information is often readily obtainable about persons who occupy such formal positions. At the same time, this approach has a great liability, because it is based on the dubious assumption that real power is directly related to formal position. There is a considerable amount of evidence that suggests this is not always the case. The "powers behind the scenes" may be instrumental in the selection of persons to occupy formal positions, as well as in the determination of what kinds of political issues shall be acted upon by government or by important political groups. The politics of many countries show the history of periodic influence of "kingmakers," men and women who never held high formal office but who are generally considered to have been crucial in shaping the histories of their nations. Similarly, powerful persons may prefer anonymity to the public attention focused on holders of formal positions. The most effective use of power may occur when power is exercised away from public scrutiny.

A second approach to identifying the powerful is to study *who participates in the activities* that are considered most important to the management of political affairs. Usually, this means studying participants in decision-making. If an otherwise uninformed observer merely looked at the formal positions held by Presidential advisers, such as President Nixon's foreign-policy adviser,

Professor Henry Kissinger, he might well not assign great importance to these individuals. But a focus on the apparent decision-
making activities that have taken place around the presidency
in recent years would suggest that some advisers, such as Kissinger, have exerted great influence on important political decisions. Of course, it must be kept in mind in using this approach
that participation in decisions does not necessarily indicate power
or influence. It is perfectly possible that a Supreme Court Justice
could participate in every decision by the Court during a given
term but always fall in the minority among his colleagues, and
thus have no discernible effect on the substance of the decision
taken or on the long-run thinking of the Justices as a group.
Similarly, the confidential secretary to the president of a Latin
American republic might well participate in nearly all decisions
made by the chief executive without necessarily having any, or
consistent, influence on the decisions themselves.

A third approach to identifying the politically powerful is to
rely on the judgments of well-placed observers. That is, the student of politics can identify individuals who presumably are
close to the activities under study and inquire in detail of them
who the really powerful participants in this activity are. Naturally, the meaningfulness of this approach depends largely on the
knowledgeability of the judges we select. It is often difficult to
know just who the most astute and candid observers of, say, the
local political scene in Council Bluffs, Iowa, might be. Simply
put, some people think they know more than they actually do.

This discussion suggests that the concrete study (*i.e.,* the
operationalization) of the important concepts of influence and
power can be rather more complicated than one might at first
imagine. This is not to say that these concepts should be rejected by students of politics. One well-known political scientist
was once quoted as saying that the concept of power is "something
we can't do much with, but we can't do without." There continues to be general support among students of politics for the
notion that power and influence are central to an understanding
of political activity. Consequently, it behooves us to be as careful
and as explicit as possible in our efforts to identify influence and
power as they appear in the political process.

DECISIONS AND POLICY

In chapter 1, we introduced the concept of decision-making. We suggested that decision-making was a process involving the selection, by persons in positions of power or influence, of a particular course of action from among two or more competing alternatives. Decisions, therefore, are the objects on which the decision-making process is focused. That is, decisions are prescriptions, or statements of commitment to action, made by persons who have power or influence.

It should be noted that decisions are not the same as policies. In chapter 4, while discussing the Spiro model, we introduced this important distinction between decisions and policies. We adopted the shorthand notion that decisions constituted acts of resolution, while policies constituted acts of attempted solution; that is, policies result from efforts to enforce decisions. The concept of policy, therefore, refers to what is actually being carried out, or enforced, in the real world.

As we have said, there can be considerable slippage between decision and policy. Even though the U.S. Congress and the Supreme Court may make decisions decreeing an end to racial discrimination in public institutions and facilities, the ability of enforcement agencies to carry out the tenets of these decisions may be limited. If we view the actual state of enforcement of authoritative decisions as constituting policy, then it cannot be said that current public policy excludes segregation and discrimination in race relations. The decisions of authoritative political bodies have indicated a commitment to an end to segregation and discrimination, but there continues to be significant slippage between decision and policy.

Students of politics have developed numerous ways of looking at the decision-making process. We will consider three of them, which can best be represented in terms of three questions:

1. What are the *steps,* or *phases,* of decision-making?
2. What are the *principles guiding* decision-making?
3. What are the *factors influencing* the nature of the decision-making process under given conditions?

Steps in Decision-Making

Many students of politics find it helpful to look at decision-making in terms of the steps or phases involved in reaching a decision. By now you have learned enough about the study of politics to guess that there must be considerable disagreement about what these most important steps or phases should be called. But it is possible to identify certain common features in the various existing lists of decisional steps. Most step or phase characterizations of decision-making suggest that the process consists of

1. the *definition* of an issue as being important enough to warrant attention on the part of decision-making groups
2. the *gathering of information* about the circumstances surrounding the issue
3. the *formulating of alternative courses of action* that might be pursued in handling the issue
4. some decisions on the *rules or procedures* that will be followed in making the final selection of a course of action (*i.e.*, decisions about who is ultimately responsible for a final decision and *how* that final decision will be reached)
5. the estimation of *likely results* of pursuing each of the possible alternative courses of action
6. the final *selection of one course of action* from among several
7. a subsequent *appraisal, or assessment of the success* of the decision, especially as reflected in enforced policy, in handling the original issue
8. the decision *to end consideration* of this issue *or to reformulate* the issue for continued action (in the case of negative evaluations of the effect that the decision has actually had in terms of policy)

In other words, students of politics now recognize that decision-making involves rather more than sitting around a table in a smoke-filled room and choosing some course of action. It also involves the careful gathering of information, the precise formulation of possible courses of action, the careful evaluation of those alternatives, the act of decision itself, and a subsequent evaluation of whether the decision, as taken, constitutes an adequate response from the decision-making group. To be sure, many political decisions are taken without the kind of care and thoroughness implied by this list of decision-making steps. Sometimes, political decisions must be made under considerable time pressure, and the information-gathering and -evaluation functions may be slighted. But, in general, these eight steps provide us with a reasonably accurate impression of the process of political decision-making.

When, for example, the President of the United States, has to make a major foreign-policy decision, he first seeks a wide range of intelligence information, both from agencies of his own government and from his country's allies. He will seek, too, the counsel of informed experts who will help him in the formulation of alternatives. These alternatives are likely to be debated by several different groups, including both formal agencies that are part of the government structure, such as the National Security Council, and informal, *ad hoc* groups summoned together by the President and including principally his foreign-policy advisers. Once a decision has been made and ordered into effect, the President and his staff will watch closely to see whether it is being carried out faithfully, or whether further action will be necessary to secure its enforcement.

Similarly, when the Congress considers action on a social issue, the proposed legislation is referred to a committee specializing in the subject matter involved. The committee staff, as well as the individual staffs of congressmen on the committee, will gather a wide range of information to assist the committee in its deliberations. The committee most likely will consider not only the specific legislative proposal before it but also alternative plans, perhaps in the form of suggested amendments to the original bill. Its ultimate recommendation to the house of which it is a part (the Senate or the House of Representatives) will itself be debated in turn, and perhaps substantially modified, by the full membership of that house. Further, once Congress has acted and the legislation has been signed into law, the congresssional committee that was principally involved in handling the legislation may wish to hold subsequent hearings concerning problems in enforcement of the law. Thus, in the cases of both presidential foreign-policy decision, and congressional action on social issues, the basic steps of the decision-making process outlined above are very likely to be followed.

Principles of Political Decision-Making

The second way to look at the decision-making process is to describe it in terms of the principles that guide, or perhaps *should* guide, decision-making. The people who write about decisions from this perspective sometimes are guilty of implicitly confusing the "is" with the "ought" of decision-making. That is, they sometimes list principles that supposedly *do* guide decision-making when, in fact, they are advancing *idealized* criteria against which the actions of decision-making groups might be evaluated. It is important, for reasons we have discussed in chapter 2, to keep these empirical and normative elements distinct, though, admittedly, this is sometimes easier said than done.

For example, one of the principles that supposedly guides governmental decision-making is the *principle of rational action*. It is sometimes asserted that actions of governmental agencies (or, indeed, of any organizational bureaucracy) are efficiently designed to achieve consciously selected political or economic ends. Whether any organization staffed with human beings will ever operate in a wholly rational way is questionable. It depends, of course, on what one means by "rational." If one means something like never engaging in behavior that is counterproductive, or which runs against the purposes of the organization, then absolute rationality is probably unlikely. Yet, it remains true that most discussions of decision-making principles depend, explicitly or implicitly, on some notion of rational behavior.

It might be interesting to examine the principles of governmental decision-making advanced by Anthony Downs.[3] Professor Downs's principles strike most people as being rather idealized. Probably they are difficult to realize in any absolute way, but they do, nevertheless, provide an interesting focus for examining the actual decision-making process in politics. In addition to the principle of rational action, Downs offers five other guiding principles:

1. *The principle of self-interest.* Professor Downs asserts that any organization or governmental agency is always ready to sacrifice the interests of any other organization or agency if there is a perceived conflict of interests. The only exception to this would be a situation in which an organization believes that its long-run existence depends on the sufferance or good will of another organization or agency.

2. *The principle of identifiable utility.* It is argued that no organization wishes to provide benefits either to its members internally or to its constituents externally unless the recipients can clearly identify the source of those benefits. In other words, political decision-making is based on the premise that you do not give someone something unless he knows exactly from where he is getting it.

3. *The principle of goal permanence.* Organizations are not expected to alter their basic goals on short notice. The tactics they use in pursuing their goals may legitimately change, but their goals do not. Part of Downs's argument is that organizations become strongly committed over time to a given set of goals, and that it is therefore extremely difficult to bring them to change their idea of what they are, and should be, doing.

4. *The principle of marginal operations.* Here, Downs, using a principle of hard-nosed market economics, asserts that governments and organizations do their best to pursue this sometimes elusive economic principle. Specifically, he argues that governments and organizations increase their expenditures only until the support-gain (*e.g.*, vote-gain) of the last dollar they spend equals exactly the support-loss (*e.g.*, vote-loss) of the last dollar they financed, that is, obtained through taxes or other assessments. To put this another way, governments or organizations spend money as long as their expenditures result in a net gain of votes or other types of support. At the point at which spending more money would result in no additional support-gain, or in support-loss, they stop spending money. From this perspective, the possible social value of the programs for which additional

money might be spent is a secondary consideration. The important thing is pay-offs in the form of political support.

5. *The principle of the rule of an articulate and concerned majority*. Downs was concerned primarily with describing decision-making within the context of a pluralistic democratic system. He was aware, however, that even under highly democratic conditions genuine majority rule is rare. Even in a democracy, he suggested, the "majorities" whose wishes are respected are majorities of articulate, concerned citizens. That is, the people who constitute "majorities" are people who feel particularly involved in certain political and social issues, and who succeed in organizing in such a way that their views are clearly articulated to decision makers. As another political scientist, E. E. Schattschneider, has suggested, a relatively small part of the population may constitute an articulate and concerned majority on any given issue.[4] Indeed, there is a considerable bias in the system of representing interests in most societies, with the result that many people are systematically excluded from opportunities to influence government decision-makers. It is possible to extend Downs's view of the nature of majority rule even to less democratic systems, by making use of his concepts of *consensus of views* and *consensus of intensities*.

On the basis of what Downs says, we can suggest that, in any political system, other things being equal, government will be likely to choose in its decision-making the alternative preferred by an articulate and concerned majority only when that majority reflects both a consensus of views and a consensus of intensities. For there to be a consensus of views, a majority of the persons affected by the issue must favor one course of action over all other possible courses of action. For there to be a consensus of intensities, the articulate and concerned citizens in the system must agree on which issues are the most important ones to be acted upon by government. Only when this articulate and concerned majority agrees both on which issues are most important and on what should be done about the most important issues is government likely to be constrained by the feelings of this group of citizens.

Obviously, much of what Professor Downs says is based on the notion that governmental and organizational decision-making consists of a series of rational acts. In fact, some people might view with alarm the hardheaded, calculated rationality implied by some of these principles. Whether they correspond closely with reality is an empirical question; that is, it should be possible with careful research to identify the extent to which political decision-making proceeds along these lines. Looked at from this perspective, the Downs scheme may be useful to students of politics regardless of whether his list of principles is thought of as a statement of what "is" or as a statement of what "ought to be."

Factors Influencing Decision-Making

A third way to look at the decision-making process is in terms of the numerous factors that influence it under different conditions. In a sense, the Spiro model introduced in chapter 4 may be viewed as such a perspective on decision-making. That is, Spiro sees decision-making as the interaction of four factors: political goals, the types of issues being processed, the nature of the political problems encountered in the pursuit of these goals, and the personal, organizational, or system styles that characterize efforts to resolve these issues.

Two other students of politics who have adopted a roughly similar perspective are Richard C. Snyder and James A. Robinson.[5] Their writings, though focusing on factors that influence decision-making, refer to a different set of concepts from Spiro's. Snyder and Robinson are interested in directing our attention to such considerations as:

1. What are the characteristics of the *unit of decision?* Who are the major participants, and what are their personal characteristics? What are the elements of the *organizational context* in which a decision takes place? How highly formalized are the relationships among the members of the decision unit? Are there formal rules and procedures that guide their deliberations? Or is the group essentially of an *ad hoc* nature, with little formal structuring in its interactions?

2. What are the characteristics of the *setting* in which the unit of decision must operate? Is the unit of decision part of a govern-

ment structure, a political party, or some other politically relevant organization? What scope will the decision have? Is this to be an authoritative decision, to be enforced by the coercive powers of government? Or is it a decision of a recommendatory nature, which may affect a small number of persons, and which will not be backed up by authoritative sanctions? In a slightly different vein, is the immediate environmental context in which the decision must be made likely to affect the nature of the decision? Is there a crisis at hand, for example? Must the decision be made in a matter of minutes, hours, or days?

3. What is the *origin* of the decision-making situation? Was the decision forced upon the decision-makers, or did they themselves initiate concern for the issue at hand? Relatedly, does the situation call for specific action, or would continued inaction be an acceptable alternative?

4. What is the pattern of *motivations* characterizing the decision-making process? What do the decision-makers consider to be the goals of the decision-making unit itself or of the organization or broader society for which the decision must be made? What personal motivations do the decision-makers individually bring to the process of selecting a course of action? What high priority values or norms do the decision-makers see as being involved in their decision?

The work done by Snyder and Robinson has been considerable, and one can identify from their writings other, more specific factors of importance in understanding the decision-making process. For our purposes, however, the above examples will serve to illustrate the way they look at decision-making. They also are particularly aware that decisions must be compared with one another. Consequently, they are interested in knowing what factors are important in accounting for differences in the content of decisions made either by different groups or by the same group operating at different points in time.

The importance of a clear understanding of the political decision-making process cannot be overstated. As we have suggested in chapter 4, several of the principal approaches used in the study of politics depend implicitly or explicitly on the concept of de-

cision-making. Surely, decision-making is one of the most important activities constituting the political process, in large part
because, as we have said, the material and human resources available to any society for the solution of its problems are always
limited. Decisions must be made on how these resources will be
allocated. Hence the importance of the concepts of decision and
policy in understanding the nature of political activity.

CONFLICT

As we have seen, conflict is one of the central features of
political life; it is a necessary characteristic of modern society.
Even the smallest political units include individuals from varying
educational and cultural backgrounds. These persons have different ideas about what should be done with the resources available in their environment. They develop and express their concerns about resource allocation in different ways and through
different institutions. Sometimes, they observe different norms, or
rules, concerning the ways in which they should pursue their
interests; they act with different degrees of feeling, different intensities of commitment. Because societies have limited resources
at their disposals, there is competition for access to, or control
over, these resources. This competition is manifested in conflicts
among individuals, groups, and organizations, such as political
parties or interest groups.

It is worth emphasizing that conflict, as a basic fact of life,
need not be violent or unstructured. For, while, to be sure, a riot
may be viewed as a conflict, so, too, may a presidential election.
A wide-scale purge of political opponents by a dictator in a less
developed nation may be viewed as a manifestation of conflict;
so may, at the same time highly civilized but persistent differences
of opinion among members of the British Cabinet about how a
dock strike should be handled.

The existence of conflict as an everyday part of life helps under-
score the fact that the efforts directed by society toward the
handling of conflict aim at conflict *resolution,* or *management,*
rather than at the *elimination* of conflict; for erasing conflict is,
for all practical purposes, impossible. We must live with conflict.

Indeed, it can well be argued that the existence of effectively managed, institutionalized conflict is the hallmark of a society that permits and encourages participation of all its citizens in the political process. Consequently, when we speak of the efforts made by societies toward the resolution of conflict, we should understand that the goal of these efforts is conflict management, and that any notion of eliminating political conflict in contemporary society is patently naïve.

One of the reasons conflict is a fundamental fact of political life is that conflict is often the product of change. It is frequently the case that technological, economic, or other environmental changes bring about redistributions of society's resources. When such redistributions occur, some people will become disadvantaged. Those who lose ground will seek to regain what they have lost and will organize their efforts toward influencing another re-allocation of resources. When this occurs, of course, there is conflict. Much of the conflict resulting from these kinds of changes, it should be emphasized, may be at least partly outside the capacity of political officials to control. The political leadership in a society must respond to such changes just as the citizenry must do, although leaders have a greater variety of resources directly at their command.

Explaining Differences Among Political Conflicts

Conflicts may vary in their specific origins, in the ways in which they are handled, in their duration, and in the intensity of feeling or commitment that they manifest or generate. Students of politics have examined numerous factors that help explain why some conflicts last only a short time, are handled through existing societal mechanisms, and do not generate intense feelings, while others are much more disruptive of society, invoke much greater intensity of feeling, and may last for what seem like interminable periods. Five sets of factors are most commonly mentioned in explaining these variations among conflicts.[6]

1. The *goals* toward which conflict behavior is directed may be significantly different: The pursuit of the presidency or of the Chancellorship, for example, may imply higher stakes to the par-

ticipants than an effort to gain a seat in Congress or in the Bundestag. The alteration of racial attitudes may be a more intensely pursued goal than the protection of gold as the basis for international monetary transactions.

2. The *resources* available to various conflicting groups are likely to be significantly different. Schattschneider has persuasively argued that the interest-group system in the United States, for example, involves a heavy bias such that a certain limited number of interests have massive resources with which either to broaden or to dampen conflict, while other interests are poorly organized and lack meaningful resources to pursue their concerns.

3. The *institutions* or *structures* through which conflict is pursued and ultimately handled may be different. As we have suggested, one of the important differences among political systems is in their ability to handle conflicts through existing institutional structures. For example, it is generally argued that legislative institutions provide particularly useful frameworks within which major societal conflicts might be resolved. One of the tests of the effectiveness of legislatures rests in the success with which they are able to deal with the major issues of conflict presented to them. Similarly, students of politics believe that the process by which conflicts are resolved varies between institutions. For example, the conflict-resolution process in the executive branch of government is likely to be closer to a command or decree style, while bargaining and compromise are perhaps more likely to characterize legislative conflict resolution.

4. The *norms* and *mores* that set the bounds on permissible conflict behavior are different, both for between political systems and for different conflicts within the same political system. The norms of fair play and societal mores on questions such as the bribery of public officials are substantially different in various cultural settings. What is corruption to one man may be the effective use of legitimate political power to another. Similarly, students of politics have sometimes asserted an inverse relationship between the magnitude of the stakes involved in a conflict and the degree to which ethical constraints limit the behaviors of the participants in the conflict. That is, the higher the stakes, the less ethically constrained conflict participants may feel.

5. The *strategies* chosen by the parties to the conflict may vary. In some cases, participants in a conflict may wish to expand the arena of the conflict to involve a larger number of individuals or additional levels of government. Other parties to the conflict may wish to limit the arena of conflict. According to Schattschneider, the conflict participant who perceives that he is losing usually wants to expand the arena of conflict. Whoever is winning would prefer to keep the conflict confined to whatever institutional framework is being used. For example, in the 1950's and early 1960's, supporters of efforts to reduce racial discrimination and segregation in the United States felt that they had to expand the arena of conflict both horizontally and vertically if they were to have a meaningful opportunity to realize their goals. They needed to involve the federal government, for state governments had failed to take adequate action; and they needed to involve persons of a variety of racial backgrounds in order to demonstrate the breadth of existing concern with the problem. In a similar vein, the strategies used in efforts to resolve conflict may vary a great deal. Because the modes of conflict resolution are so important to an understanding of politics, it is to this subject that we now turn.

Modes of Conflict Resolution. The usual eclecticism and variety prevails among students of politics when it comes to identifying the principal methods used in resolving conflicts. For our purposes, at least six distinct modes of conflict resolution need to be identified.

Two closely related modes of conflict resolution, which we shall treat as one here, are *tabling* and *displacement*. In a sense, each of these strategies is a kind of avoidance mode. It involves not actually dealing with a given conflict, but rather focusing attention on a "substitute" conflict that might be capable of draining off energies that had been devoted to the other conflict, and which might also be more easily resolved. Not only is it the case that resources available to deal with important societal conflicts are limited, but the energies and attentions of the political authorities who must ultimately deal with these conflicts can be stretched only to a point. Thus, a conflict may be tabled or displaced even though it is considered to be a high-priority problem by everyone concerned.

It is worth emphasizing that the procedure of displacing, or substituting, conflicts can have profound effects on the balance of political forces in a society. This point is argued forcefully by Schattschneider.[7]

> *The substitution of conflicts is the most devastating kind of political strategy.* Alliances are formed and reformed; fortresses, positions, alignments and combinations are destroyed or abandoned in a tremendous shuffle of forces redeployed to defend new positions or to take new strongpoints. In politics the most catastrophic force in the world is *the power of irrelevance which transmutes one conflict into another and turns all existing alignments inside out.*

He discusses, for example, the tremendous impact on American politics when the societal cleavage over the slavery issue was replaced by the conflict between agrarian and industrial interests after 1896. In a parallel way, the rising level of societal conflict in the late 1960's over American involvement in the Vietnam war, and, relatedly, over defense and space spending, undoubtedly contributed to the failure to give appropriate attention to certain other pressing issues, including environmental concerns and proposals for reform of certain aspects of the political structure.

A second and related mode of conflict resolution consists of *redefining* the nature of the conflict. According to one political scientist, Paul H. Conn, conflict redefinition usually involves getting parties to the conflict to focus on *specific* aspects of the problem rather than on the *general* issues that have been raised. Conn suggests that conflict redefinition can be particularly important in military battles.[8]

> For example, let us consider a border dispute between two countries. At first there may only be limited skirmishes. As the struggle becomes more involved, however, the original dispute often spreads to a conflict between two types of political systems. The charges multiply and the rhetoric becomes increasingly general and bitter. By this time all-out fighting has broken out, and the possibility for negotiation has decreased.

Conn suggests that the only way to resolve such conflicts is to get the involved parties to focus on the initial skirmishes and on the means by which such skirmishes might be avoided in the future. Thus, conflict resolution may rest on the extent to which it is possible to redefine the conflict in terms of specific confrontations that can be negotiated rather than in terms of fundamental problems of life-style, cultural difference, or ultimate virtue of one position or another. Such a strategy seems to have been used in winding down the Soviet-Chinese border conflicts at the beginning of the 1970's.

A third mode of conflict resolution is *resource expansion*. When a government is faced with conflicts over the distribution of scarce resources, it may find that the most efficient way of handling the problem is to divert resources that had been devoted to another kind of activity and thus make possible at least substantial satisfaction of the demands of all parties involved in this conflict. The conflicts during the 1950's and early 1960's over the funding of education in the United States and in other developed countries provides an important example of the use of resource expansion as a mode of conflict resolution. In general, national governments increasingly recognized that resources would have to be diverted from other uses to the support of educational programs. As a result, many of the potential and real conflicts among subnational government units over the allocation of national resources for education were avoided or substantially reduced, at least until the late 1960's.

A fourth mode of conflict resolution may be characterized as *imposition* or *command*. In the relatively unusual situation in which a decision-maker can threaten reprisals for a continuation of conflict, as well as allocate the resources at issue, he may utilize a command style of conflict resolution. In this case, the conflict is resolved by fiat; one point of view or another is selected as the preferable one, resources are allocated pursuant to that decision, and reprisals are threatened against the unsuccessful parties to the conflict should they choose to continue pursuing their concerns. Such circumstances are rarely found in pluralistic systems and are probably increasingly unusual even in highly structured political systems, such as those of the Soviet Union, mainland China, or Spain.

In systems where there is relatively little mass participation in politics, but where there are several competing groups of political leaders, or elites, a common mode of conflict resolution may be *bargaining*. Bargaining may be viewed as a form of reciprocal conflict management among leaders.[9] The bargaining process, which implies some compromising of partially inconsistent goals by parties to the conflict, is widespread within government structures, such as legislatures. The process of moving a proposed piece of legislation through Congress, for example, may consist primarily of a series of compromises and bargaining agreements among legislative leaders, on the one hand, and among organized opponents and proponents of the bill, on the other. In such a situation, the direct influence of the political leaders' constituencies is minimal. The essence of the process is leaders bargaining among themselves, attempting to resolve their differences through compromise, and perhaps persuasion.

A final principal mode of conflict resolution may be characterized as *competition*. In this case, there is minimal involvement in the conflict on the part of "third parties." That is, neither government agencies nor potentially concerned nonparticipants become involved in resolving the conflict. It is left essentially to the original participants to arrive at some kind of joint termination of the conflict. A neighborhood fist fight or, in some senses, a gangland war might constitute examples of competitive conflict resolution. Generally speaking, however, competition as a means of resolving conflicts is rare, indeed, in contemporary society. Precisely because such conflicts concern societal resources, there is a broadly felt need for collective social action. This exercise of social responsibility toward conflicts over resources more often than not implies governmental involvement at some level. Indeed, the very notion that a principal purpose of the political process is to resolve significant social conflicts argues that unstructured, unimpeded competition among conflicting parties is unlikely to continue for very long. Further, as we have already suggested, whichever party is not doing well in a given conflict situation is likely to seek the involvement of other groups and institutions, probably including government, in an effort to better its position. Thus, conflict resolution is deeply imbedded in the fabric of the political system.

LEADERSHIP RECRUITMENT AND BEHAVIOR

The concept of *leadership* was introduced briefly in chapter 1. Leadership consists of the ability to mobilize human resources in the pursuit of specific goals. It therefore refers to a relationship between people. This relationship may involve the exercise of influence or power as well as participation in decision-making. Since we have already discussed these concepts, we will not devote additional space here to discussing the obvious ways in which leaders engage in these activities or are part of these kinds of relationships. Instead, we shall address ourselves to three questions that have been given much attention by students of political leadership: What are the additional characteristics of leadership as a kind of relationship? What are the most important characteristics of leaders? How do people become leaders, that is, how are political leaders recruited?

Authority and Mobilization Skills

In addition to involving the exercise of power and influence and participation in decision-making, leadership also implies the presence of *authority and organizational and mobilization skills*. We have already suggested in this book that government leaders are *authoritative* political actors. The authority dimension is an important characteristic of leadership. It involves something more than simply having influence or power. It is more than simply being able to bring someone to do what you want him to do, regardless of his intentions or desires. Authority additionally implies legitimacy. An authoritative leader is one whose actions in organizing, mobilizing, and allocatng resources are accepted by the persons for whom these actions are relevant. The decisions of authoritative political actors are carried out as faithfully as possible, not merely because these decision-makers are powerful, but because it is viewed as appropriate and legitimate that they have been involved in making these decisions. It is worth emphasizing that authority is not an attribute of a leader; rather, it is a characteristic of the relationship that exists between leaders and followers. If the followers attach legitimacy to the acts of the leader, we may speak of the relationship between leader and followers as one of authority.

The other salient characteristic of leadership is the presence of *organizational and mobilization skills*. We have already suggested that such skills are crucial to political activity and to the management of public affairs. No organization or agency can exist without leaders capable of motivating members toward goal achievement and of organizing their activities in such a way that the energies of the organization are effectively directed toward the leaders' desired ends. Human resources are obviously crucial to stability and progress in human society. In a complex society, the ability to organize and direct human energies—leadership—is vital.

Personal Characteristics of Leaders

One of the questions that has intrigued both political scientists and social psychologists for a long time is whether leaders have personal characteristics that set them apart from nonleaders. In a sense, one can separate this general question into two parts: Do leaders reveal unusual personal characteristics in the actual practice of leadership? And, are there consistent features in their backgrounds and early professional careers that enable us to predict either that they will become leaders or that they will adopt particular kinds of behaviors or styles after they do become leaders?

The study of the personal characteristics and behaviors of political leaders has focused on their *values and issue orientations*, their *personalities*, and their leadership *styles*. In recent years, students of politics have come to recognize that the basic values held by political leaders must be studied separately from the positions they take on specific issues. *Values* are fundamental, general, and enduring postures toward man's relationship with government and other elements of his environment. *Issue orientations* are opinions held on issues of the moment, which, being event-related, are therefore more specific and, thus, ephemeral.[10] Consequently, it cannot be assumed that the issue orientations of elites stem entirely from the same sources as do their value orientations. Nor can one assume that the dimensions of these two types of orientations will be consistent, even for a given individual. To illustrate: The daily press is full of reports of statements by political leaders who, while professing a strong distaste for war, staunchly defend the involvement of their own country in armed conflict. Countless state governors, while expressing strong opposition to the principle of taxing consumer purchases on an across-the-board basis, are quite willing, when revenues dip, to urge state sales taxes. Similarly, numerous protestations by judges of belief in racial brotherhood and harmony have foundered when state and federal district court judges have been asked to order strict implementation of congressional and Supreme Court dicta dealing with racial segregation and integration. The values and issue orientations of political leaders assuredly must be studied separately from one another.

Students of political leadership have also been interested in looking at the *personality* characteristics of leaders. There have been several interesting, if somewhat speculative, "psychobiographies" written on prominent political leaders in a variety of countries.[11] They have tended to focus on such factors as adolescent identity crises in the lives of leaders, on the degree of sincerity of leaders' beliefs in their professed creeds, on the nature of their interpersonal relationships with close associates, on their patterns of ambition and motivation toward the achievement of high office and toward the execution of leadership tasks, and on their degrees of receptivity to new or contrary information (*i.e.*, their relative open- or closed-mindedness, or dogmatism). A parallel line of inquiry has been to ask why certain kinds of leaders are attracted to particular kinds of situations (*e.g.*, crises), while other leaders are attracted more to routine, day-to-day tasks of management and organization.

There are many difficulties, of course, with these kinds of

studies. The principal one is that reliable psychological data on prominent political personalities are often very difficult to obtain. Among many social scientists, there is considerable skepticism toward psychoanalysis from a distance. It is probably fair to say that the degree of acceptance of these personality analyses increases as the length of time from the leader's last tenure increases. That is, psychobiography appears to be accepted primarily in the context of broad historical generalization about the characteristics of certain leaders who achieved considerable historical prominence. Thus, in 1973 more credence is likely to be given a psychobiography of Adolf Hitler than to a similar study of, say, Walter Ulbricht.

Since the 1930's, a good deal of attention has been given to the study of leadership *styles*. This research has tried to learn more than simply what the styles of leaders tend to be in different kinds of situations. It has also sought to relate leadership styles to task performance as well as other reactions of followers. For example, an important question has concerned the effects of three contrasting styles of leadership—*laissez faire*, authoritarian, and democratic—on the performance of tasks by followers. The results of this research have generally been conflicting and inconclusive. Some slight evidential weight suggests that democratic leadership styles tend to result in higher morale among followers. On the other hand, a good deal of evidence suggests that authoritarian leadership styles can lead to as high a productivity as that obtained with democratic leadership styles.[12]

Some of these studies have gone further and examined the impact of *follower* characteristics on the effects of leadership style. For example, some researchers have found that bright students benefit more from permissive (*i.e.*, democratic or *laissez-faire*) leadership, whereas less intelligent students often produce more under authoritarian leadership circumstances.[13] These somewhat more rigorous studies seem consistent in their findings with some general impressions arrived at by many students of comparative political systems. There seems to be a general feeling that an essentially democratic leadership system elicits more favorable attitudes from the general population but probably does not produce any higher productivity (economic, social, political, or other) than do authoritarian styles of leadership. Similarly, some political scientists have asserted that democratic leadership systems are more appropriate when the general educational level of the population is higher, whereas authoritarian regimes may more efficiently mobilize the resources available in societies where educational achievement is low and illiteracy is relatively high. At a minimum, we can safely conclude that no single leadership style—*laissez faire*, democratic, or authoritarian—is universally functional for all types of political situations.

Leadership Recruitment and Behavior

The other central question that has interested students of political leadership is how leaders got where they are. Can one identify social-background characteristics, or career experiences, that would help us to predict a person's rise to a position of leadership? Similarly, is it possible to predict how a political leader might act, what values and issue orientations he might espouse, as a leader, by looking at his social background and early career? A very considerable part of the traditional research on political leaders has focused on these questions.

Until very recently, the belief was widespread that a man's social origins were important in explaining his thinking and his behavior as a political leader. Only since the late 1960's have political scientists begun to accumulate evidence that seriously challenges this assumption. Edinger and Searing, in a landmark study of the social backgrounds, careers, and issue orientations of French and West German political leaders, discovered that *recent* career experiences were the most useful predictors of the position taken by these political leaders on important issues.[14] Social-background characteristics were found to be generally unimportant in explaining issue orientations. Further, no readily identifiable patterns of social backgrounds were discerned among these two leadership groups. Recent research on leadership in several Communist systems by Lodge, Zaninovich, Beck, and others [15] has served to reinforce Edinger and Searing's conclusions. There now is good reason to believe that the issue orientations of political leaders are substantially influenced by their recent career experiences, and that the disparate backgrounds from which political leaders in many countries come do not exert decisive influence on the ways in which they look at important political issues.

It might be emphasized that these pieces of research have examined a considerable variety of social-background and career characteristics of political leaders. Among the social-background, or demographic, attributes of leaders that have been studied are: time of birth; ethnic background; economic and geographic characteristics of places of birth and early childhood; family social background and standing; nature and extent of family political participation; amount of formal education; and nature of special education, such as military schools, Party schools (*e.g.*, in Communist countries), or polytechnic institutes. Among the career characteristics studied are: formal positions these leaders have held in government and other political hierarchies; points in time at which positions were held; ages at which the leaders held these positions; length of time for which each position was held; nature of professional and social affiliations held; professional-skill areas (*e.g.*, industry, agriculture, communications, science, education) in which a political leader has worked; and significant adult political experiences (*e.g.*, participation in strikes, armed uprisings, detention, immigration). Thus, these studies have approached the examination of social-background and career characteristics in a very thorough way, and their findings are all the more important because of such thoroughness.

It is important to emphasize, however, that, while this discovery of the relative unimportance of social-background characteristics in influencing values and issue orientations may hold for political leaders, it may not apply to nonleaders. As we shall suggest later in this chapter, there is a growing amount of research on the process of political socialization, that is, on the process by which politically relevant values, attitudes, and beliefs are inculcated into the citizenry. This research indicates that many basic orientations toward politics have been learned by the time a young person is in the seventh or eighth grade.

This would seem to run counter to the notion that adult career experiences shape political issue orientations. What we may be discovering, however, is that the situation is different for leaders from what it is for nonleaders.

GROUPS AND INTERESTS

Political groups are collectivities of individuals who have organized for the purpose of articulating some common concern and thus pursuing some identifiable goal. These common concerns, or goals, are often referred to under the rubric of "interests," hence the phrase "interest group." Because the notion of a political group seems definitionally inseparable from the notion of an interest, even some of the strongest proponents of a group approach to the study of politics have suggested that the phrase "interest group" is redundant; that is, the phrase is saying essentially the same thing twice. For our purposes, however, the question of whether the concept of "group" and "interest" have independent meaning seems unimportant.[16] It appears reasonable to continue to use the phrase "political group" and "interest group" synonymously.

The Nature of "Group Behavior"

We have dispatched the preceding issue rather quickly. But there is another issue that, having caused the expenditure of considerable intellectual and emotional energy by some students of politics, cannot be dismissed so lightly. Let us briefly examine it, then, before going on to discuss the ways in which the group concept has been used in political science. This second issue concerns the extent to which groups have identities of their own, that is, the degree to which it makes sense to speak of groups, as distinct from the individuals composing them.

It is common, in news reports about politics, to find such statements as; "Interest group X today issued a statement of opposition to President Nixon's declared moratorium on school busing" and "Interest group Y has repeatedly maintained that legislation limiting the possession of firearms constitutes an infringement of a basic constitutional right." Yet, there is nevertheless some question whether a group actually does anything. Perhaps the predominant opinion among students of politics is that it is not groups, as such, that think and act but people, sometimes in the name of an organization or group. (The same comment might be made, by the way, about nations: Nations do not act; it is human beings in positions of power, influence, and authority who commit the resources held within the boundaries of a nation-state toward particular kinds of action.) The behaviors to be studied and explained are those of individuals. This is certainly not to deny that individual behaviors may be influenced by the patterns of interaction with other human beings that occur as part of group organization. But, at a minimum, it is important to emphasize that groups are composed of individual human beings, and that "group behavior" is, in fact, the behaviors of numerous individuals, even though those individual behaviors may be different by virtue of their taking place within some kind of organizational context.

Our discussion of this important point about the precise nature of a group should now allow us to proceed to a consideration of groups as they function within the political process. We shall succumb to the usual practice of using language that seems to suggest that groups themselves are behaving. But it should be understood that group activities are viewed here as the activities of individuals who happen to have organized in some way in an effort to pursue a politically relevant goal. While we shall speak of things that groups do, and of the functions of groups in the political process, we shall seek to avoid the problem of reification; that is, we shall avoid implying that groups have psyches, brains, or physical existence distinct from the characteristics and actions of their members.

Groups in the Political Process

Earlier sections of this chapter have already implied the importance of groups in the political process. For example, when we pointed out that a central feature of political life was conflict, we said that political groups usually represent the principal vehicles through which political conflict is carried on. Generally speaking, unorganized individuals do not have much chance of achieving significant influence in complex, modern societies. The need to organize into formal groups seems clear. Similarly, when it was suggested in chapter 1 that a common way of defining politics is in terms of the authoritative allocation of scarce resources, we said that this allocation of resources in society is, in considerable part, the result of conflict among various groups. Furthermore, it may be argued that political groups are among the principal recipients of the benefits or deprivations that result from government decisions and societal policies.

One perspective on this important role of groups is to say that interest groups perform the *interest-articulation function* for the political system. According to some students of politics, notably Gabriel Almond, interest articulation is one of the most fundamental functions, or activities, that takes place in society.[17] Indeed, without the sustained performance of this interest-articulation function, Almond believes that a political system cannot continue to function stably. Interest articulation, as the phrase implies, involves the formal expression of the collective concerns of a number of individuals and the pursuit of goals consistent with these concerns through action designed to influence decisions on the allocation of societal resources.

We cannot emphasize too strongly that focusing entirely on interest groups would yield a misleading picture, indeed, of the political process. To be sure, an understanding of interest-group activity is crucial, but a focus on groups to the exclusion of the many environmental and political factors that influence the activities of groups would be foolhardy. If, for example, we wanted to determine why some interest groups are more successful than others in pursuing their members' concerns, then we would have to look not only at the characteristics of the interest groups themselves but also at a variety of factors not connected with the nature of the groups. Students of interest-group activity have focused on a number of factors, some of the most important of which are:

1. the *membership size* of the group
2. the *scope* of activity of the group
3. the *intensity* of activity of the group

4. the nature of the *techniques* used in pursuing the group's goals and, relatedly, the nature of the *demands* made by the group (with particular attention to the relative specificity or diffuseness of those demands)
5. the *internal operating characteristics* of the group, especially its degree of cohesiveness
6. the *material and human resources*—especially those relevant to the use of techniques of persuasion—available to, and used by, the group
7. the extent to which the members of the group are simultaneously members of other politically relevant organizations; that is, the extent to which a group's membership maintains *overlapping group identifications,* and, possibly, multiple group loyalties
8. the extent to which the group's activities or goals are consistent with *norms and mores* of the political culture
9. the extent to which interest group activity is *institutionalized,* and therefore considered legitimate, in the political system
10. the degree to which the group is able to cultivate and maintain direct *avenues of communication* with those authoritative decision-makers whose behaviors they wish to influence

Obviously, the list of factors that might influence the success of an interest group could be made much longer. But the above list will serve to illustrate what must be taken in consideration in studying the impacts of political groups.

Statistical Aggregates as "Groups"

The astute reader will have noticed by now that we have excluded a certain type of collectivity of individuals, which is sometimes referred to as a "group," from our consideration. This is what might be called a statistical group or a statistical aggregate. For example, all persons of German descent living in the United States, or all persons of German descent living in Rumania, might be considered a "group." Generally speaking, however, students of politics do not treat such a statistical aggregate as a "group." Perhaps this is due, in part, to the synonymous identification of "groups" with "interest." If interests are thought of as activities in pursuit of goals, then unorganized collectivities of individuals—statistical collectivities—do not have interests.

On a more practical level, there is strong reason to believe that unorganized collectivities of individuals have minimal impact on most political outcomes. It is possible, of course, to carry that argument too far. One can argue that an electorate is an unorganized group, and that, in liberal-democratic systems, the electorate exercises considerable influence, at least on the final selection of prominent public officials. On the other hand, one can argue, in response, that the electorate (1) is, in fact, largely composed of a variety of overlapping organized groups and (2) exercises minimal influence on the selection of public officials, since the choices presented to the full electorate at the time of general election are sharply filtered and circumscribed, primarily by influential groups, chief among them political parties.

In the final analysis, perhaps we have to come back to the old cliché that "all definitions are arbitrary—by definition." There are times when students of politics need to be concerned with what the categories of individuals—statistical collectivities or aggregates—are thinking, even if they are not formally organized into interest groups. But, in order to keep such collectivities distinct from organized interest groups, we usually do not attach the term "group" to statistical aggregates.

Interest Groups and Political Parties

One final note of relevance to our discussion of groups and interests concerns the relationship between interest groups and political parties. In chapter 2, we introduced our definitional distinction between interest groups and parties. We said that political parties share with interest groups the characteristics of organizational structure and goal orientation. But political parties, in addition, offer their own candidates for public office. Thus, the providing of candidates is an important difference between interest groups and political parties.

There is another difference between the two, reflected in the functions that they perform in the political system. We have said that interest groups perform an interest-articulation function; that is, they present, in a formal way, the concerns of some set of individuals. Political parties may be viewed as performing a function that follows directly after the interest-articulation function. This is *interest aggregation,* and it involves pulling together, under a broader umbrella, a variety of different interests or sets of demands. Interest groups tend to have relatively specific foci; they are often organized to pursue a reasonably narrow set of concerns and goals. In most political systems, by contrast, political parties must have a much broader range of concerns. In order to hope for success at the polls, they must appeal to a variety of interests; hence their more general, diffuse, and aggregative posture toward the demands being made through interest groups.

It should be emphasized that the degree of autonomy that interest groups have from the political-party system varies in different political settings. In what has been called the Anglo-American type of political system the functions of political parties and interest groups are sharply differentiated.[18] In at least two other types of political systems, however, this is not the case. For example, in less developed, "non-Western" systems in Asia, the Middle East, and Latin America, neither political parties nor interest groups are particularly well developed. Indeed, the functions of interest articulation and interest aggregation may be performed by government agencies, the government bureaucracy, or even the military. Still another situation is exemplified by France and Italy. In this case, the political parties and interest groups are organized and established, but they are not independent of one another. That is, there are some parties that more or less control interest groups; this is especially true in the case of Communist and socialist political organizations. To a lesser extent, it is true, also, of the Roman Catholic Church. The point to be made, then, is that differences among political systems may have a significant impact on the relationships between interest groups and political parties.

POLITICAL CULTURE: THE
POLITICAL VALUES, BELIEFS, AND ATTITUDES
OF CITIZENS

One does not have to believe in democratic principles to recognize that politics is influenced by the ways in which citizens define their relationship with government. There is no doubt that the influence of citizen thinking on political outcomes varies a great deal in different political systems and at different points in time. We feel confident in saying that citizen opinion was more important in the United States, Great Britain, or the Federal Republic of Germany in 1972 than it was in Spain or Czechoslovakia in 1972, or in Germany in 1943. But, despite these very real variations in the importance of what citizens think, this dimension of human activity always has a sufficient measure of importance to justify the continuing attention of students of politics.

Affective, Cognitive and, Structural Dimensions

The concept of *political culture* is sometimes used to embrace the several aspects of citizen thinking about the nature of government and about the relationships between individual citizens and government. Political culture has three major dimensions: the *affective* dimension (*values*), the *cognitive* dimension (*beliefs*), and the *structural* dimension (*attitudes*). Each warrants our close attention.

The *affective* dimension of political culture consists of the *values*, or "ought" propositions, held by the citizenry. These values reflect their ultimate preferences about the form of government under which they would like to live and about the relationships that should hold between that government and themselves. These values include not only generalized and abstract feelings about the proper role of government, and of individuals in politics, but also judgments about the performance of specific individuals or organizations in the polity. Thus, the affective dimension of political culture includes not only a preference for, say, openness and democracy in government but also evaluations of whether a current administration's performance is sufficiently consistent with such ideals of openness and democracy.

The *cognitive* dimension of political culture embraces the informational *beliefs* that people have about government and politics. That is, it concerns citizens' definitions of the "is" of politics. It includes their perceptions of what is actually going on in the polity, and of what has gone on in the past. It hardly needs to be stressed that different individuals living in the same political system may define political "reality" in significantly different ways; for reality is not a fixed, determinant point. Thus, we stress that political beliefs are based on perceptions, which may be substantially variant within the same population. Is there corruption in American national government? The answer depends on whom you ask.

The *structural* dimension of political culture refers to political *attitudes*. The concept of attitude has been defined in frustratingly numerous and diverse ways by different social scientists. We choose here a definition that admittedly is not the most common, but which may be the easiest to use for purposes of distinguishing attitudes from values and beliefs. We shall view attitudes as structures for thinking—mental frameworks, if you will, within which values and beliefs are organized and set into relation with one another. From this point of view, attitudes do not have substantive content of their own. Substance is contained in values ("ought" propositions) and beliefs ("is" propositions). Attitudes are structures for interrelating these substantive notions.

For example, an important attitudinal dimension relevant to politics is the dogmatism-openmindedness dimension. We may contrast individuals according to the degree to which they are willing to accept new beliefs or new values that are, at least partially, inconsistent with ones they already have. Persons wholly unwilling to accept new values or beliefs would be classified as attitudinally dogmatic. Persons willing to reject existing values and beliefs would be thought of as attitudinally openminded.

There is no necessary relationship between any particular set of substantive values or beliefs and any particular form of political attitude. For example, there are conservative dogmatists, liberal dogmatists, and even middle-of-the-road dogmatists. There are openminded conservatives, openminded liberals, and openminded middle-of-the-roaders. Viewed this way, political attitudes are logically independent of political values and political beliefs. One of the interesting questions about any group of citizens, therefore, concerns the way in which their values, beliefs, and attitudes are related to one another: that is, the particular blend or mix of attitudes, values, and beliefs that goes to make up a particular political culture.

Orientational Dimensions

In the broadest sense, then, political culture can be thought of as the orientations of citizens toward political objects.[19] We can sharpen our focus on the concept of political culture by identifying, from the work of Almond and Verba, four types of political objects toward which citizens may have orientations. The particular pattern of orientations toward these objects determines the over-all character of the political culture of any given system. It will be recalled that, in chapter 4, in introducing Easton's input-output model, we introduced a distinction between political inputs and political outputs. This distinction is important in describing the dimensions of citizen political orientations.

The first orientational dimension consists of the *political system as a whole,* as a "general object." [20] Here, we are concerned with citizen cognitions and evaluations of the nation in terms of such things as patriotism or alienation, strength or weakness, and democracy, constitutionalism, or tyranny. The second dimension of citizen orientations concerns the *input aspects of the political process.* What information does the citizen have about how demands are made upon government or about how supports can be offered or withheld? What are the citizen's values about the input process? Does he prefer an open, pluralistic, bargaining-competitive system or, rather, an elitist and closed system? How does the citizen evaluate the performance of input functions in the system in which he lives?

A third dimension of citizen political orientations concerns the *output functions* of the polity. What does the citizen know and feel about decision-making in government and in other important political organizations? Does he understand the process of decision-making and the problems of policy enforcement? What evaluations does he hold of the individuals and institutions involved in these output functions? Finally, the fourth dimension of citizen orientations concerns the *self as active participant in politics.* How does the citizen view himself as a member of a political system? Does he have information about his individual rights, his obligations as a citizen, his opportunities to influence the actions of those who govern? How does the citizen feel about his abilities to exercise such influence?

These four dimensions of political orientations, though sometimes closely related within the psychological makeup of a given individual, are often quite independent of one another. That is, a citizen may possess very specific values and beliefs about the political system as a whole without having information, or even values or judgments, about specific individuals and institutions involved in performing input or output functions. Or an individual may have considerable information and substantial feeling along the first three dimensions of political orientations but have only a very fuzzy, and perhaps contradictory, picture of his own role in the political system. In short, a citizen may think he understands how the system works but feel he is essentially unable to do any thing about it, or that he really has no business trying to do anything about it. The feeling on the part of the individual citizen that he should and can influence those political activities that are relevant to his own existence is sometimes referred to as a feeling of *political efficacy* or *citizen competence.*[21] One of the interesting questions is the way in which the other three dimensions of political orientations are related to feelings of political efficacy or citizen competence. If we make the assumption that a relatively high degree of citizen competence is a prerequisite for sustaining democracy, then an understanding of how such a sense of competence is nurtured and maintained becomes an important issue in democratic political philosophy.

Types of Political Culture

Almond and Verba have identified three broad types of political cultures: *parochial, subject,* and *participant.* These cultures may be distinguished by the extent to which citizen orientations along each of the four dimensions described above have been developed. In a *parochial* political culture, most citizens have not developed identifiable orientations toward any of the four types of political objects—the system as a whole, the input process, the output process, or the individual as political participant. The best examples of such parochial political cultures are thought to be several African tribal societies.[22] In a *subject* political culture, there is a high frequency of orientations toward the system as a whole and the output aspects of the system, but little understanding of the input process or of the individual as a political participant. The individual is, in reality, a "subject"; hence the labeling of this type of political culture. The individual is essentially a passive object, subject to governmental authority.

In the third type of political culture, the *participant* type, individuals tend to be explicitly oriented not only toward the system as a whole and its output (decision- and policy-making) functions but also toward the input functions and effective modes of participation by citizens. In such political cultures, the level of political awareness and information is generally high, and this awareness extends to an appreciation of the ways in which individuals and groups can participate in influencing the actions of authoritative decision-makers.

The Level of Analysis Problem

There have been numerous critiques of the use of the concept of political culture. Some students of politics are enamored with it, others are skeptical of its utility. Many methodological issues have been raised about the ways in which the concept has been used. We shall mention only one here, but it is a very important one.

The careful reader will have noticed that the notion of political culture must operate at a different conceptual *level* from the one at which the concepts of individual values, beliefs, and attitudes operate. Values, beliefs, and attitudes are held by *individuals*. Political culture is a term that makes sense only as a *collective* description of the values, beliefs, and attitudes thus held. That is, political culture is a description of the political orientations of a large number of people who collectively make up the citizenry of a political system. Political culture is therefore a *system-level* concept, while values, beliefs, and attitudes are *individual-level* concepts.

For our purposes, what is especially important to note is that political cultures that are *predominantly* participant, say, will undoubtedly include many individuals whose orientations are more consistent with subject or parochial cultures. Conversely, subject political cultures (*i.e.,* those that are predominantly subject) will undoubtedly include many persons whose orientations are participant. Thus, we recognize that the concept of political culture is a general one and certainly does not purport to describe an invariant "national characteristic" of the people within that system.

One of the principal reasons that there are many variations in the political values, beliefs, and attitudes of citizens within the same system is that the processes of political socialization are not consistent, even within modern societies. These processes of political socialization affect different individuals and groups in different ways. Thus, an understanding of political socialization is crucial to an understanding of the political process. It is consequently appropriate that we turn at this point to a discussion of the concept of political socialization.

POLITICAL SOCIALIZATION

The extent to which a society maintains its existence, or the degree to which its political culture changes, may be crucially influenced by political socialization. Political socialization is the process by which an individual learns politically relevant values and attitudes (including dispositions toward behavior). This process is conducted and mediated through a variety of social agencies and institutions, including the family, peer groups, schools, adult organizations, and the mass media.

When the process of political socialization involves the essentially undistorted transmission of a particular political culture from generation to generation, political socialization becomes a vehicle for societal stability. On the other hand, when young people in a society develop political and social expectations and values different from those of their parents, the socialization process can be viewed as the basis of political and social change. Because the socialization process takes place through a variety of societal institutions, changes in any of these institutions may provide a basis for changing patterns of political socialization. Thus, the study of socialization implies specific attention to a variety of societal agencies insofar as they exert influence on the development of values and attitudes by young people.

Socialization and Levels of Analysis

It is worth reminding ourselves how political socialization fits into some of the approaches and models discussed in chapter 4. For example, political socialization is one of the principal societal functions described in the work of Almond and Powell. In their model, as in Easton's input-output model, political socialization may be viewed as an input function in the political process. The socialization process exerts considerable influence on the nature of citizen supports available to the political system and on the nature of the demands likely to be made by societal groups seeking influence on political decisions. Political socialization, similarly, is central to system maintenance, in that the sustenance of a particular political order depends, in part, on society's ability to transmit a supportive political culture across generations.

Somewhat like political culture, the concept of political socialization may be used at two distinct levels of analysis. Using the term in the same sense as Almond and Powell, and Easton do, one is led to think of political socialization as a system-level concept. That is, the focus in these models is on the role played by political socialization in the stable change and integration of political systems. At the same time, it seems clear that the empirical study of the socialization process must focus on individuals, since it is in the acquisition *by individuals* of values, attitudes, and behavioral dispositions that we are interested. Thus, although political socialization may be viewed as a factor contributing to the particular state of a political system at a given point in time, the actual study of the phenomenon of socialization must proceed at the individual level.

Elements of the Socialization Process

Although their precise conclusions have varied, students of political socialization seem to agree that, for most people, much of the basic acquisition of politically relevant values and attitudes occurs before high school. Indeed, some even argue that many of the most fundamental value postures retained throughout our lives are learned by the middle of our elementary-school experience.

Just how these politically relevant values and attitudes are developed by individuals is not yet fully clear, although an increasing amount of systematic research is being directed toward the socialization process. In general, we may say that socialization takes place through three complementary, and perhaps overlapping, kinds of processes: the *learning of particular behaviors,* the *development of psychological dispositions,* and the *learning of certain role expectations.*[23] *Learning* is a broad term that applies to all behavior deriving from training procedures.[24] It may take place as a result of direct *conditioning* and *reinforcement.* Thus, a child may be directly punished, or rewarded, for certain patterns of behavior. It may also take place through *imitation* or *identification.* A young child usually learns early that it will be to his advantage to imitate certain behaviors of the older and more powerful people with whom he interacts, while conspicuously avoiding the imitation of certain others. Similarly, young children apparently begin to identify at an early age with a limited number of adults, and to begin to internalize the values and attitudes they see manifested by those adults. Early in the child's life, these various aspects of the learning process will be focused largely on the immediate family. As the child grows older, other referents may be picked up, such as peers, teachers, and even real or imaginary distant figures, such as prominent historical figures.

There has been substantial debate concerning the relative influence of internal personality characteristics, as opposed to situational or role circumstances, in structuring a child's behavior. Much of this debate seems to have been exaggerated. It seems apparent that the significance of personality characteristics varies a good deal with the degree to which the situation in which a person finds himself is structured ahead of time. Even within a given category of situations—*e.g.,* in the classroom—there are some situations in which role constraints are very severe and other situations in which the unstructured nature of the moment permits considerable influence from the child's personality characteristics.

From the perspective of role-expectation learning, political socialization is seen as a process by which society's notions of what is appropriate behavior in particular roles, or situations, is learned. The concept of role is a kind of conceptual bridge relating the individual to his societal environment. Every position, every status, in society is surrounded by a set of expectations of appropriate behavior, which, shared by most members of that society, are then transmitted through generations. This notion of role expectations is relevant not only for an understanding of how the individual sees his appropriate activity within the polity, but also to the individual's notions of the sorts of behavior that should be exhibited by persons in positions of power and influence. Thus, political socialization includes the learning of expectations about what government officials should do as well as about how they should do it.

The Need for Longitudinal Data

A central methodological issue raised in socialization research has concerned the failure to gather longitudinal data on the socialization process. Political socialization is thought of as a process that continues over a number of years. Further, one of the most important questions in political research concerns the conditions under which early political socialization may be overcome by adult career or other politically relevant experiences. Thus, ideally, an understanding of the socialization process implies having concrete information on the development of values and attitudes over a substantial period of time by a variety of individuals.

Unfortunately, most studies of political socialization done to date have not benefited from this kind of information gathered over a period of time. They frequently are studies of groups of young people viewed at a single point in time that attempt to sort out the various influences—family, school, peer group, mass media—that seem to be affecting the values and attitudes acquired by these persons. Such data do not actually illuminate the process of socialization as it impacts upon specific individuals over a period of years. Until we have such reliable longitudinal data, our understanding of the socialization process, as important as that process clearly is for an understanding of politics in general, will be less than perfect.

THE USE OF CONCEPTS: TWO CAVEATS

This chapter has introduced seven sets of concepts frequently used in the study of politics. Obviously, there are many others that might have been presented, and which you will undoubtedly encounter as you pursue your own interests in the political process. For our purposes, there are two important general points to be made here.

First, it cannot be emphasized too strongly that how we look at something does make a difference for what we eventually see. This chapter has suggested that there are numerous ways of defining these basic concepts, both conceptually and operationally. Sometimes, these definitions may even operate at different conceptual levels. These different definitions may have considerable impact on how we see each of these concepts fit into a more general approach, model, or theory of politics. It is not enough to say merely that one is interested in power, or in decision-making, or in leadership. The serious student of politics must be explicit about how he wishes to use these important terms, for they are capable of being misunderstood. Presumably, we are not interested in accepting imposed orthodoxy about what each of these terms "should" mean; indeed, the absence of such orthodoxy is a cornerstone of scientific inquiry. On the other hand, in the absence of orthodoxy, we must be prepared to be explicit when we communicate ideas about politics. Understanding is substantially dependent upon clarity in the use of concepts.

Second, it is worth stressing that these different concepts are in no sense mutually exclusive, or contradictory, ways of looking at political activity. On the contrary, they constitute complementary ways of looking at some of the same things. That is, these concepts are at least partially overlapping. They direct our attention to certain aspects of the political process that are so closely interrelated that the concepts describing them frequently overlap in their empirical implications. Leadership may involve decision-making and the exercise of power or influence. The socialization process involves the inculcation of values and attitudes. Conflict resolution may depend, in considerable part, on the success of political socialization in a society and on the extent to which interest groups operate within institutionalized channels for handling differences of opinions. We would probably not have to try very hard to design a definition of politics that would embrace all seven sets of basic concepts used in this chapter, for these concepts are complementary and, therefore, intellectually reinforcing. An eclectic approach to politics through this or a similar set of concepts could be a meaningful way to orient oneself toward the political process.

NOTES

1. See Gordon J. Di Renzo, "Conceptual Definition in the Behavioral Sciences," in Di Renzo (ed.), *Concepts, Theory, and Explanation in the Behavioral Sciences* (New York: Random House, 1966), pp. 9–10.
2. See Robert A. Dahl, *Modern Political Analysis* (Englewood Cliffs, N.J.: Prentice-Hall, 1963), pp. 41–47.
3. See Anthony Downs, *An Economic Theory of Democracy* (New York: Harper, 1957).
4. See E. E. Schattschneider, *The Semi-Sovereign People* (New York: Holt, Rinehart and Winston, 1960), especially pp. 20–61.
5. The work done by Snyder and Robinson has been considerable. Representative contributions would be: Richard C. Snyder, "A Decision-Making Approach to the Study of Political Phenomena," in Roland Young (ed.), *Approaches to the Study of Politics* (Evanston, Ill.: Northwestern University Press, 1958), pp. 3–38; and James A. Robinson, *Congress and Foreign Policy-Making* (Homewood, Ill.: Dorsey Press, 1962).
6. See Paul H. Conn, *Conflict and Decision-Making: An Introduction to Political Science* (New York: Harper and Row, 1971), pp. 46–61.
7. Schattschneider, *The Semi-Sovereign People,* p. 74.
8. Conn, *Conflict and Decision-Making,* p. 293.
9. Robert A. Dahl and Charles E. Lindblom, *Politics, Economics and Welfare* (New York: Harper, 1953), p. 324.
10. This distinction between values and issue orientations has been drawn in William A. Welsh, "The Comparative Study of Communist Political Leadership," chapter 1 in Carl Beck, Frederic J. Fleron, Jr., Milton Lodge,

Derek Waller, William A. Welsh, and M. George Zaninovich, *Comparative Communist Political Leadership* (New York: David McKay, 1973).

11. Adolf Hitler, for example, has been the focus of several such efforts. Perhaps the best among them is Alan Bullock, *Hitler: A Study in Tyranny* (New York: Harper, 1952). See also E. Victor Wolfenstein, "Some Psychological Aspects of Crisis Leaders," in Lewis J. Edinger (ed.), *Political Leadership in Industrialized Societies* (New York: John Wiley and Sons, 1967), pp. 155–81.

12. Some of this evidence is summarized in Samuel H. Barnes, "Leadership Style and Political Competence," in Edinger (ed.), *Political Leadership in Industrialized Societies,* pp. 67–69.

13. A. D. Calvin, F. K. Hoffman, and E. L. Hardin, "The Effect of Intelligence and Social Atmosphere on Group Problem-Solving Behavior," *Journal of Social Psychology,* XLV (February, 1957), 61–74.

14. Lewis J. Edinger and Donald D. Searing, "Social Background in Elite Analysis: A Methodological Inquiry," *American Political Science Review,* LXI, no. 2 (June, 1967), 428–45.

15. Most of this research is reported in Beck, Fleron, Lodge, Waller, Welsh, and Zaninovich, *Comparative Communist Political Leadership, op. cit.*

16. For a discussion of this issue, see Charles Hagen, "The Group in a Science of Politics," in Young (ed.), *Approaches to the Study of Politics, op. cit.*

17. See the discussion of the Almond-Powell functional-developmental model in chapter 4. See also Almond and Powell, *Comparative Politics: A Developmental Approach, op. cit.*

18. These differences among the three types of political systems are discussed in Almond and Powell, *ibid.*

19. See Gabriel Almond and Sidney Verba, *The Civic Culture* (Boston: Little, Brown, 1963), p. 13.

20. *Ibid.,* p. 16.

21. *Ibid.,* pp. 171–85.

22. *Ibid.,* p. 17.

23. Kenneth P. Langton, *Political Socialization* (New York: Oxford University Press, 1969), pp. 8–16. See also Dean Jaros, *Socialization to Politics* (New York: Praeger Publishers, 1973), chapter 1.

24. *Ibid.,* p. 9.

6

Gathering Information About Politics

In the first five chapters, you have looked at politics from a number of perspectives. You have come across several ideas about what constitutes the essence of politics. You have seen the study of politics characterized in terms of the principles of science. The major subfields of political science have been introduced to you. And you have examined the content of the political process in terms of models, approaches, and concepts.

One of the impressions that probably strikes you at this point is that there is a great deal of information available that is relevant to politics. This is true partly because of the pervasive character of politics in human society and partly because of the social complexity of society. We interact and communicate with one another in a multitude of ways, and many of these social behaviors need to be included in the study of politics.

At the same time, you have also discovered that anyone who really wants to understand what politics is all about must be careful about the way he obtains and handles information. There is, indeed, a lot of information to be had, but the reliability of a considerable part of that information may be open to challenge. The serious student of politics, as we have said, is a skeptic. As he builds his understanding of the political process, and before he makes important political choices as a citizen, he will make a genuine effort to evaluate the reliability and usefulness of the information available to him.

This chapter discusses some important types of information that students of politics can gather and use. And, because there is a close relationship between how we obtain information and the use we then can make of it, this chapter also discusses some methods for gathering data about politics. Depending upon what we are trying to discover, or perhaps upon the purposes to which we want to put information, some techniques for gathering data may be more appropriate than others. Consequently, we give some attention here to the evaluation of these methods of data gathering.

One other preliminary caveat should be entered. In a very real sense, much of this chapter is about how *you* can gather information about politics. It is not just a discussion of how some other people have found out what they know about the political process. We are not talking here about political science as an abstract academic enterprise. Rather, our focus is on how people who really want to understand what the political process is like can accumulate some sound information on which understanding and evaluations can be based. Of course, it is not practical to think that every method of data gathering discussed in this chapter could actually be used by each person with an interest in politics. Some data-gathering procedures require greater time and resources than do others. Further, different sorts of data are used to answer different kinds of questions; the information you seek depends on what you are interested in. In general, however, each of these ways of acquiring information, and certainly each of the categories of information that will be mentioned, is available as a basis for enhancing the knowledge of each of us.

Types of Data and Data Gathering

There are numerous ways of gathering information about politics. Some require the direct observation of political behavior, while others may be done through secondary sources, that is, through documents and other information collections often found in libraries. Some involve gathering a few pieces of information on many subjects (*e.g.*, individuals), while others require the accumulation of much information about only a few subjects. Some of the information gathered through these various methods is susceptible to sophisticated mathematical and statistical analysis, while other information seems best treated from a nonquantitative point of view. In short, there is great variety in the information that can be gathered about politics.

We shall not attempt to cover every possible category of political data in this chapter. Rather, we shall focus on six major categories of information: data from *survey interviews*; data from the *content analysis* of documents; *biographical* data on individuals; data on certain types of political *events*; *aggregate descriptive statistics* on various aspects of social, economic, and political conditions in society; and data obtained through the *observation* of political behavior, including information obtained from experiments.

Survey Research

The purpose of survey research is to identify and explain the values, attitudes, and beliefs (including behavioral dispositions) of relatively large numbers of persons by administering questionnaires to much smaller segments, or "samples," of the larger collectivity. Thus, survey data consist of responses to carefully designed questions that have been asked of scientifically selected sets of citizens.[1]

Survey research provides a basis for understanding what people think about politics, and what they intend to do about what they think. When properly done, survey interviewing can reveal not only the values, beliefs, and attitudes of individuals but also their inclinations toward political behavior, such as voting in an election or becoming involved in local politics. Further, survey research may provide a basis for understanding what sorts of relationships exist between what people think and their personal attributes. That is, survey research can help us to understand the extent to which such factors as age, sex, religion, education, occupation, and income exert influence on the way people think about politics.

Survey research is a particularly meaningful way to obtain information about politics in systems in which public awareness of political life is relatively high, and in which the prevailing political ideology accords legitimacy to citizen participation in politics. Where political competence is low, or where citizen involvement in politics is discouraged, survey research is less useful for understanding the political process. That is, if people have only marginal knowledge about public affairs, or if they feel that they cannot or should not become involved, then their opinions will tell us relatively little about the factors influencing political outcomes.

Broadly, there are two sorts of questions confronting the student of politics who wants to do survey research. First, he must ask how he can obtain information that will permit him to make statements about a large population of persons, even though he will be able to interview only a small part of that population. That is, he must determine how to make his interview sample representative of the larger group to which he wishes to generalize his findings or conclusions. Second, he must consider carefully what information he wishes to obtain, and how he can best structure his questionnaire to obtain the needed information.

You may be aware that national polling organizations in the United States are able to make accurate statements about the political preferences of the American population as a whole on the basis of periodic interviews with fewer than 2,000 persons. Obviously, the selection of that sample of 2,000 is crucial. If the responses one obtains from those 2,000 individuals are not essentially the same as the responses that would be garnered by talking to 200,000,000, then the survey would not be of much use. Without going into the long and complex historical development of public-opinion surveying, we can simply say that this activity has become highly specialized, scientific, and precise. There is powerful evidence to suggest that very small samples, carefully selected, can yield meaningful generalizations about the political values, beliefs, and attitudes of very large populations.

There are two broad considerations that come into play when drawing a sample to be interviewed. They are the same whether we are talking about a national sample of voters or a sample of students on a small, liberal-arts campus. First, it is important that the sample be unbiased. This means that every person in the larger population must have an equal chance of being included in the sample. Generally speaking, the best way to accomplish this is to take a *random* sample.[2] This can be done by taking every twentieth or hundredth person on a voter list, for example. It can also be done by using a table of random numbers, generated by a computer and including persons whose positions on the voter list correspond to the computer-generated numbers.

A second consideration is whether the sample includes people who have the characteristics that the researcher thinks are most relevant to explaining different values or attitudes. A researcher might have an idea that orientations toward student politics vary primarily on the basis of sex, class standing, and social affiliations. Thus, it would be important that the sample include, in representative proportions, both males and females, students at all class levels, and members of a variety of social organizations. The researcher probably would want to *stratify* his sample along these dimensions, or characteristics, of individuals. If so, he would first subdivide his population by categories of sex, class standing, and social affiliations; then he would random-sample his subjects within each one of the categories he deemed important. In this way, he would be sure that the sample not only was unbiased but included the individual characteristics thought to be relevant to the problem being studied, that is, explaining differences among students in their feelings about student politics.

As you might imagine, organizing and setting up the questionnaire itself can be a pretty complicated procedure. The questions have to be asked in such a way that they are understandable to the respondent. Further, it is important that the respondent attribute the same meaning to the question as does the researcher. The questions cannot be "loaded." One of the quickest ways to "turn off" a person being interviewed or responding to a questionnaire is to phrase questions in such a way that they show a bias on the part of the person who designed the questionnaire.

Similarly, questions need to be phrased in such a way that the respondent can shape his answer out of his own experiences or feelings, rather than, for example, on the basis of what he thinks he "ought" to say, or believes the interviewer wants him to say, or thinks someone else "like himself" might say. Sometimes, it is appropriate to use what are called forced-choice questions: questions that provide the respondent a series of answers from which to choose. Other times, the purpose of the research might be to explore the subject's general frame of mind about a topic or issue, in which case open-ended questions might be used: questions the answers to which are not provided to the subject, thus compelling him to respond in his own words.

There are numerous other subtle concerns that are part of the task of constructing questionnaires. There are also numerous ways in which care must be exercised in the interview itself.[3] In general, establishing the proper rapport in a personal interview can be very important in eliciting meaningful answers from the respondent. We shall not attempt to cover the details of these sometimes complicated methodological issues here. Suffice it to say that the meaningfulness of survey-interview information about politics is very substantially dependent upon the care taken in organizing and administering the questionnaire, as it is in selecting the sample of persons to be interviewed.

Content Analysis

Sometimes it is not possible to interview the persons whose ideas are important to our efforts to understand politics. For example, it might be important to us to know, as precisely as possible, how prominent historical figures viewed certain aspects of politics. Or, perhaps we are interested in contemporary political figures but recognize that personal interviews with Leonid Brezhnev, Chou En-lai, Anwar Sadat, or even Spiro Agnew are unlikely to be granted. In such instances, the careful analysis of a leader's public writings and statements may be the best way to get at the dimensions of political thinking of our subjects.

Content analysis consists of systematically classifying the content of documents into carefully defined sets of categories. These categories reflect the themes, or ideas, that we want to identify and analyze. This process of careful classification of the content of documents permits us to determine the relative frequency and intensity with which certain symbols, words, or themes are used.[4]

Content analysis can be applied to a wide variety of political subjects. In addition to telling us a good deal about what prominent political figures have to say, content analysis may help us identify, for example, the level of friendliness or hostility in communications between nations. It may be used to study the content of various ideologies or to identify particular propaganda techniques being employed by individuals or organizations. Content analysis might also be used to improve our understanding of political socialization, through an analysis of the content of textbooks. In a historical context, content analysis has even been used to determine the disputed authorship of important political documents.[5]

We can summarize the advantages of content analysis under four general headings. First, this method of data gathering especially recommends itself in situations where there is restricted data access, that is, where direct interview access to prominent personalities is difficult or impossible. Second, content analysis is particularly salient when we are studying societies in which there is a positive relationship between the sources of public communication and the importance of these sources for societal outcomes. That is, it is especially useful to be able to study the communications of political elites when those elites seem to have a virtual monopoly on the decision- and policy-making processes in society. Third, content analysis can be crucial when the researcher feels he must have particularly large samples of communication to insure accuracy of interpretation. For one of the problems with examining ideas expressed by a person in a given five-, ten-, or thirty-minute period is that such ideas may not be representative of what he might really think over a period of weeks, months, or even years. We all recognize that our thoughts and our comments are influenced by circumstances of the moment. Therefore, content analysis is useful in situations where reliability may depend on being able to examine many statements made by a person at different points in time. Finally, content analysis can even be useful in cases where direct interview access to political leaders is possible. We may, for example, be able to interview local government officials; but it might be useful to use content analysis of the speeches of these leaders as a supplementary, or corroborative, technique. Elite interviewing probably will always be a sensitive method of data gathering, and such interviews might profitably be checked against analyses of public speeches and writings.

It is worth mentioning that content analysis can now be done partly by computers, thus relieving researchers of some aspects of what previously has been a very time-consuming method of information gathering. Of course, computers can only do what people tell them to do. Computer content analysis involves careful preparation by the researcher; but, once this preparation is completed, computers can process a great deal of information at very high speed, and with much greater reliability than individuals can hope to achieve.[6]

There are many methodological issues in content analysis. Just as with survey research, there are numerous respects in which the student using content analysis must take great care in organizing and carrying out his research. The extent of the potential methodological difficulties depends on the complexity of the analysis that is attempted. For example, it is one thing merely to *describe* the content of a communication; it is quite another to attempt to draw *inferences* from the content to such things as the motivations of the author or the communicator. Another problem is that content analysts sometimes have difficulty separating the cognitive from the affective dimensions of content. You will recall from the last chapter that the cognitive dimension refers to "is" perceptions, while the affective dimension refers to "ought" feelings. Sometimes the "is" and "ought" aspects of an individual's statements can be very difficult to separate. In particular, some common, politically relevant adjectives have strong affective significance for some people but are simply descriptive classifications (*i.e.*, cognitive) to others. Examples might be terms such as "socialist," "Communist," "authoritarian," and even "liberal" or "conservative." Separating the cognitive from the affective dimensions of such content requires careful study of the source of the communication, and even then it depends upon a certain measure of inference.

Another, more general problem is how to be sure that simple word counting, or theme counting, does not result in taking words out of their appropriate context. We have to be sure that we understand and categorize the *meaning* apparently given to a word or phrase by the person who uses it, and not merely tabulate its occurrence. For human communication is a subtle and complex process; people can give different shades of meaning to simple words by the ways in which they structure sentences or use qualifying phrases. The content analyst must be sensitive to these contextual conditions that may substantially change the meanings of words.

Biographical Data

For a long time, many students of politics have believed that an understanding of a person's social origins, conditions of upbringing, educational and professional training, and early-adult career experiences was important for explaining his involvement in the political process. Earlier, we mentioned some examples of items of personal background data that are thought to be important in understanding the thinking and the behavior of political actors. Some of the background characteristics studied are attributes acquired by an individual at birth, including sex, nationality, race, and ancestral background. Other information might be seen as relevant to early socialization, including rural versus urban upbringing, education, political involvement of family, religion, and youth memberships and activities. Numerous data on career experiences as an adult are also thought to be relevant for an understanding of perspectives toward politics. As we have indicated earlier, recent research suggests that these career experiences may be much more important than social background factors in explaining elite political orientations and behaviors. On the other hand, the social background attributes may be of greater utility in understanding the roles of the mass citizenry in politics.[7]

It is worth emphasizing that biographical data alone are not often of great significance to the student of politics. We gather biographical data to explain, so far as we can, a person's values, beliefs, and behavior. But we may wish to go further and relate such data to certain aspects of the functioning of society. In particular, we may seek to view the backgrounds of political leaders as indicators of the sorts of values held by influential people in society. Some distinguished students of social change have argued that the personal characteristics of political elites become "secondary societal values." [8] According to this view, persons who are elevated (by whatever selection methods) to positions of public prominence and trust must have personal characteristics that are respected by the people who put them in such positions. In turn, the tendency of the mass citizenry to develop, over a period of time, an identification of certain personal characteristics with the notion of public leadership further promotes the influence of these values. Thus, in the future, according to this argument, the personal attributes of a society's political leaders are likely to be emulated by new generations.

This view of the self-perpetuating tendencies of leaders' personal characteristics is based on several crucial assumptions. In particular, it assumes that public leadership is regarded in a basically favorable way by the general population. The degree to which this is true apparently varies between political systems. At the same time, there seems little doubt of the accuracy of the general proposition that the attributes reflected by persons in positions of leadership are usually highly visible and thereby acquire at least potential influence on subsequent value formation in society.

Aggregate Data

Students interested in comparing many different political systems have increasingly come to use what is called *aggregate data*. Since comparison is so important to the development of reliable understanding, any data used in comparative analysis warrant our close attention.[9]

Aggregate data, simply put, are data on aggregates. Aggregates, as we have said, are collectivities, usually of individuals. A voting district might be considered an aggregate, as might a city, a county, a state, or a nation. Aggregate data consist of

quantitative information which characterizes the entire population of the aggregate, rather than any specific individuals within
it.

As aggregate data characterize entire populations rather than
just individuals they are treated apart from the three data-
gathering methods just discussed above. In survey research, in
content analysis, and in biographical studies, information is
gathered and reported for specific individuals. (These individuals
may or may not be anonymous; in survey research, they generally will be. The relevant point is that the information is col-
lected and organized as information about individuals.) Of
course, it is possible to aggregate—to sum—responses to surveys,
data on styles of communication, or biographical information on
sets of individuals. Such information can be used to tell us something about aggregates—for example, about the political preferences of Iowans or the occupational and social-class origins of
Californians. Such data, however, are initially gathered and reported with the individual as the basis of observation. Aggregate
data, by contrast, focus on a population or aggregate.

Some examples will serve to sharpen our notion of aggregate
data. Most national governments and a great variety of private
and quasi-official institutions issue massive quantities of aggregate
statistical information each year. This information includes, for
example, census statistics, which are prominently used in social
research. The literacy rate in a population, data on educational
enrollment and achievement, and per capita income are other
examples.

Some information usually referred to as aggregate data is only
in a very limited sense a summation of individual characteristics
or performances. For example, such things as gross energy production, the value of imports, retail trade volume, the consumer
price index, and the volume of railway traffic may be useful
indicators of the *nature* of aggregates (*e.g.*, nations), but only in
a very indirect way do they amount to aggregations of individual
behaviors.

Especially for methodological purposes, we may divide aggregate information collections into two broad categories: cross-
sectional data and time-series data. Cross-sectional data consist of
information on several, presumably comparable aggregate units

(*e.g.,* nations, states, or counties) gathered at one point in time. Thus, official election returns by county in the United States for the 1972 Presidential election would constitute a collection of aggregate cross-sectional data. Time-series data deal with one or more aggregates, studied at several different points in time. A collection of data showing the distribution of votes by political party in American Presidential elections from 1848 to 1968 would be an aggregate time series. Another example of a time-series collection would be data on the number of outbreaks of civil violence in a Latin American country each year between 1935 and 1970.

In examining political circumstances in many different settings, the use of aggregate cross-sectional data is appropriate. For the advantage in cross-sectional data is that reasonably comparable information may be available on many countries for recent periods, though less consistently available for historical periods. Aggregate time-series data are especially useful when the purpose of the study is to identify and explain patterns of change, or development. But reliable time-series data on politically relevant circumstances are available for only a relatively small number of countries.

Although aggregate data are relatively easy to obtain, there are numerous problems involved in using them. Record-keeping practices are unfortunately inconsistent among different nations. Many governments have an interest either in distorting or in only partially reporting important social, economic, and political statistics. Further, even where deliberate distortion is at a minimum, record-keeping procedures may be unsystematic, inconsistent, and unreliable within the aggregate unit being studied. As a result, aggregate data are often less than fully reliable and thus can serve only as rough approximations of the conditions being studied.

It cannot be stressed too strongly that aggregate data, generally, are appropriate only for the study of aggregates and must be used with great care in describing or explaining behaviors of individuals. What is characteristic of an aggregate, as a collective whole, obviously may not be characteristic of any given individuals or groups within that aggregate. (We discussed this problem in chapter 5, in talking about the nature of political culture.) Further, *relationships* that are identified between important factors at the aggregate level do not necessarily hold true for individuals within the aggregate. For example, a classic study has shown that finding a high correlation between illiteracy levels and the proportion of blacks in the populations of the American states could lead to a substantially fallacious inference that American blacks are significantly more likely to be illiterate than American whites.[10] In the original study, the data were aggregate, reported at the state level. The information took the form, "In Alabama, *x* per cent of the population is black, and *y* per cent of the population is illiterate." The analysis of these state-level aggregate data showed a high correlation between black population and illiteracy, that is, states with more blacks tended to have more illiterates. Yet, it was discovered, by examining information on *individuals* in areas where both illiteracy and black population were high, that there was *not*, in fact, a significant correlation between being illiterate and being black. That is, the number of nonliterate whites in areas with substantial black populations was found to be high as well. As a result, the apparent relationship between illiteracy and race, which seemed to emerge by looking at aggregate data, was found to be wholly misleading and substantially inaccurate when confronted with more specific data on individual persons.

Although there are some important methodological limitations on the usefulness of aggregate data, we should not jump to the conclusion that they are not really helpful in studying politics. On the contrary, the availability of a variety of aggregate indicators for many political units, and their availability over historical time periods for several aggregates, make these data important resources for the student of politics. In addition, there are ways in which aggregate data can properly be used to make inferences about within-aggregate (*e.g.*, individual-level) characteristics and relationships, if adequate care is exercised.[11] Thus, aggregate data can contribute significantly to a broadening of our understanding of political life.

Event Data

In some respects, event statistics might reasonably be included under the previous heading of aggregate data. The sources of information on important political events, however, are often different from the sources of other commonly used aggregate information. Further, event statistics generally do not represent aggregated characteristics or behaviors of most or all of a given population, as is the case with most aggregate data. Rather, they usually refer to nonregularized activities of relatively small groups of persons. This is not always the case; civil wars may generate event statistics, and they are usually participated in by large portions of a population. Still, the nonregularized and non-mass bases of event statistics provide a useful way to distinguish them from other kinds of aggregate data.

Event statistics often are not available from official government sources and are not recorded in the usual statistical yearbooks or compendia. Apparently, this is due in part to the sensitivity of such event data to some governments. Examples of events of political importance to which students of politics recently have given attention are assassinations, strikes, demonstrations, riots, *coups d'état*, and mass resignations from high political office. More broadly, event statistics frequently focus on instances of unrest, instability, or violence.

The understanding of civil strife, and of the resulting system instability, is obviously very important for an understanding of the contemporary political world. You will recall that several of the approaches and models discussed earlier in this book gave considerable attention to the concept of system stability and to the procedures by which political systems maintain order. Consequently, event statistics can be especially helpful in making use of some of the important approaches and models used in the study of politics.

The collections of event statistics mentioned above provide information on developments within given countries. A slightly different form of event information consists of *interaction data*. Rather than describing activities *within* countries, interaction data deal with relations *between* nations. These data may refer to such events as trade transactions, intergovernmental communications, exchanges and visits of diplomatic personnel, the execution of treaties or other formal agreements, and even military skirmishes, confrontations, or war.

Event data, like aggregate data, can be of a cross-sectional or a longitudinal nature. They may describe happenings and inter-actions for numerous political units at a given point in time or for a more limited number of units over a considerable span of time. Time-series interaction and event data are particularly use-ful in describing changing trends in international relations.

Within-nation event data and between-nation interaction data can be analyzed in conjunction with one another. Such analysis helps us to understand the relationship between the domestic and international spheres of political activity. For example, some students of politics have been interested in the relationship between domestic political conflict and the involvement of coun-tries in conflicts with other nations. Does internal strife increase the likelihood that a nation will be involved in conflicts with other nation-states? Or, on the contrary, does a preoccupation with internal difficulties direct attention away from international relations, thereby "cooling off" conflict-full relations between countries? Is it possible that prolonged involvement in high levels of international conflict makes it more likely that internal turmoil will develop within a country? Or does a nation's in-volvement in international conflict solidify elements of the popu-lation behind the current leadership, thereby reducing the chance of internal unrest? The relationship between domestic-and foreign-conflict involvement is a very important one for understanding contemporary political affairs. Event statistics can be very helpful in contributing to our understanding of this relationship.

Observational Data

With each of the preceding five categories of information, the student of politics is dependent on the reporting or recording of information by others. Even in survey research, we are dependent upon the clarity and candor of the responses given by our sub-jects. There is another category of data, however, that is not dependent on information reporting or recording by others. With these data, the researcher himself is involved in some form of observation of the phenomena in which he is interested, and he is responsible for carrying out the recording of the details of what is happening. We call these categories of information *observational data.*

There are three major types of observational procedures used in gathering information about politics: direct, nonexperimental observation; "unobtrusive" observational measures; and experiments. As we shall see, these three sets of procedures vary a good deal, but they all share the advantage of not being dependent on secondhand reporting of information.

Direct, Nonexperimental Observation. Sometimes, it is possible for a researcher to observe certain types of political behavior by being or becoming a member or participant in the political unit he wants to study. Similarly, students of politics sometimes are able to make direct observations of the activities of political actors, even though the student may not be a formal part of the political situation in which that actor is operating.

The great advantage of observational studies is that they are able to examine behavior as it *occurs* rather than as it has been *reported.* We have already suggested that what people actually do and say is not always the same as what they might report that they did or said. Further, the perspective and precision that can be part of an observer's analysis of unfolding political events may be lacking in the reports of individuals who are personally, and perhaps emotionally, involved in what is going on.

There also are certain types of interesting and important questions about politics that are very difficult to study by anything other than an observational procedure. This is especially true for the study of political organizations that might be considered "radical" or even "subversive." Barber *et al.* offer the example of an interest in studying the Ku Klux Klan, the Minute Men, or the Communist Party.[12] It seems unlikely that members of these organizations would respond to elaborate survey questionnaires. Biographical data on their membership would be rather difficult to come by. Thus, although gaining admittance to meetings of these groups might be difficult, it might also be the only way to gain reliable understanding of how the organization functions, and of the kinds of individuals who are important in the organization.

Perhaps a more accessible example concerns the study of interaction among high-ranking diplomats in international organizations. Some students of international politics believe that, although formal speeches in the U.N. General Assembly are not likely to turn up great surprises in foreign policy, the observation of informal interactions among diplomats in the Assembly and in the councils of the United Nations may provide important clues to forthcoming international developments. Since these meetings are public, it is possible to chart these interactions.[13]

Another example might be the use of participant observation techniques in the study of childhood political socialization. Administering questionnaires to children is a delicate process. Getting them to talk with candor and understanding about the development of their own thinking concerning abstract objects in their environment is very difficult. But some important clues about the nature and degree of familial influence, for example, may be gained by observing the child in his home situation.

In each of these cases, there are some real difficulties involved in setting up and pursuing direct observation of politically relevant activity. But, in the absence of meaningful alternatives, such procedures assume importance for the student of politics.

"Unobtrusive" Observational Measures. Unobtrusive measures of social phenomena are methods of observation in which the observer is removed from the behavior being studied, but in which the researcher himself is still the recorder or evaluator of what is taking place.[14] Perhaps the most obvious example of this kind of procedure would be hidden mechanical observation, involving such things as secret recording devices and photographic equipment. Such procedures certainly are not in common use in political science, however, and some researchers feel ethical compunctions against their use.

The principal advantage of unobtrusive measures over direct observational procedures is that, with the former, the individual being studied is not aware that he is the target of investigation. When people know they are being studied, perhaps especially in political circumstances, they may adopt unrepresentative roles that would serve to cloud our understanding of their behaviors. With unobtrusive measures, the research or measurement act itself cannot serve as a factor that might induce artificial change in the behavior being studied.

Webb *et al.* have described a variety of unobtrusive measures used in the study of social behavior.[15] Others are summarized by Milgram [16] and by Sechrest.[17] One of the most interesting of these unobtrusive measures, and one that serves to illustrate their application, is a technique for assessing public values toward different politically relevant organizations. This is Milgram's "lost-letter" technique.[18] In this procedure, the investigator drops throughout an area a considerable number of addressed and stamped letters. People who come across these "lost" letters on the street have to decide whether to mail them, to disregard them, to destroy them, or to spirit them away. The technique proceeds on the assumption that persons are most likely to mail letters that are addressed to organizations toward which they have positive affect. That is, it is assumed that individuals will wish to "help" the organization by forwarding the letter. Thus, according to Milgram, the individual defines his values and attitudes toward an organization through the nature of his actions concerning the "lost" letter.

Unobtrusive measures can also be used to study the apparent impact of political communications, especially speeches to crowds. In this case, the observer may closely watch facial expressions and physical movements of listeners, as well as more obvious manifestations of approval or disapproval, such as applause or jeering.

While these unobtrusive measures avoid some of the difficulties involved in direct observational research, and in nonobservational studies, they have their own distinct limitations. Perhaps the most important is that the relationship between the unobtrusive measure and the concept it is supposed to reflect may be unclear or difficult to establish. It may be necessary to make several assumptions, and some considerable inferential leaps, in order to connect facial expressions with the impact of a speech. Similarly, many unobtrusive measures are difficult to judge objectively. Different observers looking at the same facial expressions, for example, might interpret them in different ways. Further, because such unobtrusive measures tend to be affected by a variety of environmental circumstances of the moment, it is difficult to know to what degree the results of such studies can be generalized to other situations or to other groups of individuals. Perhaps the most judicious attitude to take toward the use of unobtrusive measures is to suggest that they may be very helpful *supplementary* modes of study, when nonobservational, or direct observational, information may be open to challenge. In these cases, unobtrusive measures can provide an important added dimension that may help us to understand political activity.

Experiments. In most of the natural and technical sciences, experimentation has been for some time the principal way of gathering information. Students of politics have, until recently, labored under the misconception that human behavior could not really be studied by experimental methods. There is no doubt that the political researcher cannot "stop the world" or manipulate the nature of social reality. Generally speaking, we cannot bring the political world into the laboratory. And the range of interesting political circumstances that can be re-created, or simulated, in controlled laboratory settings is still modest, indeed.

Nevertheless, there is, in principle, no reason why the basic elements of experimental research cannot be carried out by social scientists. The types of political phenomena that we will be able to study by experimental methods will remain limited. But there is no question that the precision and reliability that scientific understanding requires are tremendously enhanced when we are able to do careful experimentation.

In the most general terms, in order to have an experiment, we must be able to do three things:

1. Manipulate the principal factor that we think causes the political phenomenon in which we are interested
2. "Neutralize" (or control) the effects of other factors that might be thought to have some effect on the phenomenon under study
3. Systematically observe and measure the effects of the manipulated factor (*independent variable*) upon the phenomenon being studied (*dependent variable*)

Each of these three procedures implies careful planning and

precise execution of the research. In order to be able to ascertain the effect of the independent variable, or the presumed causative factor, in an experiment, we must be able to introduce that factor when, and only when, we are prepared to measure its effects on the dependent variable. That is, we must be wholly in control of the incidence of the independent variable. In order to be able to rule out the possible effects of other factors, we must be able to isolate the subjects under study from as many contaminating environmental influences as possible. We must also be able to control (by randomizing) relevant characteristics of our subjects, such as age, sex, education, and so forth. Finally, in order to be sure that we have precisely identified the effects of the independent variable, we must be able to measure the dependent variable (the phenomenon under study) both *before* and *after* the introduction of the independent variable.

There are numerous forms of experimental and quasi-experimental designs that can be used in the social sciences.[19] A discussion of all of them does not seem necessary here. Rather, we shall mention only a frequently found version of the "classic" experimental design. This will serve to illustrate how experimental research in political science can be done.

In this common experimental situation, the basic design of the experiment involves:

1. The selection of at least two groups of subjects, whose relevant personal characteristics have been randomly distributed across the groups
2. The measurement of the dependent variable, which might be something like a particular value proposition, or attitude, in each of the groups
3. The introduction of an experimental factor or variable to one of the groups, such as a persuasive or propaganda statement considered relevant to the value or attitude being studied
4. The presentation to the other group, known as the control group, of reading material considered to be nonrelevant to the value or attitude being studied
5. A second measurement of the value or attitude under study for all members of each group, to determine whether the

introduction of the experimental material had a significant effect on the thinking of the subjects; that is, whether the propaganda statement had a greater effect than did the nonrelevant reading material on the subjects' thinking.

This basic experimental design, or some variation of it, has been used in examining the impact of a variety of factors on politically relevant values, beliefs, and attitudes. Along a slightly different line, some students of politics are now conducting experiments designed to identify the physiological correlates of political values and attitudes.[20] In this research, subjects are experimentally tested for such physiological responses as galvanic skin response and heart-rate change when presented with auditory or visual political stimuli, such as symbols, pictures, or speeches. One of the purposes of such research is to discover whether individuals actually have strong emotive responses to certain symbols, even while asserting that they are essentially unaffected.

The simulation technique mentioned in chapter 4 sometimes approximates experimentation. The basic features of this approach already have been laid out and need not be repeated. We have noted that there are difficulties with the use of simulation, principally in re-creating real-world situations in the laboratory, and that there are problems in trying to randomize or otherwise control for the effects of personality characteristics of the human participants in the simulation. Nevertheless, simulations have some of the features and advantages of experimental design and can be useful devices in generating and testing ideas about complex political relationships.

NOTES

1. For a general introduction to survey research, see Charles H. Backstrom and Gerald D. Hursh, *Survey Research* (Evanston, Ill.: Northwestern University Press, 1963).
2. There are some differences of opinion among survey researchers concerning how samples should be drawn for different research purposes. It does not seem necessary to introduce these issues here. A useful perspective on one of the most important of these issues can be found in "Conditional Universals and Scope Sampling," chapter 7 in David W.

Willer, *Scientific Sociology: Theory and Method* (Englewood Cliffs, N.J.: Prentice-Hall, 1967).

3. See R. L. Kahn and C. F. Cannell, *The Dynamics of Interviewing: Theory, Technique and Cases* (New York: John Wiley and Sons, 1957).

4. A useful, general introduction to content analysis is Ole R. Holsti, *Content Analysis for the Social Sciences and Humanities* (Reading, Mass.: Addison-Wesley, 1969).

5. For example, content analysis has been used to determine the probable authorship of some of the *Federalist Papers*. See F. Mosteller and D. L. Wallace, *Inference and Disputed Authorship: The Federalist* (Reading, Mass.: Addison-Wesley, 1964).

6. It is worth emphasizing that, contrary to the notions held by many persons, computers can recognize and process alphabetic characters, and thus textual materials, as well as numbers. Some examples of the uses of computers in content analysis are given in Holsti, *op. cit.*, pp. 150–94.

7. See M. George Zaninovich, "Party and Non-Party Attitudes Toward Social Change," in R. Barry Farrell (ed.), *Political Leadership in Eastern Europe and the Soviet Union* (Chicago: Aldine, 1970); and M. George Zaninovich, "Elites and Citizenry in Yugoslav Society: A Study of Value Differentiation," chapter 6 in Carl Beck, Frederic J. Fleron, Jr., Milton Lodge, Derek J. Waller, William A. Welsh, and M. George Zaninovich, *Comparative Communist Political Leadership* (New York: David McKay, 1973).

8. For example, see Edward A. Shls, "The Intellectuals and the Powers," *Comparative Studies in Society and History*, I (October, 1958), 5–22; and S. F. Nadel, "The Concept of Social Elites," *International Social Science Bulletin*, VIII, (Fall, 1956), 413–24.

9. A useful introduction to the use of aggregate data in studying politics may be found in Richard L. Merritt, *Systematic Approaches to Comparative Politics* (Chicago: Rand McNally, 1970), pp. 24–63.

10. For a summary of the difficulties involved in such a study, see W. S. Robinson, "Ecological Correlations and the Behavior of Individuals," *American Sociological Review*, XV (June, 1950), 351–57.

11. For an introduction to these possibilities, see Leo Goodman, "Some Alternatives to Ecological Correlation," *American Journal of Sociology*, LXIV (May, 1959), 610–25.

12. Sotirios A. Barber, Robert E. Johnston, Roger M. Nichols, and Janice B. Snook, *Introduction to Problem Solving in Political Science* (Columbus, Ohio: Charles E. Merrill, 1971), p. 36.

13. For example, see Chadwick F. Alger, "Interaction and Negotiation in a Committee of the United Nations General Assembly," *Papers of the Peace Research Society (International)*, V (1966), 141–59.

14. See Eugene J. Webb, Donald T. Campbell, Richard D. Schwarz, and Lee Sechrest, *Unobtrusive Measures: Nonreactive Research in the Social Sciences* (Chicago: Rand McNally, 1966).

15. *Ibid.*

16. See Stanley Milgram, "The Experience of Living in Cities," *Science*, CLXVII (1970), 1461–68; and Milgram, "The Lost Letter Technique," *Psychology Today*, III (1969), 30–33.

17. Lee Sechrest, "Testing, Measuring, and Assessing People," in E. F. Bor-

gatta and W. W. Lambert (eds.), *Handbook of Personality Theory and Research* (Chicago: Rand McNally, 1968), pp. 529–628.

18. See note 17, above. See also Stanley Milgram, Leon Mann, and Susan Harter, "The Lost Letter Technique: A Tool of Social Research," *Public Opinion Quarterly*, XXIX (1965), 437–38.

19. For an excellent summary of these research designs, see Donald T. Campbell and Julian C. Stanley, *Experimental and Quasi-Experimental Designs for Research* (Chicago: Rand McNally, 1966).

20. See John C. Wahlke and Milton G. Lodge, "Psychophysiological measures of Political Attitudes and Behavior," *Midwest Journal of Political Science*, XVII, 1 (February, 1973).

7

Structuring and Analyzing
Information About Politics

The focus of our treatment of information gathering in Chapter 6 was on the substance of the information itself. Now it is appropriate to discover something about how one decides in particular instances what information to gather and how it shall be organized and analyzed.

Obviously, the idle accumulation of information without some guiding design is highly inefficient, and might never yield any useful results. Before someone gathers information about politics, he must structure (or organize) his research. Hence, the proper sequence for the three broad categories of activity covered in chapters 6 and 7 is (1) structuring the study, (2) gathering information, and (3) analyzing information. This book treated step (2) first. It is worth briefly mentioning the reason for having done this.

Information gathering was treated separately because the structuring (1) and analysis (3) of information involve a number of very similar methodological issues that are best discussed conjointly. The analysis of information is directly dependent on how the study was organized, or structured, in the first place. More specifically, *the hypothesis is the common thread running through research structuring and data analysis*. The focus of structuring a study is on the *development and statement* of hypothesis. The focus of analyzing information is on the *testing* of hypotheses. Because they share this common core, so to speak, research structuring and data analysis are appropriately discussed together.

This certainly is not to suggest that information gathering does not raise methodological issues. On the contrary, a considerable part of chapter 6 was devoted to words of caution about when and how various data-gathering procedures could be used. At this point, we are nearly ready to turn from the information itself toward these practical, methodological issues that surround fitting information into hypotheses about politics.

STRUCTURING THE STUDY OF POLITICS

There are at least five sets of decisions that the student of politics must make in the course of structuring his study. Each of these sets of decisions requires careful discussion. It might, however, be useful to provide an overview of the decisions in advance.

1. The student must *select a general topic,* or problem, to be studied. This implies some criteria on the basis of which one topic is selected in preference to others.

2. He must identify a *basic strategy* for approaching the topic. In particular, he must determine whether his study will be *exploratory* or *verificatory* in nature. He also must give attention to the *deductive* versus *inductive* elements of his strategy.

3. He must decide on the *form* of the inquiry, especially whether he will explore research *questions,* explore research *problems* or test *hypotheses.*

4. He must decide how to *define* and *measure* the *variables* with which he will deal.

5. He must delimit the *scope of inquiry, i.e.* the specific cases (*e.g.,* persons, samples, aggregates, populations) that he will examine.

Selecting A Topic

It is remarkable how little attention students of politics have given to one of the most basic questions in all of social inquiry: What criteria can a person use in deciding what topic or problem to study? In some cases, we "decide" to study either what we are *told* to study (*e.g.*, by a course instructor or by the director of a research project) or else what "interests" us. Presumably, we can do relatively little about the former. But, when we have the opportunity to choose, few of us ever think systematically about why we ought to select one sort of topic or another.

Perhaps there is a prior question: Why try to have criteria to evaluate the relative importance of one project over another? Why not just opt for intellectual anarchy, and have people continuing to study whatever "appeals" to them at the moment? James A. Robinson, one of the few political scientists who have tried to deal with these issues, effectively poses—and answers—this question.[1]

> The answer to this question is that resources are scarce among students of politics. Our desire to know exceeds our capacity to learn. There are many things we do not know but would like to know. The questions we cannot answer but would like to answer, the half-formed and untested hypotheses, the merely tentative conclusions which we have about a subject—all of these add up to an imposing need and desire for more knowledge. What we would like to know is very great; our resources for knowing are very limited.

In short, intellectual anarchy might be psychologically comfortable, but it is socially wasteful. There is too much knowledge to be sought, and there are too few resources, and too little time, for the seeking.

Let us be sure that we understand Robinson's position. He is *not* urging that all of us must accept a single criterion for determining the most important topics for study. Rather, he merely wants each of us to be thoughtful and explicit about how we make these choices. Robinson would like to see each student of politics accept some notion of social or intellectual importance as a basis for his selection criteria. Perhaps even that is asking too much. But, at a minimum, each student should be conscious of why he selects a particular topic for study and should be able to defend his criteria of selection.

For our purposes, then, it is enough to summarize some of the criteria that might be used in deciding on a topic for study.

1. *Gaps in current knowledge.* One approach is to identify

subject-matter areas that are considered relevant to topics on which considerable knowledge has been accumulated, but which themselves have been given little attention. Example: Although considered relevant to the frequently discussed topic of political instability in Latin America, very little research has been done on organization and leadership in political parties in those countries.

2. *Available data.* Some researchers select topics because there are many relevant collections of reliable data available. It appears as if some research in the area of citizen opinions about politics has been encouraged simply by the availability of data from many surveys.[2]

3. *Sophisticated techniques.* Researchers are sometimes motivated toward certain topics because information on those topics can be gathered and analyzed by relatively sophisticated or powerful techniques. For example, because experimental research designs offer more precise control over the study, some researchers prefer to concentrate on subjects that can be handled experimentally. Or, some students may be inclined to choose topics on which quantitative data are available, so that relatively complex statistical procedures can be used in analyzing the data.

4. *Popular models or approaches.* The current "popularity" of certain models or approaches often exerts a great deal of influence on the topics chosen for study. For example, systems approaches and functional approaches are currently very popular in political science, and many researchers seem to rule out any research focus that cannot comfortably be fitted into one of these perspectives.

5. *Salient behavioral dependent variables.* Some researchers have adopted a strategy suggested by Robinson, namely, focusing on those political behaviors that seem most salient, or significant, in the political process. These salient behaviors are viewed as the most important dependent variables to be explained by students of politics, and research problems are formulated around efforts to explain these important behaviors. For example, Robinson identified a series of behaviors considered especially relevant in policy-making and urges that research be focused there.[3]

6. *Breadth of relevance.* Another approach is to concentrate

on those topics that are somehow related to the broadest possible range of studies now being done. For example, if a researcher felt that much of the current research being done on politics could be considered relevant to *conflict,* he would devote his energies to study topics relevant to an understanding of conflict. This strategy is based on the premise that the most efficient use of human resources can be realized by being sure that there is as much common ground as possible in our collective efforts.

7. *Personal values of the investigator.* For some students, the choice of a research topic is both individual and normative. They embrace in their topics the search for knowledge thought to be useful in solving pressing social problems or in providing a fuller understanding of how desired political conditions could be realized. Students using this sort of criterion might want to generate information about how people of different races view one another or about the social and economic conditions necessary to achieve and maintain democracy.

8. *Personal interests of the investigator.* In this case, the researcher's posture is individualistic but not normative. The criterion for selecting a topic has nothing to do with pressing social problems, but rather concerns the intellectual "appeal" of an idea. If the topic seems "interesting," or "exciting," it is worth doing. While this criterion might seem frivolous to some people, it should be stressed that there is a widespread belief that people do their best work when they are working on something that intellectually "turns them on." [4]

By now, you know that choices such as these have to be made by the individual student of politics. At least this book proceeds on the assumption that thought provoked is far better than order imposed. It is not at all clear that there is a "best" criterion for topic selection. But it is important that each of us think carefully about this issue and have a conscious position on it.

Basic Strategies of Inquiry

Research strategies may be exploratory or verificatory in nature. A project is *exploratory* if little is known about the topic, thus necessitating "starting from scratch." Exploratory studies are not guided by specific expectations about what the objects to be studied look like or how they are related to one another. Rather, such studies involve mapping the terrain—gaining some general sense of what the foci of the study are like and perhaps working in the direction of formulating some general statements about patterns of interrelationship.

Verificatory studies, by contrast, focus on topics about which a good deal has already been learned. Consequently, verificatory studies are structured around some reasonably explicit expectations about how different elements of the subject are interrelated. As the term implies, verificatory studies attempt to *verify—i.e.,* to add certainty to—our previous understanding of a topic.

Verificatory studies contribute more directly to theory building, and probably enjoy higher "status" in science, than do exploratory studies. This is true because *replication*—repeated study of the same or similar objects operating under similar conditions —is crucial to the establishment of reliable knowledge. In order to be sure that what one investigator has discovered is not a "special" or "deviant" case, repeated studies are required. Or, similarly, a large number of cases must be studied within the framework of a single research project. This is not to say that exploratory studies are not worthwhile; indeed, they are often very important in the early stages of generating information about a subject. But the *direct* contribution of such studies to science is relatively slight.[5]

The distinction between exploratory and verificatory strategies is roughly paralleled by the contrast between inductive and deductive research strategies. Broadly, *induction* involves deriving general statements from specific observations; *deduction* involves deriving specific statements from more general premises. When we structure a research project by looking at a model or theory and then deciding how its general statements can be applied to, and examined in, a specific case that we wish to study, our strategy becomes deductive. If we decide to examine specific characteristics of a given case, and then attempt to derive from that case more general hypotheses that could be examined in another research project, our strategy becomes inductive. Generally speaking, exploratory strategies are inductive in nature, while verificatory strategies are deductive. That is, exploratory research involves the study of specific cases (or, settings) in an effort to generate general statements that link political phenomena. Verificatory research usually implies testing generalizations that have already been accumulated on the basis of earlier inductive studies.

Although it is relatively easy to draw abstract distinctions between exploratory and verificatory strategies, as well as between inductive and deductive strategies, they are often used conjointly in practice. There is a persuasive reason for this, namely, that induction and deduction are inherently dependent upon one another. It is difficult, indeed, even to outline and define a research topic, let alone begin to explore the dimensions of given cases, if you do not have some general statements (*e.g.*, models or hypotheses) to guide you. Otherwise, where would the student get his ideas about what to look for, and at, in the first place? Thus, in one sense induction must have the benefit of some prior thinking from which deductions can be made. Conversely, deduction is dependent upon some prior induction, in that general statements commonly are based on accumulated and synthesized knowledge from past specific studies. Some students of politics have asserted, in effect, that they "just dreamed up" their hypotheses, or generalizations, but it seems highly doubtful that such intellectual creativity is not based substantially on what a person has learned through past experiences. In other words, even "grand theorists" have pictures of the world that reflect their own experiences and observations.

Just because deductive, verificatory studies seem to contribute more directly to scientific theory, you definitely should not conclude that exploratory studies are not worth doing. On the contrary, breaking new intellectual ground can be stimulating and rewarding. As we suggested at the beginning of this chapter, there are substantial gaps in our understanding of political behavior, and efforts to fill those gaps should be welcome. Considerable care, however, needs to be exercised if exploratory studies are to prove worthwhile. Three caveats, in particular, might be mentioned.

First, the student who plans an exploratory study should be

quite sure that the subject has, in fact, been little researched. All too often students of politics have broken "new" ground only to discover that the path was already made and marked. We must always be certain that we have carefully searched relevant bibliographic sources to make sure that our view of the current state of research on a given subject is accurate. Second, it is especially important in exploratory research that the student adequately prepare himself by doing extensive general background reading about the cultural setting in which his study will be done. For example, if a student were interested in studying political leadership behaviors in Latin American dictatorships, he should be quite sure that he knew a good deal about the political and cultural characteristics of the countries in which political leadership would be examined. Finally, exploratory strategies require the conscious use of criteria of relevance in deciding what information to gather and analyze. Exploratory studies lack the coherent structure provided by the generalizations with which deductive, verificatory studies begin. Consequently, exploratory studies must, at a minimum, make use of some criterion by which it can be decided what kind of information is most relevant to the subject at hand. Generally speaking, the most effective way to handle this is to focus your topic as specifically as possible, and then to think of whatever aspect of the topic seems to represent a *dependent variable*—a phenomenon you want to explain—even though you do not have specific ideas about how other variables can be used to understand that dependent variable. Deciding on what you want to explain should, in turn, suggest, at least broadly, what sort of information should be gathered about the topic in order to insure that you have everything you need to conduct the study.

Form of the Inquiry

Studies of politics can assume one or more of three basic forms: (1) the exploration of research *questions,* (2) the exploration of research *problems,* and (3) the testing of *hypotheses.* The form chosen for a study has important implications for how the study will be carried out.

Research *questions* are descriptive, nonrelational inquiries.

They take the form of "What are the characteristics of object X?" An example of a research question would be, "To what extent is frustration with political authority present among the citizens of system X?"

Research *problems* are relational but nondefinitive inquiries. They take the form of "What is the relationship between phenomenon A and phenomenon B?" (Note that the *expected shape* of the relationship is not specified.) An example of a research problem would be, "What is the relationship between frustration with political authority and violent, politically relevant behavior?"

Hypotheses are conjectural statements specifying a particular relationship between phenomena.[6] They may take one of several slightly variant forms of the statement "As phenomenon A increases, phenomenon B increases." (We shall discuss these slightly variant forms shortly.) A hypothesis might state, "As frustration with political authority increases, the likelihood of violent, politically relevant behavior increases."

In a very general way, we can say that research questions and problems provide form for inquiries in which the investigator essentially does not know what his data will look like. In this sense, research questions and problems are exploratory forms of inquiry. Hypotheses, by contrast, embody specific expected relationships and thus are used in verificatory research.

In another sense, we may view research questions and problems as preliminary and intermediate steps along the way toward the development of hypotheses. The examples used above, dealing with frustration and violence, illustrate this point. A student interested in this topic might well begin by trying to learn something descriptive about frustration with political authority, and then about violent, politically relevant behaviors, in a few societies. His initial exploratory efforts might lead him to anticipate some sort of linkage between frustration and violence, but the likely shape of that relationship could be unclear. At this point, he would shift his research from exploring the nature of frustration and the nature of violence and begin to explore the nature of the relationship between the two phenomena. Researching this problem should ultimately lead the student to identify some fairly specific dimensions to the frustration-violence relationship. These specific relational dimensions would provide a basis for the formulation of hypotheses.

We suggested above that hypotheses can be stated in several slightly different forms. The basic nature and purpose of a hypothesis are the same, regardless of the specific form to express the statement. The form may be varied to facilitate the use of certain techniques of analysis, or simply to suit the personal preference of the researcher. Four variations of the basic form of hypotheses can be identified: (1) the literary alternative, (2) the operational alternative, (3) the literary null, and (4) the operational null. To put this in another way, there are two dimensions to the expression of hypotheses: They may be stated in the null form or in the alternative form: and they may be stated in the literary form or in the operational form.

The *null* form of a hypothesis states, in effect, that the researcher does not expect to find the relationship he is looking for. It indicates that the independent variable will have no effect on the dependent variable. The *alternative* form does just the opposite; it states the relationship you expect to observe. Or, the alternative form states the hypothesis you will accept *if* the null hypothesis is *rejected*. Thus, a null hypothesis might state that increasing frustration will not increase the likelihood of violent behavior. The alternative form would state that, as frustration increases, the likelihood of violent behavior increases.

It is entirely reasonable to wonder why anyone would ever want to state a hypothesis in a form contrary to what he actually expects to discover, that is, in the null form. Why not simply put one's expectations in a straightforward, positive way?

The answer to this question has to do with the problem of how a researcher decides whether he has "significant" findings, or conclusions, in his study. We shall take up the difficulties involved in deciding what is "significant" at greater length in chapter 8, but some consideration of this issue is necessary here.

In a sense, the crux of the "significance" problem is the obvious fact that reality is a blend of shadings and degrees, not stark contrasts and absolutes. Strictly speaking, whether something is "true" or "fact" is a question of degree, or probability, or tendency. Let us look at our example of a hypothesized relationship between frustration and violent behavior. Does frustration lead to violence? It is awfully difficult to answer yes or no. In particular, we must decide *how much* effect frustration would need to have on violent behavior before we can assert that there is a relationship between the two. Further, we would need to decide with what *probability* (*i.e.,* degree of certainty) the relationship would have to hold in order to justify the conclusion that a relationship exists.

Whenever we start talking about such questions of *degree,* we are implicitly saying that we have a *fixed base point* from which we can assess those degrees—degrees of difference, degrees of change, or degrees of probability. And this is where the null hypothesis form becomes useful. Saying that there *will* be *some* difference (some change, some effect)—*i.e.,* using the alternative form—is ambiguous. How much change is "some"; how much effect is a "significant" effect? There really is only one level of effect, or difference, that is reasonably unambiguous. That level is *none.* Thus, stating hypotheses in the null form provides a basis for determining the *extent* to which an effect, or difference, can be identified. To be "significant," a difference must be significantly *different from something,* or some level. The level commonly chosen in science is zero.

Let us emphasize that not every effect or difference that is greater than none is considered "significant." On the contrary, scientific procedures are clearly conservative in assessing significance. The criteria invoked usually require a considerable magnitude of difference from zero, and a high probability that the results could not have occurred by chance, before significance is attributed. The point is that the null hypothesis form states the relationship under study in such a way that rigorous procedures can be used to determine the "significance" of our research results.

Hypotheses also may be stated in literary or operational forms. Actually, we have already introduced a similar distinction in chapter 5, when we contrasted conceptual and operational definitions. *Literary* hypotheses state relationships in terms of *concepts.* *Operational* hypotheses state relationships in terms of the actual *research procedures,* or operations, necessary to test for the existence of the relationship. Thus, the literary form represents a more direct link between the hypothesis and our more general model or theory, whereas the operational form links the hypothesis with the actual conduct of a particular piece of research. A literary hypothesis might state that increased frustration toward political authority will lead to an increased likelihood of politically relevant violence; while the operational form might state that a decrease in caloric intake per capita will lead to an increase in the number of violent deaths from riots and political assassinations. In this case, the researcher would be operationalizing "frustration" in terms of caloric intake and operationalizing "politically relevant violence" as deaths from riots and assassinations.[7]

As we suggested above, the null alternative dimension and the literary operational dimension of hypothesis-statement are necessarily combined, giving us four distinct hypothesis forms. The *literary null* related concepts in a "no-difference" form; the *literary alternative* relates concepts through a positive statement of expected association; the *operational null* relates research operations in a "no-difference" form; and the *operational alternative* relates research procedures, but in terms of a positive statement of expected relationship. As we have implied, the literary alternative form is probably the most common way to state a hypothesis for purposes of telling others what you are doing. The operational null form is frequently required as a basis for the actual execution of research, especially the analysis of your data.

Hypotheses are of crucial importance to a systematic understanding of any subject—and, hence, to science.[8] Hypotheses permit us to go beyond mere description and to examine relationships among social phenomena. They link our specific research projects to a broader body of knowledge, partly because they often are deduced from, or suggested by, our models or theories, and partly because they are the vehicles through which our tentative understanding of specific situations can be pulled together and generalized for examination in other settings. And hypotheses in operational form can be tested, thus providing a basis for verification, that is, adding greater certainty to our knowledge about our political environment.

Through our examples, we have implied that hypotheses link phenomena that may vary—increase, decrease—in their manifestations. We have talked, for example, about frustration *increasing*, and how it might lead to an *increase* in violence. At this point, we should make explicit the important point that *hypotheses relate variables*—things whose characteristics or manifestations vary in different settings or at different points in time. After all, if the level of frustration were always the same everywhere, or if the level of violent, politically relevant behavior were uniform and unchanging, there would be no sense in trying to establish a *relationship* between the two. Another way to put this is that hypotheses state how *variations,* or *changes,* in one phenomenon are related to *variations,* or *changes* in another phenomenon. If there are never any variations, or changes, in something, you cannot incorporate that thing into a hypothesis. Because variables are central to the use of hypotheses, we now turn our attention to a, definition and discussion of variables.

Variables

A *variable* is a property that takes on different values, or assumes different characteristics, that is, *varies*. Usually, a variable can assume one of several values. Thus, there are many possible levels of frustration, violence, political participation, power, influence, conflict, and so forth. Depending on how precisely we want to look at our variables, the levels of these phenomena might be a potentially infinite set of values on a very detailed scale, or might simply be grouped into categories of, say, "very high," "high," "medium," "low," and "very low." (We shall shortly say more about the precision of different levels of measurement.) But, generally speaking, variables may take on one of several values. Usually, these values are part of a single scale, and we can refer to these variables as being *continuous* variables, that is, the scale underlying the measurement of the variable consists of a continuous series of values that have an identifiable relationship with one another.

In some cases, however, variables may take on only two values.

We refer to these variables as *dichotomous* variables, or *attributes*. Sex, for example, is generally considered to be a dichotomous variable; since sex is usually thought to have only two categories, researchers speak of it as a *natural* dichotomy. There are numerous other variables, however, that could assume several different values, but which the researcher may wish, for a variety of reasons, to treat as if they were dichotomies. We refer to these variables as *analytic* dichotomies. Variables may be *dichotomized* to show *presence or absence* of a property, or to distinguish two *different levels* of the presence of a property. For example, data on levels of citizen participation in politics might be dichotomized to distinguish voters from nonvoters, "gladiators" from "spectators," or strong party identifiers and supporters from weak party identifiers and supporters. In each of these cases, the student of politics could devise more precise, continuous scales to use in distinguishing several different levels of these variables. For purposes of simplicity, however, or in order to use certain specific procedures of analysis, he might wish to treat these variables in a dichotomous fashion.

A second "special case" of variables consists of those that take several values, but which cannot reasonably be viewed as being based on a single, continuous dimension. They have several different categories, but also reflect more than one underlying scale, or dimension. We refer to these variables as *polychotomous* variables. For example, the variable of occupational background has been used in several studies of political leadership. There is a notion that leaders recruited into politics from different sorts of professional training and experiences—law, corporate business, education, banking and finance, and so on—may think and behave differently as political leaders. Occupational background, therefore, usually is treated as a polychotomy. Thus, the variable of occupational background has several possible "values," or categories. But these categories cannot be ranged along any one dimension. We cannot say that a background in law, for example, is "occupationally" "more" or "less" than a background in banking and finance. Viewed merely as occupational categories, these different backgrounds have no necessary relationship, quantitative or logical, with one another. In a sense, each occupation represents a separate dimension of activity. When we use variables such as education, frustration, or intelligence, it is easy to visualize different levels of the variable. But the notion of different "levels" or "degrees" of occupation makes little sense.[9]

Thus, variables can be separated into three subtypes: continuous variables, dichotomies (attributes), and polychotomies. As we have suggested, the distinctions among these three subtypes of variables are based substantially on the *level of measurement* used by the researcher. Indeed, the measurement process is exceedingly important in any careful effort to find out more about reality, since measurement is the basis of our operational definitions of our concepts. A few words about *levels of measurement* are in order at this point.

Levels of Measurement. Social scientists conventionally distinguish four levels of measurement. These different levels of measurement, as we have suggested above, are reflected in four types of scales, having different degrees of precision. Nominal and ordinal scales are often characterized as "qualitative" scales, whereas interval and ratio scales are described as "quantitative." Each type of scale involves measurement in the most general sense, that is, measurement as the assignment of numbers. These scales differ considerably in their degree of precision and thus in their usefulness to students of politics.

Nominal scales are, in fact, nothing more than classifications to which numbers have been assigned. The numbers on a nominal scale have no consistent relationship to one another. The numbering system used on the jerseys of an athletic team is an example of a nominal scale. In football, a running back may wear the number 25, and the center, the number 50, but one cannot infer from this that the center is twice as talented, fast, large, or bright as the running back. Similarly, a student of Bulgarian politics might be interested in studying the effects of nationality (*i.e.,* national background) on the behavior of political leaders in that country. His classification of principal national backgrounds among Bulgarian leaders might include Bulgars, Turks, Macedonians, and Gypsies. For purposes of encoding his data for computer analysis, he might assign numbers (say, one through four) to these national groupings. Clearly, the numbers would have no significance other than to provide a kind of shorthand numerical designation for each category of the polychotomy, national background. To put this another way, no *ordering* is implied by the numbers used in a nominal scale. Thus, when a researcher has no single dimension for ordering the categories of his variable in relation to one another, his measurement must make use of nominal scales. Generally, this is true of most polychotomies and some dichotomies.

Ordinal scales are based on the notion that a single dimension exists along which categories of a variable can be ranked; that is, there is a property that the categories exhibit "more" or "less" of. Further, ordinal scales have transitivity: If A is greater than B, and B is greater than C, than A must be greater than C.

Occupational status is a frequently cited example of a variable that can be measured at the ordinal level. Armed with the appropriate data from survey research, we can determine that some occupations are more prestigious than others in given societies. Using such information, we can construct an ordinal scale ranking occupations from the highest to the lowest in terms of status or prestige. Note, however, that it is extremely difficult to determine *how much* more status inheres in one occupation as compared with another. This *absence of consistent intervals* between the rankings of an ordinal scale is what distinguishes such scales from higher levels of measurement. A ranking of the "top 10" college football teams or the "top 20" political science departments in the country might purport to tell us who is best, next best, and so on, but it would not tell us *how much* better, say, number 3 was than number 6. Indeed, there might be very little difference between number 3 and number 4, but a very great difference between number 4 and number 5. Ordinal scales do not have equal (or, indeed, determinate) intervals between ranks. When a researcher is using polychotomies or dichotomies for which he can reasonably assume a ranking among the categories, he may make use of ordinal scaling. Or, if he has a continuous variable, but cannot really be certain that the intervals between ranks or categories of that variable are equal, he may feel constrained to use ordinal measurement.

Interval and *ratio* scales are "quantitative" scales. They are used when the numerical size of the differences between categories, or scores, is known and consistent. Generally speaking, this is possible when standard units of measurement, such as monetary units, units of time, or proportions of persons in a population, constitute the basis of categorization of a variable. Thus, governmental expenditures for specified categories of activity can be measured with precision. The amount of education achieved by a political leader can be viewed as a quantitative variable, as can the proportion of the labor force engaged in farming, or the per capita caloric intake of a population.

Interval and ratio scales are similar, but they can be distinguished from one another. The difference is that ratio scales have nonarbitrary zero points. When we talk about variables such as, for example, amount of education and amount of government expenditure, there is a meaningful zero point—no education, no money. When we have such a meaningful zero point, we can compare ratios; that is, we can say that government expenditures for activity A are twice those for activity B, or that leader X has twice as much formal education as leader Y.

Blalock provides what is perhaps the most familiar example of an interval scale that is not also a ratio scale.[10] This is temperature, measured in terms of Fahrenheit or centigrade scales. As Blalock points out, the zero points on both of these scales are arbitrary. Consequently, it is not reasonable to say that a temperature of 30° is twice as hot as a temperature of 15°, so that these temperature scales are not ratio scales. But it is possible to say that, on either scale, the magnitude of the difference between 30° and 15° is the same as that between 60° and 45°. The scales do qualify, therefore, as interval scales.

Many of the continuous variables used by social scientists can be measured at the interval or ratio level. Variables measured at these levels are—other things being equal—more useful to the student of politics than are less precisely measured variables. This is true because more precise, quantitative scales tell us more about the relationships between categories of a variable, and because their precision enables us to be more exact in exploring the impact of one variable upon another. The greater the precision with which we can identify variation in the occurrence of our variables, the greater our capacity to identify co-variation, that is, to trace connections between the patterns of variations in each variable.

It is worth emphasizing that the level of measurement used by a researcher is dependent as much on his own ingenuity, and his measuring instruments or procedures, as on the "inherent nature" of the objects he is studying. Many students of politics used to believe that quantification had little relevance for their field, simply because there were very few political phenomena susceptible to quantitative measurement. Fifty years ago, the notion that interval scales of political influence, or politically relevant violence, could be devised would have been considered laughable by all but a handful of political scientists. Today, while there remain meaningful disagreements about the overall usefulness of such scales, it is nevertheless the case that the major dispute is over *which* interval scale of influence or violence ought to be used. It is not that the basic nature of influence or violence has changed; rather, it is that students of these phenomena have become both more imaginative and more precise in the way they conceptualize and measure influence and violence. To put this point in the context of one of the basic messages of this book, problems of measurement of political phenomena have to do both with what is being measured and with how we go about doing the measuring.

Indirect Measurement, Validity, and Reliability. It is well and good to talk about the importance of having precise measurement of our variables. There are compelling reasons for valuing such precision. At the same time, achieving precise, quantitative measurement may be more easily said than done. One of the principal reasons for this is that measurement in the social sciences is, in important respects, *indirect.* Two elements of this indirectness of measurement should be mentioned here.

In the broadest sense, *all* measurement is indirect. Even when a physicist measures a quantity such as mass, his measurement is indirect in the sense that the measurement is "filtered" through several conditions and devices that can distort the "true" quantity of mass. These "filters" include (1) the gravitational pull of the earth, (2) the properties of the measuring device (*i.e.,* a metal spring of some sort), and (3) the characteristics of the researcher himself.[11] If the force of gravity is not constant, if the measuring device is not highly accurate, or if the researcher has poor eyesight or poor powers of concentration, then the measurement recorded may not correspond exactly with the "true" quantity.

It is much the same with our measures of political phenomena. Our "readings" of the occurrence of politically relevant violence are similarly indirect and may be distorted by a variety of factors. These distorting influences may include (1) an inadequate theoretical-conceptual base, such that we are not always sure whether a given event fits our definition of "politically relevant violence"; (2) an operational definition that has dubious correspondence with the conceptual definition, that is, an invalid measure; (3) a measure that, though in valid correspondence with the conceptual definition, is not consistent, or reliable, in identifying real-world events; (4) inconsistent or inaccurate recording of violent events by observers in different places; or (5) inconsistent or insensitive handling, combining, or analysis of the data by the researcher. In a broad sense, then, there is an indirectness to all measurement, and this indirectness may produce distortion.

There is a closely related, but more specific, sense in which social-science measurement may be indirect. It is often the case that we are unable to observe directly, or to gather data that directly reflect on, certain important political phenomena. We made this point in chapter 6, and we shall return to it in chapter 8. We cannot interview high-level political leaders, so we *infer* their values and issue orientations from selected public speeches and writings. We cannot sit in on meetings of the Cabinet, the National Security Council, or the Supreme Court, so we *infer* the influence of different individuals, or groups, by comparing the decisions of these bodies with the positions espoused previously by their members or by those who have tried to influence them. We cannot interview enough people in the less-developed countries of the world to ascertain their degree of psychological frustration with political authority, so we resort to highly indirect measures of frustration, such as caloric intake per capita.[12]

The logical process of inference is crucial to such efforts at measurement. That is, in order to make use of such *indirect indicators* of phenomena in which we are interested, we must make certain assumptions about the relationship between the occurrence of the phenomenon itself and the occurrence of the indicator. If frustration does not go up as caloric intake goes down, then the indirect measurement of frustration through the indicator of caloric intake would not be *valid*.

In the preceding paragraphs, we have introduced two terms, validity and reliability, that are very important to the student of politics. We have illustrated the nature of validity and reliability by example, but this is not enough, given the centrality of these notions to the study of politics. More formal treatment is called for.

Validity refers to the adequacy with which we measure what we think we are measuring. We suggested above that some of the measures, or operational definitions, used in studying politics may have challengeable correspondence with the concepts to which they refer. Just as educators sometimes challenge the meaningfulness of certain test scores as measures of intelligence, or achievement, students of politics sometimes challenge the correspondence of the measures used in studying political phenomena. For example, not a few political scientists have wondered aloud whether caloric intake is a meaningful measure of "frustration," whether palace *coups* are useful measures of "revolution," or whether congruent behavior really measures "influence."

When we raise questions about the meaningfulness of a measure in telling us something about a concept, we are raising issues of validity. Because of the indirectness of measurement in the social sciences, validity is a very important consideration for the student of politics. We need to do everything possible to insure that our measures have a high degree of validity. But how? What are the procedures by which we ascertain validity?

As Kerlinger points out, the subject of validity is complex and controversial.[13] You will undoubtedly hear a good deal more about it as your study in the social sciences progresses. For now, we shall distinguish briefly among four types of validity and among the validation procedures associated with each type.

Content or *face validity* refers to the representativeness or sampling adequacy of the content of a measure. That is, content validity revolves around whether the substance of a measure appears to be "representative" or "typical" of the substance of what is supposedly being measured. Suppose you design a survey questionnaire to measure (among other things) the "conservatism" of the person responding. Content validation would refer to the extent to which the substance of your questions actually represents, or typifies, what might generally be thought to be "conservative" points of view.

Already, you probably have a hunch why content validity is often called "face" validity. The reason is that content validation usually is very judgmental and is based on the impressions of "experts," or trained researchers, concerning the representativeness of the measure. In other words, such validation is based on an evaluation of the measure on its "face," that is, in terms of a researcher's judgmental response to the over-all nature of the measure.

Predictive validity and *concurrent validity* are very similar. Both refer to the correspondence of a measure to some *outside criterion*. The predictive validity of a measure consists of its ability to predict (i.e., identify and project), say, an individual's score on another measure thought to be indicative of the same dimension of behavior. For example, aptitude tests are used to predict achievement in various fields; the scores of young people on a conservatism scale might be used to predict their subsequent involvement in conservative political organizations in college. Concurrent validity differs from predictive validity only in that the other measures to which we are "predicting" are being taken at about the same point in time, that is, concurrently. Thus, some colleges may use two or more entrance examinations and check the validity of one against the other. Or students of politics may have several indicators of political instability and may evaluate the validity of a "new" indicator in terms of the extent to which political units that are scored "high" in instability on the new indicator also score "high" on previously used and accepted measures.

Construct validity is the most complicated and, in some ways, the most difficult type to grasp. Construct validity refers to the contribution made by a measure to the *theoretical context* in which a study is being conducted. The construct validity of a measure is high when that measure helps us understand *why* a person, or a political system, scores as he does on the measure. Construct validity goes beyond the correspondence of scores on different measures; it has to do with our ability to understand the real-world relationships among phenomena that result in different scores on the measure. If different political units score differently on a measure of political instability, for example, does our measure help us *explain* these different scores? To put it another way, does the measure help us to separate the different dimensions of the concept being measured, so that we might see how those dimensions are affected by various events and conditions? Does our measure of political instability help us to recognize that instability may be a complex, multidimensional concept, and that numerous factors contribute to variations in a society's level of political instability? Does the measure help us to relate our particular study to other research that has shed light upon factors related to instability? In short, does our measure help us to imbed our own work into a broader framework of relevant theory and research?

The specific procedures by which researchers have attempted to establish construct validity for their measures are varied and numerous. Some useful discussions of this problem are available,[14] and it is unnecessary to repeat their thrust here. For our purposes, what is important to remember is that construct validity calls attention to the importance of a broad perspective toward measurement. It is important not only that we measure as faithfully as possible what we think we are measuring, but also that our measures be designed with an eye to learning as much as possible about how a given phenomenon can be explained, that is, related to other social phenomena.

Earlier, we stressed the importance of comparison to the development of a sound understanding of politics. If we do not study political phenomena in a variety of cultural, social, and economic settings, we cannot develop certainty of knowledge about politics. The need for comparative cross-cultural studies presents the student of politics with a special validity problem. This is the problem of making sure that his measures are *cross-culturally valid*.[15] That is, we must ask whether our measures mean the same thing, or are measuring the same thing, in different settings. This is a difficult task, and there is strong reason to believe that many measures commonly used in comparative research are not cross-culturally valid or, at least, have not been subjected to careful evaluation of their cross-cultural validity. For example, voting is often used as a measure of "political participation," or of the nature of citizen evaluations of government, in cross-cultural studies. But does a vote in a national election mean the same thing in, say, Great Britain as it does in France? In Great Britain, for example, there are two long-established major parties, which represent a relatively narrow ideological spectrum; the Prime Minister is selected by leaders of the majority party. In France, political parties have been short-lived, and their ideological orientations are spread over a broader range; the President of the Republic is elected by popular vote. Is a citizen's vote, then, a cross-culturally valid measure of his evaluation of government? There is some dispute about this. Further, suppose we wanted to extend our research to cover the Soviet Union, where voter turnout is extremely high, but where there is only one political party and, until recently, there were few choices of candidates on the ballot. Or, perhaps, we might wish to extend our comparison to such countries as Spain and Portugal, where elections have been irregular in occurrence and the roles of political parties sharply circumscribed. Is voting a valid indicator of citizen evaluations of government in these systems? We suspect not.

The debate over how one goes about devising cross-culturally valid measures of important political phenomena is relatively new, but it has already grown sufficiently complex to be reserved for a later stage in your development as a student of politics. The basic issue is clear, however, and it is obvious that we need to be sensitive to the possibility that some measures that seem useful in studying our own political system may not be valid for an understanding of politics elsewhere. Since an understanding of politics as a generic type of human behavior depends substantially on our ability to compare political activity in a variety of settings, the cross-cultural validity of our measures is vitally important.

Reliability has to do with the consistency—or dependability or stability—of a measure. If we measure the same phenomena repeatedly with the same or similar measures, will we get the same or very similar results? To the extent to which we do, our measures are reliable. Take, for example, the case of our survey instrument designed to measure "conservatism." If we administered these questions on several occasions to the same or similar persons, we should obtain essentially the same results, that is, the same or similar individuals should have the same or very similar "conservatism" scores. If they did, our measures of "conservatism" could be considered reliable.

Of course, we recognize that the stability of results using a given measure will be affected by factors other than the nature of the measure itself. In the case of responses to survey instruments, we know that people are affected by such diverse factors as fatigue, impatience, conditions in the immediate environment, fluctuations of memory or recall, presence or lack of rapport with the interviewer, and even "learned" response inclinations resulting from having been interviewed before. In addition, there are random, or chance, errors present in all measures, due simply to unknown causes.

To a substantial degree, such factors are beyond the control of the researcher. At the same time, we must design our measures in such a way that this random, or chance, error is minimized. That is, it is important that our measures have precision and clarity such that they are minimally distorted by random factors. For example, survey questions should be carefully structured and worded, so that interviewees would tend to give the same responses, regardless of the nature of psychological and situational conditions of the moment. Similarly, we would want to choose measures of, say, "frustration" that are not subject to substantial random fluctuations. The use of caloric intake per capita, for example, might be found to be unreliable as a measure of frustration because of difficulties involved in compiling accurate statistics on caloric intake in some societies, or because caloric intake was shown to fluctuate as a result of factors essentially unrelated to feelings of psychological frustration.

Validity and reliability, then, are crucial to measurement and, more broadly, to understanding. If our measures are not valid, that is, if we are not measuring what we think we are measuring, then our "knowledge" will be distinctly misleading and distorted. Similarly, without reliable measures we are likely to generate more confusion than understanding. Further, it is clear that neither validity nor reliability alone is a sufficient condition for meaningful results, although both are clearly necessary conditions. Valid measures are not very useful if they are unreliable; reliability in the absence of validity leads to the accumulation of precise nonsense. Serious efforts at understanding require careful attention to both validity and reliability.

We said above that variables are related through hypotheses. At this point, we should look more carefully at the ways in which researchers fit variables into hypotheses—that is, at the functions performed by variables in hypotheses.

Variables and Hypotheses

Hypotheses state relationships among variables. More specifically, hypotheses relate an *independent* variable to a *dependent* variable. The distinction between independent and dependent variables was introduced in chapter 2. There, you discovered that the dependent variable is what we are trying to explain, and the independent variable is what we are using to do the explaining. That is, we attempt to see how much of the variation in the values of the dependent variable can be accounted for by variations in the values of the independent variables. The in-

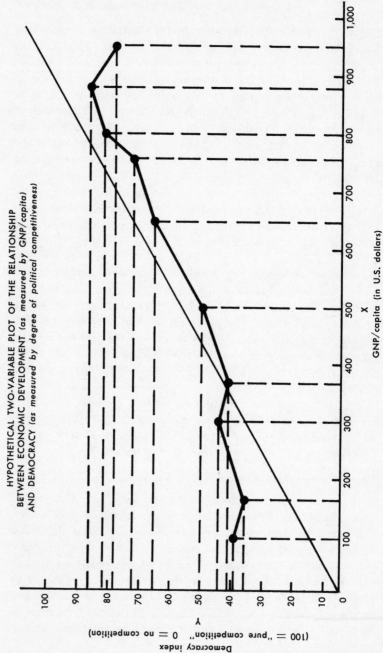

FIGURE 7.1

HYPOTHETICAL TWO-VARIABLE PLOT OF THE RELATIONSHIP
BETWEEN ECONOMIC DEVELOPMENT (as measured by GNP/capita)
AND DEMOCRACY (as measured by degree of political competitiveness)

X
GNP/capita (in U.S. dollars)

Y
Democracy index
(100 = "pure competition" 0 = no competition)

dependent variable is the presumed "cause," or antecedent, whereas the dependent variable is the presumed result, or effect.

For example, a researcher might be interested in studying the relationship between income and voting for given political parties in Great Britain. One of his hypotheses might be, "As income increases, the likelihood of voting for Conservative Party candidates increases." The independent variable would be income; the dependent variable, party vote preference. Income would be hypothesized to affect party vote preference. The higher a person's income, the greater the presumed likelihood that he will vote Conservative. Or a relationship might be hypothesized between economic development and democratic political arrangements, for instance, "The higher the level of economic development, the greater the degree of democracy present in the political practices of a system." Here, economic development would be the independent variable, and democratic practices would be presumed to result from the attainment of higher levels of economic development.

A useful way to visualize the notion that hypotheses stipulate covariation—that is, the link between variation in the values of the independent variable and the dependent variable—is through two-variable plots. Figure 7.1 presents a hypothetical plot of the relationship between economic development and democratic political practices. Suppose we have operationalized economic development through the measure of per capita gross national product (GNP), and democratic practices through some sort of combined index of competitiveness and openness in the polity. Suppose, further, that we have gathered the appropriate data on 100 political units around the world. The values of the independent variable (for which social scientists commonly use the notation X) are arrayed along the horizontal axis (the abscissa) of Figure 7.1. In our illustration, these are values of economic development, in this case GNP per capita. The values of the dependent variable (commonly noted as Y) are arrayed along the vertical axis (the ordinate). In our illustration, these are scores on our "democracy" index. We can plot the relationship between economic development and democracy by locating on the graph each of the political units studied.

That is, each dot on the graph represents a political unit (probably a country), whose location is determined by the intersection of lines drawn from its scores on the X and Y axes. In this hypothetical illustration, there appears to be a distinct relationship between economic development and democracy, since the dots that reflect high scores on the independent variable also reflect high scores on the dependent variable. Conversely, low X scores generally are linked with low Y scores. In other words, as X increases, Y also seems to increase.

To the extent that the dots representing our cases, or observations (in this case, political units), fall on, or very close to, a straight line drawn out at a 45° angle from the intersection of the X and Y axes (*i.e.*, bisecting the area between the two axes), the relationship between the independent and dependent variables is very strong, indeed. In fact, if all the dots fell precisely on that line, the relationship would be perfect, that is, each unit increase in X would be associated with a unit increase in Y. Rarely do we find such perfect relationships in studies of social phenomena. One of the tasks for social scientists is to determine the precise extent to which relationships between variables deviate from this perfect, straight-line relationship (usually called a *linear* relationship). Various statistical techniques can be useful in making such determinations, and you will learn about some of these techniques as you pursue your studies in political science.

You may have recognized already that there is nothing about two-variable plots that demands that one of the variables be a presumed antecedent and the other, a presumed effect. We can plot the relationship between two variables even if we do not have a basis for presuming that changes in one variable are "causing" changes in the other. This point, in turn, emphasizes the fact that the exploration of research *problems*, as well as the testing of hypotheses, involves the examination of relationships between variables. Two-variable plots can be used to aid in the exploration of the nature of the relationship between variables, in the absence of formal hypotheses. In fact, these plots should help the researcher to convert his tentative exploration of a problem into more definitive testing of hypotheses.

It is also worth mentioning that a given variable might be an independent variable in one study but a dependent variable in another. For example, students of political leadership have, until recently, tended to view the issue orientations of leaders as a dependent variable, to be explained with reference to such independent variables as the social origins of leaders, the nature of their education and professional training, and the nature of their adult political experiences. Now, however, these same researchers are beginning to use leaders' issue orientations as an independent variable, useful in explaining dependent variables such as the decisions made by authoritative groups of which these leaders are members. In other words, having arrived at some reasonably sound notions of why individual leaders take the issue positions they do, the next step might be to find out how much effect these individual issue orientations have on group decision-making.

In short, the thing that makes a variable "independent" or "dependent" is the nature of research in which the variable is being used. No variable is "intrinsically" independent or dependent; those terms describe the function of a variable in a proposed pattern of explanation and have nothing to do with the nature of the variable itself.

Scope of the Inquiry

Once the student of politics has formulated his questions, problems, or hypotheses and decided on measures for his variables, he has one important task remaining with regard to the structure of his study. This is the determination of the *scope* of his inquiry—that is, deciding how many cases to examine, and which cases those should be.

Generally speaking, we refer to the cases that we will study as "units of observation" and "units of analysis"; literally, they are the units, or entities, on which we will accumulate and analyze information. These units may exist at different *levels* of human activity. For example, our units of observation may be the behaviors of specific *individuals*, the characteristics of *groups* or organizations, the characteristics of larger social *aggregates* such as nation-states, or the characteristics of *inter-*

actions among social aggregates. We refer to these four levels as, respectively, the *individual* level, the *group* level, the *system* level, and the *intersystem* level.

Actually, it can be argued that, in the end, all the observations in which social scientists are interested consist of the behaviors of individual human beings. We have noted already that groups and nation-states do not "act"; strictly speaking, it is rather individuals who act *collectively* to commit the resources of groups and larger social aggregates, such as nations. Yet students of politics sometimes are interested in focusing on, and comparing, the various structures within which human beings act, as well as the individual behaviors themselves. Thus, for purposes of our analysis, we may wish to aggregate data on individuals, as we noted in chapter 6. This gives rise to a distinction made by some social scientists between *units of observation* and *units of analysis*. In this context, units of observation are the behaviors or properties being observed, that is, that constitute the bases of our information. Units of analysis are the entities we will ultimately use in analyzing our observations. For example, a study of differences among political parties in various political systems might be based on *observations* about the individuals who are party leaders and followers, but would use the political party as the unit of *analysis*. The characteristics and behaviors of individuals (the units of observation) would be aggregated and treated as characteristics of the political parties (the unit of analysis). In a sense, we would be "observing" individuals in order to "analyze" political parties.

How Many, and Which, Cases? One of the issues that must be faced by a researcher is how many cases to examine. Roughly speaking, we can respond in one of three ways to this question: (1) One may study the entire *population*, or *universe*, of the units in which he is interested; (2) one may study some sort of *sample* of that universe; or (3) one may focus intensively on a *single case*.

Studying an entire universe of cases may or may not be practical, depending on what that universe consists of. If we are interested in the opinions of Frenchmen on a set of political issues, interviewing the population (*i.e.*, all Frenchmen) would be impossible. On the other hand, if we are studying political party leadership, it might be possible (though clearly difficult) to accumulate the appropriate information on all, or nearly all, political parties in the world; and, if our "universe" consisted only of Latin American political parties, the task would be even more manageable.

There is an important message implicit in what we have just said. The notion of a "universe" is relative to a given study. Its scope depends on the *generality* of the research questions, problems, or hypotheses with which we begin, as well as of the sorts of statements we hope will emerge from our study. If we are working with hypotheses about political party leadership in Latin America, and if we wish to generalize our findings only to Latin America, then our "universe" will consist of political parties in Latin America. If we wish to make statements of more generality, say about political party leadership in "developing countries," our universe will be correspondingly broadened.

A great deal of political research deals with *samples* of populations. Survey research provides a clear-cut case for the necessity of using samples, but there are other kinds of research on politics that regularly focus on relatively small subsets selected from a much larger universe of units. Especially when the research design is complex—*i.e.*, involves the accumulation and interrelation of a great deal of information about each case to be studied—researchers tend to select a smaller, more manageable number of units to examine. A student interested in the relationship between economic development and democracy, for example, might feel that he could draw meaningful conclusions without accumulating information on every political system in the world.

Naturally, the crux of any sampling procedure is the need to be certain that the units selected for study are appropriately "representative" of the larger universe of such units. We discussed the nature of sampling in chapter 6, in the context of survey research. The point to be made here is that it is by no means certain that the appropriate sampling procedure for a study such as one relating economic development and democracy is random sampling (*i.e.,* sampling such that every political unit in the world has an equal chance of being included in the sample to be studied). Perhaps the more appropriate procedure would be, in effect, to sample the *variables,* rather than sampling the *universe of units.*[16] That is, the most important requirement of "representativeness" would seem to be that the political systems selected for study reflect the different levels of economic development and democratic practices actually found in the world. Thus, the researcher might feel that he should include in his sample several countries at each of several distinct levels of democracy. Otherwise, he might discover that he could not ascertain the extent to which, say, high, medium, and low values of economic development were linked with high, medium, and low levels of democracy, respectively.

Not only must sampling give attention to the *representativeness* of the sample; it also must be concerned with the *proportion* of the universe that needs to be included in the study. Fortunately, statisticians have given a great deal of attention to this problem and have come up with some standard guidelines showing the appropriate relationship between population size and sample size. A researcher should give attention to these guidelines, which are provided in handy tabular form in various statistical texts and handbooks, in the course of structuring his study.

Case studies reflect, in a sense, a disinterest in these issues of generality of results, and problems of sampling, that we have just discussed. As the label implies, case studies focus intensively on a single unit—*e.g.,* on leadership in the British Labour Party or on the influence of political constraints on the professional activities of members of the Bulgarian Academy of Sciences. As a result, the findings emerging from case studies cannot be generalized to any broader universe of units. Further, the case study approach can be very time-consuming, especially in view of its inherently limited pay-off in terms of broadly applicable knowledge. For these reasons, case studies in political science are pursued distinctly less often today than twenty years ago.

At the same time, case studies can make some contribution

to our understanding of politics. Especially where little prior information has been gathered on a particular political unit or on a relationship between two variables, case studies can be useful in an exploratory fashion in examining research questions or problems. Thus, the apparently sublime (if not ridiculous) example of a study dealing with the relationships between certain variables measuring political and scientific activity in Bulgaria turns out to have been an exploratory effort to find out something about the science-politics nexus in Communist systems, a much-discussed but little-researched topic.[17]

Another sense in which what might be thought of as case studies can be useful is in *deviant case analysis.* All too often students of politics have been willing to sweep "deviant cases" under the rug.[18] That is, when a few exceptions to an apparently general rule are found, the tendency has been to say that the exceptions are statistically insignificant and, therefore, can be discarded as "fascinating," but still "meaningless," oddities.

The difficulty with this sort of intellectual majoritarianism is that it leads us to ignore cases that might have helped us to refine and make more precise our generalizations. If certain cases are exceptions to a generalization, there might well be some identifiable reasons (other than mere chance) for their "deviancy." By examining these cases closely—*i.e.*, by doing case studies of exceptions—we often can discover *conditions* that "intervened" in the relationship under study and thereby brought about the "deviancy." For example, a researcher might discover a positive relationship between economic development and political stability in Latin America for the period 1945–60—except for Argentina. That is, he might find that, generally speaking, the higher the level of economic development, the higher the level of political stability—except that Argentina scored high on economic development, but was politically very unstable. Rather than simply brushing the Argentine "deviant case" aside, the more appropriate procedure would seem to be to examine closely the economic and political history of Argentina for the period 1945–60 and see whether an explanation for the "deviancy" from the generalization might be found (*e.g.*, in the degree of emotionalism in politics that surrounded the rule and subsequent ouster of Juan D. Perón).

Analyzing and Interpreting Information About Politics

Once a research project has been structured, and the appropriate data have been gathered, there remains the task of analyzing and interpreting the information that has been obtained. Broadly, the purpose of analysis and interpretation is to provide substantive answers to research questions and problems and to test hypotheses.

Although analysis and interpretation are closely related, they can be distinguished from one another.[19] *Analysis* involves the ordering of data—the breaking down, aggregating, and refinement of the data so that they are capable of providing answers to one's questions, problems, or hypotheses. *Interpretation* involves taking the results of analysis, making inferences, attributing meaning, and drawing conclusions about the topic under study. Aggregating or tabulating characteristics of individual leaders in order to make statements about political groups or structures (*e.g.*, political parties, legislatures, cabinets) of which they are members is a simple act of analysis. So is the act of arraying the observed values of two variables in a two-variable plot, as was illustrated in Figure 7.1. Any manipulation of our data that orders the data so that we can answer our research questions or problems, or test our hypotheses, can be considered part of analysis.

Interpretation may involve two types of procedures. First, in a narrower sense, interpretation takes place *within* a given study. The researcher looks at the results of his analysis and brings to bear some sorts of guidelines—one hopes explicit and precise rules—in deciding whether his hypotheses have been confirmed, or what he can say in response to his research questions or problems. Is there, in fact, a relationship between economic development and democracy? Does an increase in frustration lead to an increase in violence? At some point, the researcher must decide how his particular collection of data impacts upon the issues with which he began his study.

Second, interpretation involves seeking the broader meaning, or significance, of the research analysis. This implies comparing one's own results with the results of similar research conducted by others. It also implies fitting one's own findings into the relevant theory or theories, especially those that influenced the structuring of one's research in the first place. It is in this broader sense of the interpretive process that we recognize the self-maintaining, self-energizing character of research. Theoretical notions beget research, which in turn generates findings that refine and develop theories. The process is self-perpetuating, almost by definition; one of our tasks as students of social phenomena is to see that this process is maximally self-improving, as well.

Some Basic Procedures of Analysis

One of the most important changes in the last thirty years in the discipline of political science has been the great increase in the number and sophistication of techniques of analysis used in studying politics. As political science begins to come of age as a scientific discipline, students of politics are being called upon to arm themselves with an ever widening array of analytic skills.

This book, however, is an introduction to the study of politics, and no purpose would be served by lining up dozens of sophisticated carts before we have finished harnessing the first horse. We will content ourselves here by discussing briefly three types of analytic procedures. Most of the more specific techniques for analyzing political data, which you may wish to learn later,[20] can be subsumed under one of these three broad types.

Establishing Two-Variable Relationships. Most of the illustrations of research topics used so far in this book have referred to some sort of relationship between two variables. It is probably the case that most political research is structured around hypotheses that relate two, or a limited number of, variables. Following Kerlinger, we can view relationships as consisting of sets of ordered pairs.[21] That is, a relationship is defined by the paired

FIGURE 7.2

HYPOTHETICAL RELATIONSHIP BETWEEN
ECONOMIC DEVELOPMENT AND DEMOCRACY PRESENTED AS
A SET OF ORDERED PAIRS

Case (country)	X Economic Development (GNP/capita in U.S. dollars)	Y Democracy Index
Ruritania	100	40
Colonius	180	36
Dependus	300	45
Emergus	380	43
Transitia	500	50
Imperia	650	67
Assimila	750	72
Tranquilia	800	82
Megalopolis	890	85
Omnipitus	950	80

values of X (the independent variable) and Y (the dependent variable) for each case being studied. All values of X for the group of units under study constitute a set, as do all the Y values. An ordered pair consists of the X and Y values for any given unit, or case. (The pair of values is "ordered" in the sense that, for all cases, the members of the pair are always presented in the same order, that is, the X value is given first, then the Y value. This amounts to nothing more than saying that we shouldn't mix up the values of X or Y, which seems to be evident from common sense.) When we have a set of ordered pairs (*i.e.*, a set of X,Y pairs for the units being studied), we can define the nature of the relationship between X and Y.

Actually, we already have illustrated the definition of a relationship through a set of ordered pairs, in Figure 7.1. In Figure 7.2, the same information contained in Figure 7.1 is presented, this time in the form of a set of ordered pairs. Thus, establishing a relationship between two variables involves looking at the X,Y pairs—the conjoint values of the independent variable and the dependent variable—for a set of cases.

But, when we "look at" these X,Y pairs, what are we looking for? And how do we find it? Generally speaking, we are trying to ascertain the *direction* and the *strength* of the relationship. By *direction* we refer to the extent to which increases in the independent variable occur in the same pair as increases in the dependent variables, and the extent to which decreases in X and Y are similarly found in the same pair. Are higher values of X associated with higher values of Y, and are low X's found conjointly with low Y's? If Y is high when X is low, and vice versa, the direction of the relationship is *inverse*. If Y is high when X is high, and vice versa, the relationship is *direct*, or positive. In Figure 7.1, the line running from the lower left to the upper right corner of the two-variable space shows that the relationship described is direct. If the line through the points ran from the upper left to the lower right, the relationship between the variables would be inverse.

The *strength* of the relationship refers to the extent to which the magnitudes of X and Y covary, directly or inversely. That is, if a unit increase in X is accompanied by a unit, or proportionally identical, increase in Y, the relationship would be very strong, indeed. To the extent that the increases and decreases in X and Y do not have the same relative magnitude, the relationship is weaker. Thus, if we discovered that large increments in X were accompanied by small and inconsistent increases in Y, the relationship between X and Y would be direct but weak. Note also that large increases in X accompanied by large decreases in Y would indicate a strong (inverse) relationship.

By now you have progressed far enough in this book to know that the answer to a question such as "How do we determine the direction and strength of a relationship?" is likely to be something like "By applying certain precise, rigorous procedures of analysis to the data." That is indeed what we do. The actual application of these techniques has filled a very large number of statistics textbooks and is, therefore, beyond the presumptions of this volume.[22] It is worth mentioning, however, that the statistical procedures used depend on several considerations, including, especially, the assumptions we are willing to make about the reliability and comprehensiveness of our measures and the level of measurement of our variables. There is no single procedure used to determine the strength and direction of relationships among variables; rather, such procedures are many and varied.

Explaining Variations. For any given set of values—*e.g.*, the scores of a group of college students on a "conservatism" scale —a mean ("average") score can be calculated. Knowing the average score of a group on such a scale might be interesting, for it would permit us to compare the group's performance with that of other groups that might have responded to the same questionnaire. We could then use a difference-of-means test to discover whether any two groups were significantly different in their average degree of conservatism.

Rather more interesting than such a comparison of mean scores would be efforts to explain differences between the groups by accounting for *variations* in their respective levels of conservatism. The notion of variation refers to the sum of the squared deviations from the group mean.[23] That is, in order to calculate the variation in conservatism for our group of college students, we would (1) calculate the mean score by adding all scores and dividing by the number of group members, and (2) calculate the difference between each score and the group mean, square each of these deviations, and sum all of them. The resulting sum of squared deviations from the group mean would be the variation of the variable of conservatism.

Closely related to the notion of variation is *variance*. *Variance* is simply variation divided by the number of cases—for example, the number of students in the group. Although these two measures are not identical, and although some statistical procedures focus on one rather than the other, we shall not distinguish between them further here. These two terms, variation and variance, are appearing with increasing frequency in analyses of data on politics. Their increasing popularity is based on their usefulness in helping political scientists to develop meaningful *explanatory* statements. It is worth taking a moment to consider why these measures are especially useful for explanatory purposes.

When we talk about "explaining" something about a political variable, what we actually are referring to is *accounting for variation in that variable*. We are saying that we want to know why the values of the variable fluctuate in different situations or at different points in time. What accounts for the fact that some observations of that variable are close to the mean, while others deviate substantially; or that some deviations are well above the mean, while others are well below it?

Thus, it is variation in the dependent variable for which we want to account, that is, that we hope to explain. We try to do this by examining the effect of one or more independent variables on variation in the dependent variable. Furthermore, variation in the independent variable provides the basis for our efforts to forge the explanatory link. That is, establishing an explanatory tie between X and Y depends on the extent to which X and Y covary, that is, vary jointly. Generally speaking, correlational measures are based on the amount of variation explained.[24]

It might be mentioned that there is another set of techniques that are based on correlation, but which are more "powerful" in terms of providing explanatory linkages between variables, and which generate explanations of a slightly different form. These are regression techniques. Rather than focusing on accounting for variation in the dependent variable, regression shows *how much change* in the dependent variable can be traced to a standardized change in the independent variable.[25] Regression addresses itself more specifically to the *effects* of the independent variable than do other techniques of analysis. Consequently, regression techniques are especially appropriate for the testing of hypotheses. Regression is less directly useful in the exploration of research problems.

To this point, we have talked about explaining variation, and accounting for change, in a dependent variable when there is a single independent variable. In many respects, of course, such a picture of real-world political relationships is decidedly oversimplified. We live in a complex environment, and there is every reason to expect that important political events and behaviors have multiple "causes," antecedents, or explanations. In other words, in order to account for a satisfactory amount of variation in most dependent variables, we should expect to employ two or more independent variables.

As you might imagine, introducing additional independent variables can complicate our analysis a good deal. Two of the complications warrant brief comment here: the problems of multicollinearity and interaction effects. *Multicollinearity* refers to a situation in which the independent variables themselves are highly interrelated. Each is presumed to be related to the dependent variable, but each also is highly related to other independent variables. The problem is that the separate effects of the independent variable are difficult to sort out. Blalock offers the example of trying to explain high crime rates (the dependent variable) in terms of low education, low income, unemployment, broken families, and low aspiration levels.[26] All these variables seem to be interrelated as part of a poverty 'syndrome. But are some of these factors having an independent, direct impact on crime rates, while others are merely impacting indirectly, that is, "acting through" other variables? How can the separate effects of each independent variable on the dependent variable be inferred?

The problem of *interaction effects* is that the nature of the relationship between X and Y may be different at different levels of a third variable. For example, we might discover a strong, positive relationship between income and tendency to vote for conservative political candidates at low and moderate educational levels, but a weak relationship, perhaps even negative, between income and conservative voting at higher educational levels. That is, we might find conservative voting increasing with income among persons with low or moderate educations, but discover that the relationship did not hold true among the highly educated. In this situation, the relationships among income, education, and voting tendency are relatively complex, and our explanations of them are also necessarily more complicated.

Social scientists have been working for some time now on finding ways to handle these and other complexities introduced by multivariate (*i.e.*, multiple-variable) analysis. They have had a good deal of success, although our techniques are by no means perfect, or even highly refined. However, the specific techniques used in handling problems such as multicollinearity and interaction cannot be treated here. The complexity of these solutions, however, in no sense reduces the importance to the student of a basic understanding of the problems. We need to develop early a sensitivity to the principal issues that must be confronted in the process of analyzing data.

Identifying Patterns. In exploratory research, we may have only a limited *a priori* notion of what the data relevant to our selected topic will look like. In order to be able to do any sort of meaningful analysis and interpretation of our data, we may need to call upon analytic techniques that facilitate identifying the basic dimensions and patterns present in the data. That is, we may need first to "map the data terrain"; to reduce the dimensions of unwieldy data collections; to chart the patterns present in potentially complex interrelationships among many variables; to develop bases for classifying and scaling the data observations; to identify the "basic structure" of a set of data.[27] Such pattern-identifying procedures may fruitfully precede the formulation of explicit hypotheses.

It is important to stress that the notion of variation is central even in these exploratory phases of research activity. For, when the social scientist speaks of "patterns," more likely than not he is referring to *patterned variation*. Indeed, the notion of a "pattern" in a set of data is sometimes defined in terms of uniform covariation, or "interdependence," among several variables.[28] When we discover, for example, that education, income, and occupational status covary—*i.e.,* increase or decrease conjointly—we may reasonably speak of these variables as representing a "pattern." This pattern is often referred to as "socio-economic standing" or "socio-economic status."

It is possible to sharpen our notion of what is involved in pattern identification. Broadly, the researcher who sets out to identify patterns in a collection of information probably will ask one or more of three sets of questions:

1. What does phenomenon A look like? What are its characteristics? How can I *classify*, or type, this phenomenon?

2. What variables are related to what other variables? Are there *clusters* of variables that seem to be mutually interdependent? What underlying *common dimension*, or *common factor,* seems to be "holding them together"?

3. What are the most *salient* dimensions of this collection of data? What kinds of information can I discard, and what should I retain, perhaps even refine, for purposes of further analysis?

In posing these three questions, we have raised two important issues that have been mentioned only very briefly earlier in this book, but which deserve some modest elaboration at this point. These issues concern classification, or typology construction, and the identification of underlying dimensions of multivariate data.

In chapter 2, we noted that *classification* is an important early step in theory-building. When we talk about the various structures and institutions in which political activity takes place, for example, we need to identify important dimensions of those institutions that permit us to draw distinctions among them.

When we distinguish among pluralistic, quasi-competitive, authoritarian, and totalitarian political systems, we are making use of a four-category classification scheme, or typology. When we differentiate radical, liberal, moderate, conservative, and reactionary political groups, we are applying a five-category typology to the universe of political groups.

Setting up the categories of a classification scheme is an important act, one that influences much of the rest of the research process. Consequently, it is important that the basic rules of categorization be adhered to. These rules appear in several slightly different forms in various texts, but their basic thrusts seem pretty generally accepted. For our purposes, four such rules governing categorization, or typology construction, can be mentioned:

1. The categories (or types, or classes) should be appropriate to the purpose of the research in which they are to be used. The notion of a "universal" set of classifications of, say, political parties is highly dubious. How we categorize something depends very much on how we are hoping to analyze it.

2. The categories should be exhaustive. They should be capable of embracing all the known instances of the phenomenon being categorized.

3. The categories should be mutually exclusive and independent. No instance of the phenomenon being classified can fall into more than one category, or class.

4. The principles guiding categorization must be applied consistently for all categories in the scheme; the same dimension(s) must be used as a basis for all categories. For example, suppose we were classifying political parties on a two-dimensional basis: the nature of their campaign appeals, and the substance of their platforms. To simplify our example, suppose the campaign-appeals dimension were dichotomized into two categories, "pragmatic" appeals and "ideological" appeals, while the platform-substance dimension were dichotomized into "conservative" and "liberal" categories. This fourth rule of categorization simply says that both dimensions must be applied in classifying each political party studied. This means that we

would be classifying parties into one of four possible categories: (a) liberal pragmatic, (b) liberal ideological, (c) conservative pragmatic, and (d) conservative ideological.

Especially in exploratory research, identifying *underlying dimensions* in a collection of data can be very helpful in making subsequent research on the topic more efficient and more meaningful. Finding these underlying dimensions should aid in formulating research questions and hypotheses about how variables are interrelated. It should also provide a basis for systematic *data reduction,* that is, for discarding information not centrally relevant to an understanding of a particular topic.

Imagine yourself, for a moment, in a data-rich, theory-poor environment—a veritable paradise for someone interested in inductive pattern-mapping. That is, suppose you were confronting a broad subject-matter area in which there was a great deal of available information, but little prior theorizing or research. Let's say you are interested in the ways in which nation-states interact with one another. There are all sorts of relevant data available—data on diplomatic representation, tourism, scientific communication, trade, aid, official governmental messages, armed conflicts, and so on—but (we shall hypothetically stipulate) there is little prior work on the subject to serve as a guide. The task of developing some meaningful statements about international relations out of the morass of data represented by, say, 100 types of interactions among 100 nation-states might seem overwhelming. It would help a great deal if you could discover a limited number of dimensions underlying those 100 types of interactions, so that you could focus on perhaps half a dozen dimensions instead of 100 discrete behaviors. Similarly, it would be nice if you could discover clusters of nation-states that had frequent and consistent patterns of interaction with one another, so that you could subsequently focus at least some of your analysis on a few clusters of international actors, rather than on every nation-state, viewed discretely.

Fortunately, social scientists do have available to them some analytical techniques designed to identify underlying dimensions in large sets of data and thereby to contribute to the goal of reducing large data collections to more manageable size.

Broadly, these procedures are called *factoring,* or *clustering,* techniques. One of the most common of these techniques is called *factor analysis,* and is based on the assumption that, if several variables are closely interrelated (*i.e.,* have high common variance), a general "factor," or dimension, may underlie all of these variables. Factor analysis attempts to identify clusters of closely related phenomena. Actually, depending on the type of factor analysis used, the researcher can identify clusters of either cases (*e.g.,* nations) or variables. Consequently, factor analysis is a very useful tool in identifying patterns in large collections of data.

Again, with regard to specific statistical techniques, the purpose of this book is to suggest *why* they are needed, and *when* they are used. The specific procedures involved in using a technique such as factor analysis are best left for a later time. It is appropriate here, however, to enter an important caveat concerning the sort of data "exploration" about which we have just been talking.

Tiptoeing aimlessly through the data can be wasteful and even counterproductive. There are, sadly, some students of politics whose basic approach seems to be, "Here are lots of data (preferably quantitative); if I toss them all into one big analytical pot, and stir vigorously, I wonder what I'll end up with?" Clearly, that is not the most efficient way to develop an understanding of what the world is like; it certainly is not the way to build on the knowledge that already has been generated. As far as possible, a given piece of research should be guided by an appreciation of the accomplishments (and the mistakes) of those who have previously done relevant work. When little relevant prior work has been done, the student of politics should, at a minimum, apply common sense and uncommon care in deciding what to study, and how to study it. The more thoughtful and focused a research project is at the outset, the more precise and meaningful will be the process of analyzing and interpreting the data at the conclusion of the project.

Interpreting the Results of Data Analysis: An Introduction

Earlier we noted that analysis and interpretation are closely related. In a sense, much of what we have been saying about procedures of analysis has had to do with giving "meaning" to our data, since interpretation is based on what comes out of our analyses. There are, however, three additional topics having to do with interpretation that deserve attention. Two of these, having to do with *causal inference* and the definition of *"significance"* for our findings, will be treated as part of the more general methodological discussion in chapter 8. The third topic relevant to interpretation concerns decisions to accept or reject hypotheses and will be discussed at this point. As usual, our strategy does not include a presentation of how to use complex techniques or, in this case, a synopsis of probability theory. Rather, the task at hand is to understand the basic issues surrounding the testing of hypotheses.

The most fundamental point about hypothesis testing is that all *procedural* decisions concerning acceptance or rejection of the hypothesis must be made *before* the test is conducted. That is, the researcher must have decided ahead of time exactly what his data will have to look like in order for him to accept the hypothesis, and what configuration of results would cause him to reject the hypothesis. In the absence of such a prior decision, it would be possible to retain our hypotheses indefinitely simply by changing the rules as we went along. Further, if reasonably standardized criteria are not used in accepting and rejecting hypotheses, the results of different studies could not be compared, or accumulated. This would be true because some researchers might be inclined on subjective grounds to accept hypotheses that would be rejected by other researchers applying more rigorous standards. Fortunately, there are some commonly used statistical procedures that facilitate specification and standardization of the criteria by which hypotheses are evaluated.

The best way to understand hypothesis testing is to talk about the mistakes we can make in doing it. There are two errors that a researcher might make in testing a hypothesis:

1. He might reject a hypothesis that was actually true (statisticians refer to this as a "Type 1" error)
2. He might fail to reject a hypothesis that was false (a "Type 2" error)

The key to eliminating Type 1 errors rests in the notion of

probability. We have to ask ourselves, "How probable is it, if our hypothesis is actually true, that our evidence would be incompatible with the hypothesis?" That is, we need to establish the probability that such a misleading finding could have occurred by chance.

Type 2 errors stem from the purely logical fallacy of "affirming the consequent," that is, concluding from evidence supporting a hypothesis that the theory underlying a hypothesis is correct.[29] Blalock provides an illustration of this logical fallacy,[30] which we shall recast slightly to increase its relevance to politics. Suppose we have a theory based upon three propositions: (1) all public officials conform to societal norms; (2) it is a norm of society X that public officials may not accept bribes; and (3) Percy Fairweather is a public official in society X. If all elements of this theory were correct, we could deduce the statement that Fairweather will not accept bribes. Suppose that, for some reason, we are unable to verify the truth or falsity of the theory directly, but that we are able to gather evidence on Fairweather's behavior and, thus, to test the hypothesis deduced from the theory. Suppose, further, that we observe that Fairweather does not, indeed, accept bribes. From this, we certainly should not conclude that the theory itself was correct. In fact, any of the propositions in the theory could be false, even though Fairweather turns out to be an honest public servant. On the other hand, the theory could be true. But, then, there also could be *alternative* theories explaining Fairweather's honesty, as, for example, a theory focusing on his strict childhood upbringing.

Generally speaking, eliminating *all* possible alternative explanations for a finding is impossible, perhaps especially in the social sciences. Thus, it is usually not possible to show that a given theory, or hypothesis, is *necessarily* true. We can, however, demonstrate that a hypothesis is *false*. That is, by making some assumptions about the nature of chance events, and by applying the mathematical apparatus of probability theory, we can greatly minimize the risk of making Type 1 errors (rejecting true hypotheses). Consequently, social scientists must proceed by eliminating hypotheses rather than by establishing or "proving" them. Our purpose in accumulating knowledge is to find hypotheses that *resist elimination*.

One of the implications of what we have just said is that, strictly speaking, we can never "prove" a hypothesis to be true. We can find hypotheses that are supported by the available evidence; some social scientists even go so far as to use words such as "confirmation" when their evidence seems to be consistent with a hypothesis. But such "confirmation" is tentative, and residual, in that "confirmation" consists of being unable to *dis*confirm. Rejection, or disconfirmation, is the basis of hypothesis testing.

At this point, your thoughts, it is hoped, are racing back to an earlier point in this chapter, where we distinguished among four forms in which hypotheses can be stated. You will recall that the operational null form is the form that best facilitates the actual testing of hypotheses. Why this should be so may now be a little clearer. Consider what we are doing when we state a hypothesis in the operational null form and then seek to test—reject—it. In effect, we are seeking to reject the "negative" form of the hypothesis, which amounts to seeking to provide support for the alternative, or "positive," form. Thus, if we can *reject* the notion that "frustration toward political authority has no effect on the likelihood of politically relevant violence," we have some basis for continuing to entertain the possibility that frustration *does* lead to violence. If, on the other hand, we could not reject the null hypothesis, we would be led to reject the alternative form, and thus to discard the notion that frustration leads to violence.

This discussion of hypothesis testing has some practical implications for the ways in which students of politics approach their work. Each of these implications is, perhaps, obvious but nevertheless deserves explicit mention. First, all knowledge, and perhaps especially in the social sciences, is very tentative. The search for reliable knowledge is based on healthy skepticism, in that what we "really" know consists of hypotheses that have been disconfirmed, while hypotheses that have been supported by our research will forever remain conjectural statements. Second, students of politics should not be discouraged by what some people call "negative" findings, that is, disconfirmed hypotheses. On the contrary, a research paper that challenges a conventionally assumed relationship is at least as valuable as one that supports a hypothesis. Third, the foregoing emphasizes the point that the form in which hypotheses are stated does make a difference. We need to be thoughtful and precise in formulating the statements around which our research is organized. And, finally, the preceding paragraphs highlight with regard to hypotheses a more general point that this book has tried to make with respect to every aspect of the process of acquiring knowledge about, and developing an understanding of, politics: that the many elements of understanding are closely interrelated. From the beginning of this exciting—and vitally important—process, when we select broad topics to think about and words to use, to the conclusion, where we subject the data we have gathered to analysis and interpretation, each step is affected by what has already been done. The interdependence of these steps toward understanding is clear, and it demands that each of us proceed along the way with self-conscious attention to the meshing of what we know and how we find out.

NOTES

1. James A. Robinson, "The Major Problems of Political Science," in Lynton K. Caldwell (ed.), *Politics and Public Affairs* (Bloomington: Indiana University Press, 1962), p. 161.
2. *Ibid.*, p. 163.
3. *Ibid.*, pp. 168–82.
4 W. I. B. Beveridge, *The Art of Scientific Investigation* (New York: Random House, 1957), p. 13; James McCormack and Vincent A. Fulmer, "Federal Sponsorship of University Research," in the American Assembly, *The Federal Government and Higher Education* (Englewood Cliffs, N.J.: Prentice-Hall, 1960), p. 87.
5. A useful discussion of exploratory studies is to be found in D. Katz, "Field Studies," in L. Festinger and D. Katz, *Research Methods in the Behavioral Sciences* (New York: Holt, Rinehart and Winston, 1953), pp. 75–83.
6. Fred N. Kerlinger, *Foundations of Behavioral Research* (New York: Holt, Rinehart and Winston, 1964), p. 20.
7. This and similar approaches to studying the relationship between frustration and politically relevant violence are reported in a collection of studies edited by I. K. Feierabend, R. L. Feierabend, and T. R. Gurr, *Anger, Violence, and Politics: Theories and Research* (Englewood Cliffs, N.J.: Prentice-Hall, 1972). See especially chapters 2 and 8. It should be

noted that researchers who have used caloric intake as an indicator of frustration have also used other indicators, in order to decrease their reliance on any single indicator.

8. See Kerlinger, *op. cit.*, p. 22.
9. However, if our interest were in occupational *status*, we could meaningfully talk in terms of degrees, or levels. In a given culture, different occupations will enjoy different degrees of status approval; for example, judges and scientists might have higher occupational status than school teachers. In this case, occupational *status* could be thought of in terms of levels, or degrees, even though *occupation* itself could not.
10. See H. M. Blalock, Jr., *An Introduction to Social Research* (Englewood Cliffs, N.J.: Prentice-Hall, 1970), p. 39.
11. *Ibid.*, p. 90.
12. See Feierabend, Feierabend, and Gurr, *op. cit.*, especially chapters 2 and 8, for a discussion of the use of such indirect indicators. See also T. R. Gurr, *Politimetrics: An Introduction to Quantitative Macropolitics* (Englewood Cliffs, N.J.: Prentice-Hall, 1972), chapter 5.
13. Kerlinger, *op. cit.*, p. 444.
14. *Ibid.*, chapter 25; E. J. Webb, *et al.*, *Unobtrusive Measures: Nonreactive Research in the Social Sciences* (Chicago: Rand McNally, 1966), pp. 12–34; Gurr, *Politimetrics*, chapter 3.
15. The best discussion of this problem is found in A. Przeworski and H. Teune, *The Logic of Comparative Social Inquiry* (New York: John Wiley and Sons, 1970).
16. See D. W. Willer, "Conditional Universals and Scope Sampling," in Willer, *Scientific Sociology* (Englewood Cliffs, N.J.: Prentice-Hall, 1967), pp. 97–115.
17. See W. A. Welsh, "Politics and Scholarship in Bulgaria," *Balkan Studies*, VIII, no. 1 (1967), 138–49; and A. M. Hanhardt, Jr., and W. A Welsh, "The Intellectuals-Politics Nexus: Studies Using a Biographical Technique," *American Behavioral Scientist*, VII, no. 7 (May, 1964), 3–7.
18. See P. L. Kendall and K. M. Wolf, "The Two Purposes of Deviant Case Analysis," in P. Lazarsfeld and M. Rosenberg (eds.), *The Language of Social Research* (Glencoe, Ill: The Free Press, 1955), especially p. 167.
19. Kerlinger, *op. cit.*, pp. 603–4.
20. For an introduction to techniques of political analysis, written for undergraduate students, see G. Robert Boynton, *Political Inquiry* (New York: Praeger, in press).
21. Kerlinger, *op. cit.*, pp. 21–22.
22. See, for example, H. M. Blalock, Jr., *Social Statistics*, 2d ed. (New York: McGraw-Hill, 1972).
23. *Ibid.*, p. 319.
24. *Ibid.*, p. 378.
25. *Ibid.*, pp. 364–66.
26. Blalock, *An Introduction to Social Research*, pp. 73–74.
27. R. J. Rummel, *Applied Factor Analysis* (Evanston, Ill.: Northwestern University Press, 1970), pp. 3–4, 29–32.
28. *Ibid.*, p. 14.
29. Blalock, *Social Statistics*, pp. 112–14.
30. *Ibid.*, pp. 113–14.

8

Some Methodological Issues
in Political Science

By now you have been armed with considerable evidence of
the close relationship between *how* we learn and *what* we know.
Presumably, you can demolish the arguments of those who
want "just the facts, please," and who ignore the importance
of methods and theory. Similarly, you should be able to provide
intellectual embarrassment for those who might immerse themselves in abstract theoretical discussions without exhibiting
some concern for what their theories or methods tell us about
political reality.

To put this another way, an important message of this book
has been that understanding is a subtle, complex process. Having access to information does not necessarily yield increased
understanding. Having a mind that is creative and rigorous will
not necessarily deepen one's grasp of reality. There are some
very practical and compelling reasons why every responsible
citizen (certainly a student of politics) must be explicitly concerned with evaluating the origins and substance of the information he obtains, with carefully assessing the significance or
meaning of what he has found out, and with recording and
reporting what he has learned in such a way that others can
benefit from his experience.

One of the important implications of what we have just said, and of what we have been trying to say throughout this book, is that this thing called "methodology" is not merely the abstract mastery of techniques for gathering and analyzing information, such as survey research, computer content analysis, or statistical techniques (*e.g.,* correlation). It is also the careful evaluation of the usefulness of these techniques in helping us to understand what the world really is like. Further, and perhaps even more important, methodological concerns imply using thoughtful common sense in asking and answering some fundamental questions about the study of politics. The purpose of this chapter is to discuss briefly some of those fundamental questions.

As you might imagine, the content of any such list of "fundamental" issues confronting a field of study is likely to vary a good deal, depending upon who is doing the listing. It would be foolish to claim universality for the modest number of issues that are raised in this chapter. Many other issues could be mentioned, but these seem to be of recognized significance.

Now that you have mastered at least a basic grasp of what the study of politics is all about, and of some of the approaches, models, and techniques that are used in trying to get at the reality of political activity, it is appropriate to do a little free-wheeling contemplation of some of the underlying issues involved in putting together the "what" and the "how" of political science. Our strategy shall be to enumerate these issues under three broad interrogative headings:

1. Where do we start; that is, what are the most troublesome "givens" facing students of politics?
2. What do we think we *are* doing?
3. Have we really thought about what we *should be* doing?

Under each of these headings we will discuss several more specific issues. In the case of each of these issues, what is important is not how invigorating or how stifling the issue itself might seem, but rather what implications the issue has for the relationship between *how* we learn and *what* we know. That is, each of these methodological issues has to do with the relationship between *political science* and *politics* and should be viewed in that light.

Another way to put this is that, to different degrees and in varying ways, we try to use the apparatus of political science in an effort to understand the reality of politics. The mesh is sometimes imperfect, and our understanding, as a result, is similarly imperfect. Presumably, one of our most important tasks is to improve the contribution of political science to our understanding of politics, especially by better understanding and refining our methods of inquiry.

WHERE DO WE START?: SOME INITIAL PROBLEMS FOR THE STUDENT OF POLITICS

This book has identified many problems encountered by students of politics. Our purpose in this chapter is not to repeat or summarize what already has been said but, rather, to attempt to tie together some of these problem areas. Four general issues will be mentioned, involving, respectively, (1) limitations on access to important information, (2) limitations on our ability to control or manipulate behavior in the real world, (3) limitations imposed by our parochialism, that is, our narrow perspectives, and (4) difficulties involved in achieving "objective," communicative language.

Limited Data Access

One of the "givens" with which students of politics must work is that some of the data they consider important are difficult to obtain. There seems little doubt that the decision-making behavior of political leaders is important in shaping the nature of political activity. Unfortunately, however, while we can amass considerable information about the outputs of the decision-making process, the process itself usually cannot be observed. For social scientists, as a rule, are not invited to sit as observers of Cabinet meetings. Similarly, we may be interested in the values and issue orientations of prominent political personalities, but these individuals may or may not be available for the kind of interviewing that would give us confidence that we really had identified what they thought.

In a slightly different vein, there are innumerable research situations in which a given investigator cannot obtain relevant information, even though the data themselves are not wholly inaccessible. For example, as a practical matter we recognize that acquiring information costs money. It may require travel to distant points, as well as special skills, such as language competence. Thus, researchers interested in understanding the processes and problems of upheaval and change in less-developed countries might not be able to obtain the information they need, for want of the necessary travel funds or knowledge of the local language; further, it might be that trained research collaborators are not available, or cannot be identified, in the settings in which the research might most appropriately take place. The needed information may be "available," in the abstract, but not accessible to the researchers who need it.

There are numerous examples of situations in which a given student might not be able to obtain all the information he needs to complete meaningfully a project he has undertaken, or wishes to undertake. Because we do not always have an ideal set of data with which to work, students of politics often must use indirect *indicators* in an effort to understand inaccessible political phenomena. This can be a problem, because it is not always clear that our indicators have a close correspondence with what we are trying to study. That is, it is not always certain that our indicators are *valid*.

For example, several students of politics are interested in the causes of civil strife and violence. They believe that the presence of strife and violence can be explained in terms of what is sometimes called the "frustration-aggression" hypothesis. It is sometimes thought that, as the frustration of citizens increases, the likelihood that there will be civil strife and violence also increases. One of the difficulties with this sort of research is that we lack reliable direct evidence about the level of frustration felt by large numbers of people in different societies. Survey research on this question has not been conducted in very many settings. Lacking such direct evidence, students interested in this problem have been forced to use indirect indicators of frustration. For example, one researcher has used caloric intake per capita, measured for an entire national population, as his indirect indicator of frustration.[1] The use of such an indicator must rest on the highly problematic assumption that the lower the per capita caloric intake, the greater the felt frustration. The link between this indicator and the phenomenon to which it presumably refers may seem tenuous; at the same time, critics of such research are hard-pressed to come up with a better indicator. That research on the causes of strife and violence is significant, and should be pursued, seems to be generally accepted. Just how we might meaningfully identify and analyze variables such as personal frustration, especially when such research needs to include a variety of political systems, is a much more difficult issue to resolve.

Nonmanipulability of the Environment

According to some observers, the inability of social scientists to manipulate those elements of the real world in which they are interested, and their parallel inability to "recreate" reality in a laboratory, are the most important factors distinguishing the social sciences from the natural and technical sciences. We briefly treated this issue earlier, when we talked about the need for experimental research in political science. As you will remember, the problem is that political reactions cannot be controlled or recreated in quite the same way as can, for example, chemical reactions. We can observe a variety of political behaviors in the real world, but it is very difficult for the observer even to be aware of, let alone control for, the influence of the many environmental or situational factors that may be influencing the behavior under study.

Conversely, when we attempt to bring the real world into the laboratory, we are often unsure that we are introducing all the factors that may be relevant to explaining what we are trying to understand. Similarly, it is difficult to identify the extent to which a "laboratory culture" is having its own artificial effect on our subjects. Do participants in laboratory simulations of foreign-policy decision-making really view the decision to go to "war" in the same way as would real-world decision-makers? To what extent do participants in experiments of various kinds act as they do because they see themselves as 'performing" in a kind of "game" in which they themselves are being evaluated as "game players," rather than their behaviors being studied as representations of what goes on in the real world? It is difficult to answer such questions precisely, but students of politics who use experimental techniques believe that they have accumulated some evidence that the laboratory setting does have an effect on the behaviors of participants in these experiments. To the extent to which this laboratory effect cannot be carefully specified, we run a great risk in such research of studying artificial, rather than real, behavior.

Parochialism and the Need for Broader Comparative Perspectives

As we have suggested, every human being is a product of the multitude of experiences in his past. The increasing "cosmopolitanism" of many people in industrialized societies notwithstanding, each of us is, to some degree, a parochial being. Out of necessity, we have learned to define, relate to, and understand our environment in terms of what is previously known to us. We are distressingly quick to decide that that which is unfamiliar is somehow inherently difficult to understand. Similarly, we tend to define that with which we are familiar as being "normal" or "usual." Things that are different too often are assumed to be aberrations from normality, "deviant cases" whose characteristics are to be explained within the framework of "deviancy" rather than as part of a possible pattern of regularities in human experience.

This inherent parochialism has some obvious implications for the study of politics. Political scientists presumably do their best to avoid analyzing the behaviors of others simply in terms of those behavior patterns that are most familiar to them. That they do not always succeed seems clear. Numerous examples of parochial perspectives in the study of politics could be given, but we shall content ourselves with one only.

A real impediment to our efforts to understand political activity in non-Western, less-developed systems has been our tendency to view some of the things that go on there as deviations from a presumed "norm" represented by experiences in the industrialized systems of Europe and North America. Thus, it is presumed that political violence and extralegal seizures of the institutions of government are disruptions of the political process, exceptions to the "rule," irregularities in the "established pattern" of political activity. We have been painfully slow in recognizing that street violence and *coups d'état* may, in fact, be the "established" patterns in some Latin American systems. Extralegality may be "business as usual," and there may be no necessary relationship between *legitimacy* and *legality*. Because citizens of the United States appear to attach great respect to our basic constitutional documents, and hesitate to make fundamental alterations in them, we seem to assume that all political participants, in all cultures, naturally think the same way. That such parochial assumptions are highly dubious should be obvious.

A related tendency, and one that is in some senses even more dysfunctional for a sound understanding of political behavior, has been our propensity to assume that "developing" countries were, of course, developing in directions similar to those sought or achieved by the "advanced" nations of the world. Thus, "political development" all too often has been equated with "democracy," and economic development frequently has been linked with industrialization toward mass consumption. That participant democracy might be an unlikely (or even dysfunctional) condition to be achieved by many polities seems to be a remarkably difficult proposition for many of us to grasp. That some of the socio-economic characteristics of our mass-consumption societies might be neither attainable nor desirable in the minds of citizens and leaders elsewhere also seems difficult for us to understand.

It seems clear that such parochialism can be severely damaging to a genuine understanding of political activity. There are two implications of this point. First, we need to approach the study of politics with a recognition that unfamiliarity means neither intellectual inaccessibility nor deviancy or abnormality. We cannot approach the study of Latin American politics, for example, with the assumption that several of these political systems are somehow "out of kilter" (in disequilibrium, as some political scientists might say), and that the task of explanation is to discover how they came "untracked" and how they are going to get back to "normal." Second, and relatedly, we need to collect and analyze information about many different political systems before we can begin to make general statements about how human beings react to different political, social, and economic circumstances. Only by studying political behavior in a variety of settings can we have some confidence that our understanding of this important aspect of human existence is based on some semblance of reality, rather than on the limits imposed by our own unavoidable parochialism.

Developing "Objective" and Communicative Language

Not surprisingly, the form of language used by most people most of the time is words. Words are convenient, mostly because lots of people know lots of them. (To be sure, some people know more of them than do others, but that really is a problem only when erudition becomes obfuscation.)

Unfortunately, words have distinct liabilities as vehicles for communication. In the first place, many words mean different things to different people. We tried to illustrate this point at several places in this book, especially in chapter 5, where we talked about the importance of defining as precisely as possible central concepts used in studying politics. It can be very helpful to use careful, explicit definitions of the terms we want to employ. There are, of course, reasonable limits on this; if we felt it necessary to define essentially every term that appeared in our discourse, we would spend most of our time providing definitions. Furthermore, words are often defined in terms of other words. This may help matters somewhat, but even the words used to define other words may have ambiguous meanings.

A related problem with words is that we often have difficulty separating their cognitive and affective dimensions. The cognitive dimension of a word refers to its factual or, "perceptual" component, while the affective dimension refers to its "emotive" component. For reasons mentioned earlier, we know that it is important to keep the affective and cognitive dimensions of discourse separate from one another. Unfortunately, however, this is more easily said than done; for there are many words that have essentially cognitive meaning for some people but largely affective impact for others.

Words that have to do with contemporary ideologies are good examples. The term "socialism" may simply describe a particular form of economic organization to one person, but may immediately evoke in another vague but still powerful images of a world force for evil. Similarly, the term "elite" may simply denote a holder of a position of authority, or it may suggest an unjustifiable, and perhaps dangerous, concentration of power in the hands of one or a few at the expense of the many. In short, words may be seen as primarily descriptive of the shape of reality, or they may be viewed as primarily emotional judgments about the degree of good or evil around us.

Thus, words can be confusing in at least two related ways. First, even within a given dimension (cognitive or affective), they may mean different things to different people. Second, the matter is further confused by the fact that some words evoke primarily affective responses from some people but cognitive responses from others.

While this discussion of the limitations of words as vehicles for communication is doubtless fascinating, it may seem a trifle futile. Words, like motherhood, have problems, but both seem likely to be around for some time. Actually, there can be no dispute that, for the foreseeable future, human communication will continue to be based on words. Yet, it is probably highly desirable that, for purposes of understanding, we reduce the extent to which we are dependent on words to exchange information and understanding. Indeed, it is not unreasonable to argue that one of the basic thrusts of science is toward reducing our degree of dependence on words.

Apparently, the way to reduce our degree of dependence on potentially ambiguous words is to define words in terms of operations and numbers rather than in terms of other words. That is, the idea assuredly is not to eliminate words, but to specify the content of our verbal discourse in terms of things that are more susceptible to precision, namely, research operations and quantitative symbols.

Some examples should serve to illustrate that operations and numbers are for everybody, not just for college professors. A characteristic that most people seem to want, and which everyone seems to expect each of us to exhibit, is intelligence. Defining intelligence in terms of being able to solve problems or to master new skills, of creativity, or of simply being "bright" seems intuitively satisfying but is highly imprecise. The situation, however, improves somewhat if we give intelligence an *operational* definition, say grade-point average or performance on the Stanford-Binet Test. Such an operational definition not only gives precision to the notion of intelligence but provides a quantitative basis for making comparative statements about the intelligence of many different individuals. We cannot stress too strongly that a person may legitimately dispute the meaningfulness of either grade-point averages or performance on specified tests as indicators of intelligence. Such disputes about the validity of our operational definitions are numerous, and appropriate. But the point is that, given a quantifiable operational definition of the term "intelligence" that can be accepted by people who communicate with one another, discussion can proceed with precision and clarity.

A slightly different example of how operations and quantification can improve our communication concerns words that are designed to assess the meaning or importance of findings. For example, a fundamental question facing everyone who does any sort of study is: What *significant* conclusions can I derive from my work? What have I discovered that is sufficiently important that it bears reporting and elaboration? If, in a study of the political preferences of campus Young Republicans, I discover that males prefer Spiro Agnew over Charles Percy as the Republican Presidential nominee in 1976 by a margin of 53 per cent to 47 per cent, whereas females prefer Percy by a margin of 51 per cent to 49 per cent, have I discovered something significant? Are the preferences of male Young Republicans "significantly" different from those of female Young Republicans? Or, if I am attempting to identify the factors that explain career success in the Communist Party of the Soviet Union, is the fact that twice as many members of the highest councils of the Party now have a technical higher education than was the case fifteen years ago a significant finding? For some people examining these two hypothetical findings, the results would seem "significant" on their face. For others, the differences or increases described might seem trivial, or might appear to be a product of chance, rather than a really "significant" observation.

For the social scientist, as we said in chapter 7, one solution to this very important problem of determining the "significance" of findings is to apply certain quantitative procedures (which we may loosely refer to as "theoretical statistics") that permit us to state whether observed differences between groups, or changes over time in the characteristics of groups, are likely to have occurred by chance. As we pointed out earlier, the use of these statistical tests of "significance" clearly rests on some assumptions about the importance of chance happenings. Thus, while it is conventional to assert that a between-group difference that could have occurred by chance fewer than five times out of 100 is a "significant" difference, the selection of this 95 per cent nonchance level is wholly arbitrary. There is no logical reason why we could not accept 90 per cent probability as a basis for assessing "significance."

Let us be explicit in acknowledging that *statistical* "significance" and *social* "significance" are not necessarily the same thing. Findings that are statistically "insignificant" might be viewed by a researcher as faint but identifiable indications of the beginnings of change, for example. Even the smallest differences or changes observed in political phenomena might be considered important, depending on the interests and perspectives of the student. At the same time, such subjective impressions of what is or is not significant are likely to vary considerably between researchers. What is significant to one man might be monumentally unimpressive to someone else. The notion of statistical significance, because of its quantitative precision, carries much greater clarity. Still, what is gained in precision might be outweighed by what is lost in terms of sensitivity to the subtleties and nuances of the information we have at hand. If students of politics discarded every finding that was not buttressed by some indication of statistical significance, our storehouse of information would be spare, indeed. And that is the essence of the problem with which the student of politics must deal: On the one hand, he distinctly needs to use language that is as objective, as precise, as explicitly communicative as possible; on the other hand, he cannot permit precision to produce sterile artificiality, or "objectivity" to eradicate an important part of the subtle process of understanding what the world is about. Finding a workable blend of these elements can be difficult, indeed.

WHAT DO WE THINK WE ARE DOING?

If you asked a random sample of political scientists to tell you, in very general terms, what they and their professional colleagues were up to, you would doubtless receive a considerable variety of responses. There are many issues having to do with what might seem a profoundly simple matter, namely, the characterization of the sorts of things that students of politics are trying to do. We shall focus on only three of these issues. First, we shall distinguish among three commonly mentioned purposes of social inquiry—description, explanation, and prediction—and ask to what extent each of these contributes to an understanding of politics. Second, we shall take up briefly the notion of *causation* and try to pinpoint the importance of efforts to establish cause-and-effect relationships among political phenomena. And third, we shall focus on the concept of *change*—the one great constant—and ask whether students of politics are doing an effective job of recognizing and acting upon the prosaic truism that everything is always changing.

Description, Explanation, and Prediction in the Study of Politics

Philosophers of science—who should know, if anyone should know—have never really agreed on whether, or how, one can separate the three principal purposes of inquiry, namely, description, explanation, and prediction. Of course, intellectual disagreement can be taken as either encouragement or discouragement of the expression of one's own opinion. In this case, we shall reason that the prevailing disagreement on the matter justifies going out on a limb. Thus, distinctions among these three purposes of inquiry will be attempted.

It can reasonably be proposed that *description* involves *identifying* something and stating that it has certain *characteristics* of interest. The statement that a national legislative structure is bicameral, and has popularly elected representatives, would be a descriptive statement. *Explanation* involves the specification of *antecedent conditions* to which the characteristics of a political phenomenon can be attributed. Explanatory statements have explicit or implicit "because" clauses. Statements indicating *why* or *how* national legislative structures came to be organized as they are would be explanatory statements. *Predictive* statements are attempts to *project* and to *generalize* explanatory statements. Predictions involve projection, in that they embrace circumstances that have not yet occurred or have not yet been studied. Predictions involve generalization, in that they imply a test of the generality, or breadth of applicability, of the explanation from which they are generated. Thus, explanations will tell us why or how something came to be; in effect, explanations will specify the conditions under which events seem to have occurred. Predictions involve stating the likelihood that certain types of events will occur, given specific sets of conditions. For example, if it has been found, with a substantial degree of regularity, that young people acquire their political party identifications primarily from their parents and other significant adult reference figures, it can be said that the political party identifications of youth can be *explained* in terms of these familial and other adult contacts. Such an explanation would permit the prediction, for example, that there is a high degree of likelihood that a group of young people whose parents were both Republicans will themselves identify with the Republican Party.

It is not hard to see that explanation and prediction are very close to one another. It may be the case, in fact, that they are different only in the ways in which they are stated. Explanations refer to existing studies, while predictions refer to future states of affairs or to circumstances that have not yet been studied. Many social scientists argue that, if a person has a good explanation, he automatically has a useful prediction. On the other hand, it seems clear that explanation and prediction are quite distinct from description. For description characterizes, but does not account for, political phenomena; it is in no sense projective or generalizing. Of course, there is little doubt that description must precede explanation or prediction, since it is difficult to explain something if you are unable to characterize it in the first place. But, despite the importance of accurate description to explanation and prediction, description itself is something rather different from the other two.

We need not shy away from making an evaluative judgment about the relative importance of these three kinds of inquiry. In so doing, we shall tie each to the notion of *understanding*. As a practical matter, after all, we are ultimately interested in understanding what the world is like. And it seems clear that description makes a significantly smaller contribution to understanding than does explanation or prediction. Indeed, explanation and prediction are the cornerstones of understanding. They permit us to relate phenomena to one another and to specify the nature of those relationships in such a way that we can anticipate certain events from the knowledge of other happenings. Knowing what factors influence electoral behavior, for example, permits us to anticipate the distribution of votes for different candidates in elections. Discovering that dissatisfaction and frustration yield aggression and violence would permit us to anticipate social disorder under given conditions. Since explanations and predictions are *relational*; they help us to get a handle on the complex social and political reality in which we all must operate. By contrast, while descriptive statements permit us to identify the characteristics of things around us, they do not, of themselves, permit us to anticipate changes in our environment (or, for that matter, to attempt to bring about changes in that environment). Thus, descriptive statements contribute less to human understanding.

We have said that prediction and explanation are closely

related to one another, and we have mentioned that many people believe that a good explanation is a sufficient condition for a meaningful prediction. Consequently, it might be assumed that explanation and prediction would have equal status in science and would contribute equally to our efforts at understanding. Ultimately, we may all decide that they do, in fact, enjoy equal status. At the present time, however, there is considerable disagreement on this point among students of politics. This disagreement is considerably more than mere semantic shadowboxing. The crux of the problem is that, while explanation may be a *sufficient* condition for meaningful prediction, it may not be a *necessary* condition. That is, it sometimes seems that we can predict certain types of events with considerable accuracy without really being able to explain them. A crude sort of example of this kind of thing is the use of the "bellwether" precinct to predict the outcome of an election. In this case, a researcher may identify a precinct that has given a plurality of its votes to the winning candidate in every Presidential election since 1856 and predict that whichever candidate carries that precinct in 1976 will win the Presidential election. Such a prediction would not be based on any notion that the precinct was "representative" in terms of the background characteristics of the voters living in the precinct. It is usually the case that these "bellwether" precincts do not have identifiable characteristics upon which one could base an *explanation* of any vote outcome. Still, they can be used as a basis for accurate *predictions*.

In a sense, one can also argue that earlier econometric models of certain advanced Western economies had predictive accuracy in the absence of explanatory richness. The predictive accuracy was based primarily on finding statistical correlates (in a sense, statistical "predictors") of important economic indicators, such as gross national product or industrial output. These statistical correlates, or "predictors," could not always be linked in a satisfactory explanatory statement to the indicator that was being "predicted." Nevertheless, the "predictions" worked; that is, they were consistently right and with a considerable degree of precision. In such situations, we may say that prediction was accomplished without adequate explanation.

In this special sense, then, it can be argued that explanation is more important than prediction for the process of understanding. Predictive statements may simply state that, when we have factor A, we will have factor B. Explanatory statements purport to tell us *why* or *how* it is that B comes to follow A. In the apparatus of science, it may be the case, as many argue, that prediction is our ultimate goal. This is debatable. But there is a strong basis for arguing that explanation is more critical than prediction for the development of a sound, general understanding of our political environment.

Causation and Explanation

We suggested above that explanation involves the search for *antecedents*—events that occurred before the phenomenon in which we are interested, and which can be incorporated into a reliable statement of how or why that phenomenon took place. To use some of the terminology discussed in chapter 7, we are interested in identifying independent variables that seem to be *antecedent* to our dependent variable. It might legitimately be asked why we seem to avoid using the word "cause." At least in common usage, the notion of "cause" is synonymous with the notion of "antecedent." And, in a general sense, it can be argued that the purpose of explanation is to establish causation, to determine what events or conditions bring about other events.

It is interesting that references to "causation" in the literature of the social sciences have decreased precisely as those fields of study have become more scientific. This may seem paradoxical, since, in the view of many, science seeks to establish causation by developing rigorous explanations. Upon closer examination, however, the reason for the hesitancy of social scientists to use causal terminology is understandable. We now recognize that many earlier studies of politics that casually referred to "causes" often were not done with sufficient methodological care and thus did not establish "causation" in any rigorous sense. Indeed, we can go further than this and suggest that, strictly speaking, no proof of causation is ever possible. Hubert M. Blalock, a sociologist who has contributed a great deal to social scientists' understanding of causal explanation, puts the point directly: [2]

It is important to realize that, strictly speaking, *no proof of causation is ever possible,* since there is no way that an investigator can guarantee that there is no variable producing a spurious relationship. This is another way of saying that there is no way of deciding that all possible causes have been controlled. . . . this also applies to experimental designs and is a fundamental limitation of *all* scientific research.

In short, Blalock is suggesting that the strict establishment of what causes something else is impossible in the social sciences, simply because we can never be sure that we have controlled for all possible causes of whatever it is we are studying. This is a reason for caution but not for despair. For, while we may not be able to prove causation, we are able to make *causal inferences,* if we have the appropriate data and tools of analysis at hand. Making causal inferences always involves making simplifying assumptions about possible causes that cannot be controlled.[3] In this sense, as Blalock has noted, causal inferences always have something of a "hypothetical" nature, since we can talk about a change in A producing a change in B *only if* we assume that no variables beyond our study are impacting upon B. To put this another way, causal inference, like much of the activity of science, involves simplifying reality. The issue is not whether we must engage in such simplification, but rather how far this simplification can go without distorting our understanding of the real world.

Another way to highlight the difficulties involved in talking about causation is to think about causation in terms of a process of "producing," or "forcing." [4] If we assert that X is a cause of Y, we are saying that a change in X produces a change in Y and not merely that a change in X is followed by, or is associated with, a change in Y. Association, or constant conjunction, may be part of our notion of causality, but it clearly is not sufficient to distinguish a causal relationship from other types of relationships. For example, Blalock cites the common-sense notions that night follows day and adolescence follows childhood, but notes that it is not meaningful to think of day as "causing" night or of childhood as "causing" or "producing" adolescence. These pairs of phenomena are found together, and one follows the other. But the notion of production or forcing is absent, and, thus, causation is absent, as well.

Thus, a fundamental task for social scientists who wish to make causal inferences is to be able to separate mere association or conjunction from relationships that might reasonably be viewed as involving "producing" or "forcing" or "causation." Accomplishing this can be a complex undertaking, the details of which are well beyond the scope of this book, and which are in any case unnecessary at this point in your development of skills as a student of politics. For our purposes here, two general points about causal inference need to be stressed. In the first place, as we have said, making causal inferences involves making simplified assumptions about the phenomena we are studying. In particular, we must be prepared to assume that the relationships at which we are looking are not meaningfully affected by factors of which we are not aware. Second, as Blalock emphasizes, precision and quantification are necessary accompaniments of efforts to make causal inferences.[5] Making sure that we have ascertained precisely what effects given phenomena have on others, and, especially, being sure that we have excluded spurious associations, requires that we have precise, quantifiable information, and that we be able to use the tools of theoretical statistics in sorting out these complex interrelationships. In his important sense, then, making the most useful kinds of explanatory statements (*i.e.*, making causal inferences) is substantially dependent upon the use of that "objective," communicative language to which we referred in an earlier section of this chapter. That is, meaningful explanation may depend substantially upon our ability to use quantitative methods in the study of politics.

Studying Political Change

Change, as someone once sagely observed, is the one great constant. Most of the elements in our environment are changing and are doing so at an increasing rate. The impact of both social and material innovation and technology has been very considerable in most societies in the last hundred years. These changes have brought about significant modifications in the political arrangements used in managing public affairs. The relations of influence among different branches of government, for example, seem to have altered preceptibly in many countries during the twentieth century. The scope and nature of political participation has changed, sometimes drastically. The technological possibilities for the control of many people by few have increased tremendously and seem to have been, at least in part, responsible for the emergence of new forms of political authority in the twentieth century.[6] Fundamental political changes are all around us and are affecting the lives of each of us.

In the face of this apparently obvious significance of the process of political change, it is remarkable how little careful attention students of politics have given to the subject. To be sure, many people have written about the important subjects mentioned in the last paragraph, but most of them have done so in a casual way, usually without attempting to identify carefully the nature of the *change process* itself. Little careful attention has been given to the rates, directions, sequences, and patterns of political change.

This problem is very much related to our discussion of causation and explanation. One of the reasons why the study of political change is so important is that a focus on change has great promise for yielding especially meaningful explanations of political phenomena. That is, looking at the relationships between events over a period of time makes it easier for us to identify a *process* by which these events are related to one another. Similarly, causal inferences are easier to make when we know that some events occur *prior to* other events that are presumed effects of the former.[7]

We noted earlier in this book that an increasing number of studies of political phenomena are comparative in nature. You will recall that, in the broadest sense, comparative studies can be divided into two categories: cross-sectional studies and longitudinal studies. Cross-sectional studies involve looking at a variety of different systems, at the same point in time; longitudinal studies involve looking at one or more polities over a substantial period of time (*i.e.*, at several different time points). While cross-sectional studies can provide important findings about politics, longitudinal studies probably have greater potential for causal explanation. This is the case because cross-sectional studies cannot yield scientifically acceptable conclusions about the *process of change*, since they do not include observations on given political phenomena at different points in time.

To be sure, some researchers who have done cross-sectional studies have tried to draw inferences about the process of change from their data. They have said, for example, that it is possible to talk about the "development process" (presumably, a process of change), even though they have information on political, social, and economic arrangements in several countries at only one point in time. They have asserted that explanations of change are possible from these data because the societies at which they are looking are, in fact, at different stages, or levels, of development. That is, when we look at a variety of systems, we find some that have very low levels of development, others with modest development, and others still that are highly developed. By looking at the characteristics of systems at different levels of development, students with cross-sectional data have *inferred* a picture of change. They have identified a supposed series of steps, or stages, through which societies move in the course of social, economic, and political development. The characteristics of less-developed countries are presumed to represent an early stage of development, while the characteristics of more developed countries are assumed to be associated with later stages of development. It is then assumed that the less developed countries eventually will pass through the stages represented by the current characteristics of successively more developed nations.

There are, of course, some very substantial difficulties with this kind of inference. In particular, any such inference of a change process from cross-sectional data involves the crucial assumption that the temporal context of an observation is irrelevant. It is necessarily assumed that the less-developed countries today look essentially as the currently highly developed countries looked when they were less developed. Or, similarly, it must be assumed that underdevelopment for Kenya in 1973 looks pretty much as underdevelopment must have looked for Japan in 1873. The historical context of the observation is considered to be irrelevant. Since cross-sectional studies lack data for earlier points in time, they must assume that, in this case, the less-developed societies of today are existing in an environment essentially comparable to that in which the then-less-developed countries existed at earlier points in time. Most historians would join most political scientists in suggesting that this is a dubious assumption that places the inference of change from cross-sectional data on shaky ground, indeed.

On the other hand, it is unhappily true that reliable time-series data—*i.e.*, data over substantial periods of time on the same systems—are generally unavailable.[8] The number of different societies for which such time-series data can be obtained is relatively small. As a result, longitudinal studies generally do not embrace a wide variety of societies and are of less generalizability, or breadth of relevance, than are many cross-sectional studies.

The dilemma is real, with no easy answers. That students of politics must focus on the explanation of change seems clear. But rigorous explanations of change require carefully gathered data characterizing a variety of political systems over substantial periods of time—and such data are difficult to come by. Yet, until we develop such longitudinal information collections, our understanding of one of the most fundamental aspects of human existence—the pre-eminent influence of change—will be considerably less than complete.

WHAT *Should* WE BE DOING?

The preceding section of this chapter has suggested that students of politics are engaged in describing, explaining, and predicting political activity. In several senses, explanation seems to be the core of this effort at understanding. And explanation seems to imply attempts to establish, or infer, causation and a more rigorous concern for the study of change. We have suggested that our efforts are identifiably imperfect along each of these dimensions of activity. Such imperfection is to be expected, of course, especially in view of the relative infancy of political science as a field of study. Inadequacies of our past efforts notwithstanding, our courses of action seem reasonable. But are they "just"?

There are several questions being raised by some students about the current and future course of the field of political science. It makes no sense to attempt to cover all of these issues here, despite the considerable importance that many of them have for the future of political research. Yet, two of these contemporary issues have assumed sufficient importance among students of politics to warrant attention. While these are essentially normative issues (*i.e.*, deal with what students of politics *should* be doing), they are perhaps best introduced as factual questions: (1) Is political science simply demonstrating the obvious and/or the trivial, albeit with increasing rigor? (2) To what extent does the study of politics reflect a sense of social commitment and responsibility? How students of politics resolve these two issues will have a great deal to do with the future shape of political science.

Significance and Relevance in the Study of Politics

One of the accompaniments of recent emphases on rigorous, systematic procedures in political science has been a tendency to focus on research topics that are amenable to empirical treatment. Similarly, some of what has been written lately by students of politics seems to emphasize rigor of method rather more than interesting findings. Further, some critics of these recent trends in political research have suggested that much of what is being "discovered" is already known, indeed was discovered years ago by persons equipped with less impressive methodological tool kits. To put this otherwise, some recent emphases in political research have been characterized as rigorously establishing the trivial or, figuratively speaking, reinventing the wheel. Although they are in some respects part of the same tendency, these two dimensions, asserted triviality and unoriginality, may be discussed separately.

At the beginning of chapter 7, we talked about the issue of problem selection in the study of politics. This issue really is at the heart of the controversy over whether some recent political research is "significant" or not. It is difficult to say how one decides that research is "trivial." Doubtless, one could select extreme cases of trivia and innovation, but extreme cases are not the problem. One of the difficulties, of course, is that students of politics may select important subjects but come to unimpressive conclusions at the end of their research. Thus, a focus on the political implications of interracial strife in urban areas would be pretty generally acknowledged as significant. But concluding, at the end of such a research undertaking, that blacks and whites do not always have the same political and social priorities, and that political cleavages in large urban areas are sometimes racially defined, might not be seen as an important contribution to our knowledge.

Unless we have some reasonably well-agreed-upon criteria for problem selection, any discussion about the significance of research foci is likely to be confused and essentially unrewarding. If one accepts a specific criterion, say relevance to contemporary social problems, then it becomes somewhat easier to sort out the "important" from the "unimportant" subjects. But, being explicit about one's criteria of problem selection is a prerequisite for this kind of agreement.

Separating the obvious from the nonobvious, or the original from the unoriginal, may be even more difficult. Here, the crux of the problem lies in determining what we *really* know at the moment. Many traditional scholars of politics who are not particularly enamored of recent trends toward empirical research have suggested that they "already knew" much of what has been "found out" in recent political research. For example, some of these traditional scholars have criticized the massive amount of research that has gone into establishing parental party identification as the major predictor of an individual's own party preference. The argument is that any darned fool could have told you that; why waste valuable time and resources "proving" something that, while admittedly important, is nevertheless quite obvious?

A frequent response to this sort of criticism has been to suggest that much of the "conventional wisdom" on the basis of which we have operated for some time may be less obvious, and indeed less accurate, than we have supposed. Without doubt, rigorous scientific research may confirm what common sense tells us. Empirically oriented students of politics would argue that there is nothing wrong with this. Indeed, it would be alarming if our common-sense notions were regularly found to be wrong. The confirmation of what was "known" (or, perhaps, suspected) is justified on the ground that some of what has been "known" will be discovered to be incorrect to varying degrees. The argument is that, if only a small percentage of our conventional wisdom is denied through the process of more systematic, rigorous research, then the painstaking effort will have been justified. Indeed, there are numerous examples of widely accepted ideas that have been shown to be substantially incorrect through recent empirical research. Just one example is the finding, which has emerged since 1967, that the presumed close relationship between the social-background characteristics of political leaders and their values, issue orientations, and attitudes does not appear to hold true.[8] The finding that recent career positions, or political roles, have much more decisive impact on leaders' stands on important issues has been an important one and has substantially reoriented a good deal of the research on the dynamics of political leadership behavior. Of course, we might merely have accepted what was generally "known" about these background-thinking linkages and devoted our energies to researching important questions on which conventional wisdom had not accumulated. But, then, had we done so, we would have continued to base our discussions of one aspect of political leadership behavior on an inaccurate premise.

Again, there is no simple, black-and-white resolution of this issue. We have already suggested, especially in chapter 7, that the replication of findings is important to science. Common sense and strong hunches simply are not adequate bases for reliable knowledge. At the same time, there is no doubt that, despite the limited resources available in political science, we have already committed "overkill" in some subject-matter areas. That is, there are already some things that have been "established" many times over. Drawing the line between useful verification or replication of what has been believed or discovered earlier, on the one hand, and the wasteful application of energies to the "solution" of intellectual issues that have already been resolved, on the other hand, is very difficult. Undoubtedly, we will never come to a universal meeting of minds on how to draw such distinctions. At a minimum, however, we need to be sensitive to the issue.

Empiricism and Values in the Study of Politics

In chapter 2, we introduced the distinction between empirical and normative concerns in the study of politics. We pointed out there and subsequently that, in the strictest sense, there is no such thing as a field of study that wholly excludes normative concerns (values) from its practice. We have already noted that even the initial choice of a research topic involves the application of selection criteria, which is ultimately a question of normative evaluation. Indeed, whenever criteria are used in selecting one object over another for attention, it becomes a matter of evaluation. Further, we have noted that students of politics understandably have personal preferences about the subject matter they are studying. This book has taken the position that such personal political values must be, and can be, excluded from the actual conduct of political research. That is, it seems possible for us to identify the shape of political reality without being identifiably influenced by what we might like that reality to look like. Nevertheless, it may require considerable intellectual discipline to keep personal values out of some kinds of research. Finally, we have recognized that values are very relevant to the *use* of scientific research. "Knowledge for what?" is an important question, notwithstanding the general agreement that a legitimate answer to that question is, "Knowledge for its own sake."

A related controversy that, until recent years, consumed considerable intellectual and emotional energy among students of politics concerns whether political scientists ought to be involved in seeking, clarifying, or defining the goals to be sought through social institutions. There seems to be growing recognition that this controversy is at once significant and meaningless. It is significant because the search for an understanding of where the human order ought to be going is clearly important and probably should be engaged in by every human being who feels so disposed. On the other hand, it is meaningless, because it seems to make little difference whether such an issue is treated as part of something called political science or is merely engaged in by political scientists acting as responsible citizens. There is no doubt that such clearly normative concerns as the determination of what is "good" for human beings are expressly excluded from scientific inquiry. Science deals with what is and not with what ought to be. At the same time we have specifically noted that scientific research can help us to identify appropriate paths to take in trying to realize given goals, once these desired end states have been defined. In short, empirical research can contribute to the realization of a normative good, once that normative good has been defined. The determination of the goals must rest outside the competence of science; the realization of the goal, once given, may be substantially aided by scientific research, which can clarify the most efficient ways to reach that goal.

In a sense, all this sounds satisfyingly simple. The scientist as citizen participates in the definition of goals for society, dons his cap and gown, and marches through the portals of science, where he exchanges that cap and gown for a laboratory coat and conducts rigorous research that will aid in the realization of those goals which he has helped to define. Unfortunately, reality is rather more complex than would be suggested by this serene scene, and the student of politics, like other social scientists, may find himself troubling a good deal over the normative implications of the research in which he engages. There are numerous examples of such soul-searching by social scientists in recent years; one general kind of example can be offered here. Broadly speaking, much of the research now being done by social scientists could be viewed as contributing to a more precise understanding of why human beings behave as they do. On the positive side, improving our understanding of one another might imply increasing rationality, as well as compassion, in the management of interpersonal relationships. It might suggest that some of the prominent social ills with which we are confronted can be at least partially resolved through an increased understanding of the origins of these problems.

On the other hand, some social scientists have pointed out with alarm that increasing knowledge about the antecedents of different human behaviors implies the increased likelihood that human behavior can be controlled. After all, if we can explain and predict what people will do under certain circumstances, then such information in the hands of persons capable of manipulating those circumstances might permit them to structure and control certain human behaviors. Coupled with the increased technological capabilities of governments, which permit them to obtain and process an increasing amount of information about the activities of individuals, as well as to exercise coercive force toward large numbers of people with a relatively small investment of resources, this expanded understanding of human behavior could present frightening possibilities, indeed. It has always been a fundamental tenet of science, especially of academic science, that scientific information is in the public domain. But if it is public, anyone can make use of it, presumably for whatever purposes he might choose.

Again, there are no easy answers to these kinds of problems. No one seriously proposes that we stop accumulating information about ourselves. There are both practical and ethical reasons why such a course is highly unlikely. Further, no one seriously suggests that students of human behavior could or should individually or collectively set themselves up as judges of the propriety of how scientific information is used. Apparently, we must confront this problem with a kind of openminded anxiety, and with faith that man's increasing understanding of himself will more likely than not result in a declining propensity to misuse what he has discovered.

NOTES

1. Actually, as we have noted earlier, caloric intake per capita usually has been combined with other indicators of frustration, so that the research has not been wholly dependent on the validity of this indicator. See Ivo K. Feierabend and Rosalind L. Feierabend, "The Relationship of Systemic Frustration, Political Coercion, and Political Instability: A Cross-National Analysis," in J. V. Gillespie and B. A. Nesvold (eds.), *Macro-Quantitative Analysis* (Beverly Hills, Calif.: Sage Publications, 1971), pp. 417–40.
2. Hubert M. Blalock, Jr., *An Introduction to Social Research* (Englewood Cliffs, N.J.: Prentice-Hall, 1970), p. 70.

3. For a discussion of this and other assumptions necessary in causal inference, see Hubert M. Blalock, Jr., *Causal Inferences in Non-experimental Research* (Chapel Hill: University of North Carolina Press, 1964), especially pp. 11–26.

4. *Ibid.*, pp. 9–11.

5. Blalock, *An Introduction to Social Research*, pp. 71–78.

6. This argument is expressed, for example, in Carl J. Friedrich and Zbigniew K. Brzezinski, *Totalitarian Dictatorship and Autocracy*, 2d ed. (New York: Praeger, 1966), especially pp. 15–27.

7. See Blalock, *An Introduction to Social Research*, p. 65.

8. Actually, the extent to which reliable time series are available depends on one's definition of "reliable" and "time series." A more optimistic view of what is available can be found in Wolfgang Zapf and Peter Flora, "Some Problems of Time-Series Analysis in Research on Modernization," *Social Science Information*, X, no. 3 (June, 1971), 53–102.

9. This finding was first reported in a study of French and West German elites by Lewis J. Edinger and Donald D. Searing, "Social Background in Elite Analysis: A Methodological Inquiry," *American Political Science Review*, LXI, no. 2 (June, 1967), 428–45. Similar results are reported in Carl Beck, Frederic J. Fleron, Jr., Milton Lodge, Derek Waller, William A. Welsh, and M. George Zaninovich, *Comparative Communist Political Elites* (New York: David McKay, 1973).

Bibliography

The following listing represents a selected set of books that should be useful to undergradate students interested in pursuing the study of politics along the lines suggested in this book. The books listed below reflect, for the most part, a concept-based approach to politics; that is, they provide perspectives useful in studying politics in a variety of cultural and institutional settings. Relatedly, these references have been selected because they show a concern for the important link between what we know and how we find out—between methods of study, on the one hand, and substantive conclusions, on the other.

These books have been grouped by level of difficulty. The point of reference for categorizing a book as "introductory," "intermediate," or "advanced" is the unfamiliarity of the material to undergraduates who have just begun formal course work in political science. Naturally, different people might view the degree of difficulty of some of these materials differently; such classifications are bound to be arbitrary. Further, the difficulty of the material obviously depends on the nature of the student's prior training in related subjects. But the following classifications should provide some general guidance in selecting references through which students can further develop their skills as critical observers of politics.

I. General Conceptual Introductions to Politics

Brief Characterizations

Murphy, Robert E. *The Style and Study of Political Science* (Glenview, Ill.: Scott, Foresman, 1970).

Sorauf, Frank J. *Perspectives on Political Science* (Columbus, Ohio: Charles E. Merrill, 1966).

Concept-based Surveys

Conn, Paul H. *Conflict and Decision-Making: An Introduction to Political Science* (New York: Harper and Row, 1971).

Merkl, Peter H. *Political Continuity and Change* (New York: Harper and Row, 1967).

Rasmussen, Jorgen. *The Process of Politics: A Comparative Approach* (New York: Atherton, 1969).

Wahlke, John C., and Alex N. Dragnich (eds.). *Government and Politics: An Introduction to Political Science,* 2d ed. (New York: Random House, 1971).

II. MAJOR CONCEPTS IN THE STUDY OF POLITICS

Introductory

Friedrich, Carl J., and Zbigniew K. Brzezinski. *Totalitarian Dictatorship and Autocracy,* 2d ed. (New York: Praeger, 1966).

Jaros, Dean. *Socialization to Politics* (New York: Praeger, 1973; London: Nelson, 1973).

Lane, Robert E., and David O. Sears. *Public Opinion and Ideology* (Englewood Cliffs, N.J.: Prentice-Hall, 1964).

Milbrath, Lester W. *Political Participation* (Chicago: Rand McNally, 1965).

Schattschneider, E. E. *The Semi-Sovereign People* (New York: Holt, Rinehart and Winston, 1960).

Wootton, Graham. *Interest Groups* (Englewood Cliffs, N.J.: Prentice-Hall, 1970).

Intermediate

Charlesworth, James C. (ed.). *Contemporary Political Analysis* (New York: The Free Press, 1967).

Edinger, Lewis J. (ed.). *Political Leadership in Industrialized Societies* (New York: John Wiley and Sons, 1967).

Fagen, Richard R. *Politics and Communication* (Boston: Little, Brown, 1966).

Feierabend, I. K., R. L. Feierabend, and T. R. Gurr. *Anger, Violence, and Politics: Theories and Research* (Englewood Cliffs, N.J.: Prentice-Hall, 1972).

Gamson, William A. *Power and Discontent* (Homewood, Ill.: The Dorsey Press, 1968).

Pye, Lucian W. *Aspects of Political Development* (Boston: Little, Brown, 1966).

Roseman, Cyril, Charles G. Mayo, and F. B. Collinge. *Dimensions of Political Analysis: An Introduction to the Contemporary Study of Politics* (Englewood Cliffs, N.J.: Prentice-Hall, 1966).

Wright, William E. (ed.). *A Comparative Study of Party Organization* (Columbus, Ohio: Charles E. Merrill, 1971).

Advanced

Dahl, Robert A., and Charles E. Lindblom. *Politics, Economics and Welfare* (New York: Harper, 1953).

III. APPROACHES AND MODELS

Introductory

Merritt, Richard L. *Systematic Approaches to Comparative Politics* (Chicago: Rand McNally, 1970).

Parsons, Malcolm B. *Perspectives in the Study of Politics* (Chicago: Rand McNally, 1968).

Weinstein, Michael A. *Systematic Political Theory* (Columbus, Ohio: Charles E. Merrill, 1971).

Intermediate

Almond, Gabriel, and G. Bingham Powell. *Comparative Politics: A Developmental Approach* (Boston: Little, Brown, 1966).

Almond, Gabriel, and Sidney Verba. *The Civic Culture* (Boston: Little, Brown, 1963).

Ball, Howard, and Thomas P. Lauth, Jr. *Changing Perspectives in Contemporary Political Analysis* (Englewood Cliffs, N.J.: Prentice-Hall, 1971).

Charlesworth, James C. (ed.). *Contemporary Political Analysis* (New York: The Free Press, 1967).

Easton, David. *A Framework for Political Analysis* (Englewood Cliffs, N.J.: Prentice-Hall, 1965).

————. *A Systems Analysis of Political Life* (New York: John Wiley and Sons, 1965).

———— (ed.). *Varieties of Political Theory* (Englewood Cliffs, N.J.: Prentice-Hall, 1966).

Guetzkow, Harold, *et al. Simulation in International Relations: Developments for Research and Teaching* (Englewood Cliffs, N.J.: Prentice-Hall, 1963).

Haas, Michael, and Henry S. Kariel (eds.). *Approaches to the Study of Political Science* (Scranton, Pa.: Chandler, 1970).

Raser, John R. *Simulation and Society* (Boston: Allyn and Bacon, 1969).

Young, Oran R. *Systems of Political Science* (Englewood Cliffs, N.J.: Prentice-Hall, 1968).

Young, Roland (ed.). *Approaches to the Study of Politics* (Evanston, Ill.: Northwestern University Press, 1958; London: Stevens & Sons, 1959).

Advanced

Deutsch, Karl W. *The Nerves of Government: Models of Political Communication and Control* (New York: The Free Press, 1966).

Downs, Anthony. *An Economic Theory of Democracy* (New York: Harper, 1957).

Golembiewski, Robert T., William A. Walsh, and William J. Crotty. *A Methodological Primer for Political Scientists* (Chicago: Rand McNally, 1969).

Rapoport, Anatol. *Two-Person Game Theory: The Essential Ideas* (Ann Arbor: University of Michigan Press, 1966).

Riker, William. *The Theory of Political Coalitions* (New Haven, Conn.: Yale University Press, 1962).

IV. Philosophy of Social Inquiry

Introductory

Frohock, Fred M. *The Nature of Political Inquiry* (Homewood, Ill.: The Dorsey Press, 1967).

Meehan, Eugene J. *The Theory and Method of Political Analysis* (Homewood, Ill.: The Dorsey Press, 1965).

Intermediate

Graham, George J. *Methodological Foundations for Political Analysis* (Waltham, Mass.: Xerox College Publishing, 1971).

Meehan, Eugene J. *Explanation in Social Science: A System Paradigm* (Homewood, Ill.: The Dorsey Press, 1968).

Advanced

Di Renzo, Gordon J. (ed.). *Concepts, Theory, and Explanation in the Behavioral Sciences* (New York: Random House, 1966).

Kaplan, Abraham. *The Conduct of Inquiry: Methodology for Behavioral Science* (San Francisco: Chandler, 1964).

V. INTRODUCTION TO POLITICAL RESEARCH

Introductory

Barber, Sotirios A., Robert E. Johnston, Roger M. Nichols, and Janice B. Snook. *Introduction to Problem Solving in Political Science* (Columbus, Ohio: Charles E. Merrill, 1971).

Blalock, H. M., Jr. *An Introduction to Social Research* (Englewood Cliffs, N.J.: Prentice-Hall, 1970).

Dahl, Robert A. *Modern Political Analysis,* 2d ed. (Englewood Cliffs, N.J.: Prentice-Hall, 1970).

Janda, Kenneth. *Data Processing,* 2d ed. (Evanston, Ill.: Northwestern University Press, 1972).

Merritt, Richard L., and Gloria J. Pyszka. *The Student Political Scientist's Handbook* (Cambridge, Mass.: Schenkman, 1969).

Wallace, Walter. *The Logic of Science in Sociology* (Chicago: Aldine-Atherton, 1971).

Intermediate

Anderson, Lee F., Meredith W. Watts, Jr., and Allen R. Wilcox. *Legislative Roll-Call Analysis* (Evanston, Ill.: Northwestern University Press, 1966).

Backstrom, Charles, and Gerald D. Hursh. *Survey Research* (Evanston, Ill.: Northwestern University Press, 1963).

Dexter, Lewis Anthony. *Elite and Specialized Interviewing* (Evanston, Ill.: Northwestern University Press, 1970).

Eulau, Heinz. *The Behavioral Persuasion in Politics* (New York: Random House, 1963).

Festinger, L., and D. Katz. *Research Methods in the Behavioral Sciences* (New York: Holt, Rinehart and Winston, 1953).

Gurr, T. R. *Politimetrics: An Introduction to Quantitative Macropolitics* (Englewood Cliffs, N.J.: Prentice-Hall, 1972).

Hayes, Louis D., and Ronald D. Hedlund (eds.). *The Conduct of Political Inquiry* (Englewood Cliffs, N.J.: Prentice-Hall, 1970).

Holsti, Ole R. *Content Analysis for the Social Sciences and Humanities* (Reading, Mass.: Addison-Wesley, 1969).

Isaak, Alan C. *Scope and Methods of Political Science* (Homewood, Ill.: The Dorsey Press, 1969).

Kahn, R. L., and C. F. Cannell. *The Dynamics of Interviewing: Theory, Technique and Cases* (New York: John Wiley and Sons, 1957).

Lazarsfeld, P., and M. Rosenberg (eds.). *The Language of Social Research* (Glencoe, Ill.: The Free Press, 1955).

Madron, Thomas Wm. *Small Group Methods and the Study of Politics* (Evanston, Ill.: Northwestern University Press, 1969).

Phillips, Derek L. *Knowledge from What? Theories and Methods in Social Research* (Chicago: Rand McNally, 1971).

Webb, Eugene J., Donald T. Campbell, Richard D. Schwarz, and Lee Sechrest. *Unobtrusive Measures: Nonreactive Research in the Social Sciences* (Chicago: Rand McNally, 1966).

Wike, Edward L. *Data Analysis* (Chicago: Aldine-Atherton, 1971).

Advanced

Golembiewski, Robert T., William A. Welsh, and William J. Crotty. *A Methodological Primer for Political Scientists* (Chicago: Rand McNally, 1969).

Kerlinger, Fred N. *Foundations of Behavioral Research* (New York: Holt, Rinehart and Winston, 1964).

Przeworki, Adam, and Henry Teune. *The Logic of Comparative Social Inquiry* (New York: John Wiley and Sons, 1970).

Willer, David W. *Scientific Sociology: Theory and Method* (Englewood Cliffs, N.J.: Prentice-Hall, 1967).

Index

Affect, 161

Affirming the consequent (logical fallacy of), 213 (*see also* Error, Type 2)

Aggregate data, 146, 153–55, 157; cross-sectional, 154, 155; relation to data on individuals, 155, 156; time-series, 154, 155 (*see also* Time-series data)

Aggregates, 11, 129–30, 153, 168, 195, 196

Aggression. 220, 230

Alienation, 134

Almond, Gabriel P., 79, 83, 94, 128, 134, 135, 138

Almond and Powell model, 83–86

American politics, 39, 40, 43, 44

Analysis: of data, 200–210; levels of, 136–37, 141, 196; units of, 195, 196

Analytic construct, 9

Antecedent, in two-variable relationships, 193, 206 (*see also* Causation)

Apathy, 30, 31

Approaches, 18, 37, 55, 56, 60–78, 79, 95, 138, 141, 144, 157, 170, 217; behavioral versus institutional, 62–64; concept-based, 65–73; role of, in studying politics, 60–62, 94; technique-based, 73–78 (*see also* Communication approach; Developmental approach; Functional approach; Game theory; Simulation; Systems approach)

Assassinations, 157, 178

Association as form of relationship between variables, 233–34

Attitude, defined, 133

Attitudes, 12–14, 23, 67, 84, 85, 92, 93, 125, 132–42, 146, 147, 153, 163, 164

Authoritarian political systems, 101, 209

Authoritarianism, 4, 151 (*see also* Leadership, styles of)

Authority, 4, 7, 9, 10, 11, 12, 15, 18, 20, 65, 68, 71, 77, 82, 83, 91, 93, 101, 105, 112, 120–21, 127, 136, 175, 178, 186, 195, 214, 225, 235 (*see also* Power)

Ballot, 23, 189 (*see also* Elections; Voting)

Barber, Sotirios A., 159

Bargaining, 18, 77, 119; bargaining-competitive system, 134; as mode of conflict-resolution, 119

Behavior, 62, 63, 65, 79, 83, 146

Behavioral perspective in studying politics, 62–64 (*see also* Approaches)

Beliefs, 13, 84, 85, 92, 93, 125, 132–37, 146, 147, 153, 164

Bibliographies, important in exploratory research, 174

Biographical data, 146, 152, 153, 154, 159 (*see also* Leaders)

Blalock, H. M., Jr., 183, 206, 213, 232, 233, 234

Boundaries of system, 9

Bribes and societal norms, 213

Bundestag, 115

Bureaucracy, 29, 50, 51, 62, 108

Cabinet, 185, 200, 219; British, 113

Candidates, 72, 85, 130, 189, 207, 230

Case studies, 196, 198, 199 (*see also* Deviant case analysis)

Cases, selection of, in political research, 195–200

Categorization: rules of, 209–10; of variable, 183

Causal inference, 212, 233–34 (*see also* Inference)

Causation, 163, 193, 206, 212, 232–37

Census statistics as aggregate data, 154

Chance in analyzing data, 213, 227 (*see also* Hypotheses; Probability; Significance of findings)

Chancellor, 103, 114

Change, 4, 66, 72, 73, 85, 87, 100, 114, 138, 153, 155, 177, 179, 220, 227, 228, 234–37; directions of, 235; economic, 66, 114; patterns of, 235; problems in study of, 234–37; rates of, 235; sequences of, 235; technological, 66, 91, 114, 234

Circumstantial issues, 90, 91 (*see also* Spiro issue-processing model)

Citizens: competence of, 135; opinions of, 170; roles of, in politics, 114, 125,

251